FUNDAMENTALS OF PETROLEUM MAPS

FUNDAMENTALS OF PETROLEUM MAPS

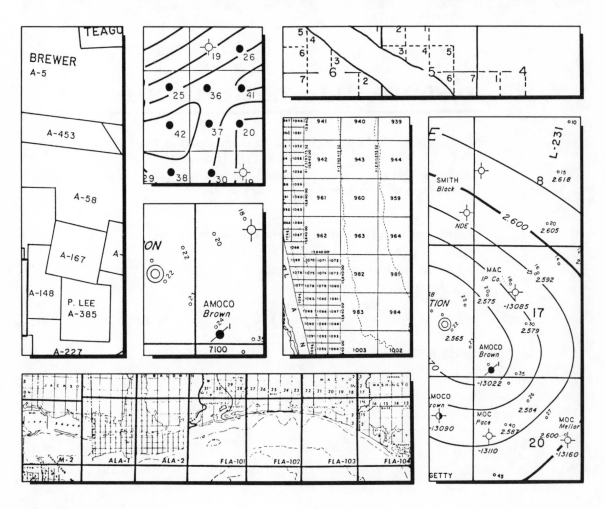

D. P. McElroy

Gulf Publishing Company
Book Division
Houston, London, Paris, Tokyo

FUNDAMENTALS OF PETROLEUM MAPS

Library of Congress Cataloging-in-Publication Data

McElroy, D. P.
  Fundamentals of petroleum maps.

  Includes index.
  1. Oil Fields—Maps.   I. Title.
TN871.M3925 1986   912′.15532′82   86-22920

ISBN 0-87201-494-0

Contents

Acknowledgments

I would like to thank Robert Neely of Neely Reprographics in Jackson, Mississippi, and New Orleans, Louisiana, who helped me start the course on mapping that led to this book and who provided most of the information in Chapter 8. I would also like to thank my family for their encouragement.

Preface

This book will introduce the reader to the fundamentals of petroleum mapping—how to make maps, how to read them, how to use them. It covers well spotting, lease posting, ink drafting, contouring, hanging cross sections, and other requirements related to geological, geophysical, and land maps used in the petroleum industry.

The glossary, abbreviations and background material covered will help readers understand why certain features are shown as they are and not merely how to depict them. The book will give nontechnical personnel a basic grasp of equipment use and care as well as information on reprographic processes that can save time and money while producing professional results. How to locate and use information sources is also covered.

Although it is not intended to teach drafting, the book will prove helpful to those with limited training called upon to prepare material for presentation. "Old hands" will learn faster or cheaper ways to get the same job done, independents with limited staff and resources may avoid some expensive drafting bills, and new employees and new graduates will learn basic and practical methods of petroleum mapping.

The industry has long needed a manual that would answer questions, show a better way to accomplish goals, standardize methods, and train new personnel. I hope those needs are fulfilled in this book.

Dorothy ("Dot") P. McElroy

1
Basic Drafting Principles

This chapter is not intended to teach "drafting." It is included as a reference source only, but it might prove helpful to one with limited training who is called upon to prepare material for presentation. "Old hands" might learn a faster or cheaper way to get the same job done, and independents with limited staff and/or resources may avoid some expensive drafting bills.

EQUIPMENT

Triangles and T-Squares

These are used as straightedges. Some have beveled edges to prevent ink blots. They should be stored flat or hung up to prevent damage. Never use these as cutting guides; even steel edges can be nicked. (If you need a cutting guide, use the edge opposite the beveled edge.) Drafting triangles are right triangles (one 90 degree angle) and come in two shapes: 30°-60° and 45°. The size is determined by the length of the longest side adjacent to the right angle.

Compasses

These are used to draw circles.

- *Beam compass*—Has two independent legs that can be loosened and moved along a bar to new positions. It has no parts to wear out and no matter how far apart the legs are, the points are always vertical to drawing. It is used for very large circles. (See Figure 1-1A.)
- *Bow compass*—Name for a group of compasses whose legs are held together by a clamp or screw.
- *Center bow compass*—Variation of bow compass with control mechanism located between the legs. This construction provides the most accurate and durable positioning. (See Figure 1-1B.)
- *Drop bow compass*—Used to draw very small circles. Has a pivoting leg that is free to move up and down. (See Figure 1-1C and D.)

Note: Take care not to punch holes in the drawing or carve out the circle.

Dividers

These are like compasses without a pen or pencil attachment. (See Figure 1-1E and F.) They are used to transfer dimensions from one source to another for direct comparison.

- *Proportional dividers*—X-shaped device with movable legs marked with a scale and joined by movable set screw. The opening of one pair of legs will be proportional to the opening of the other pair. They can be set at different ratios. (See Figure 1-1G.)
- *Spacing dividers*—Also called contour spacers, they have eleven points that always divide to precision settings at ten equal spaces. (See Figure 1-1H.)

Erasers

While their function is obvious, they are good only if the end result is not worse than the original error. There are many different kinds, and the differences and limitations of each should be analyzed before choosing one.

- *Pencil erasers*—Soft pink is most common. These come in various degrees of hardness. Use the softest eraser that will do the job.
- *Artgum and kneaded erasers*—So soft they leave the surface almost untouched. They are used primarily for cleaning.
- *Ink erasers*—Because ink will penetrate the surface of paper and go into the fibers and because ink will react with film surface, it is very important to use the correct erasing method for the particular situation. (Refer to the detailed explanation in "Erasing Ink Details.")

Pen Points (Drawing and Lettering)

The simplest and most common pen point is a curved piece of metal shaped to a point and slitted. It is sometimes called a *crow quill*. Some pen points are relatively stiff; others very flexible. Lettering points are bent at an angle and are usually larger than quill pens. (Speedball™ is the name of a familiar kind.) New nibs may fail to

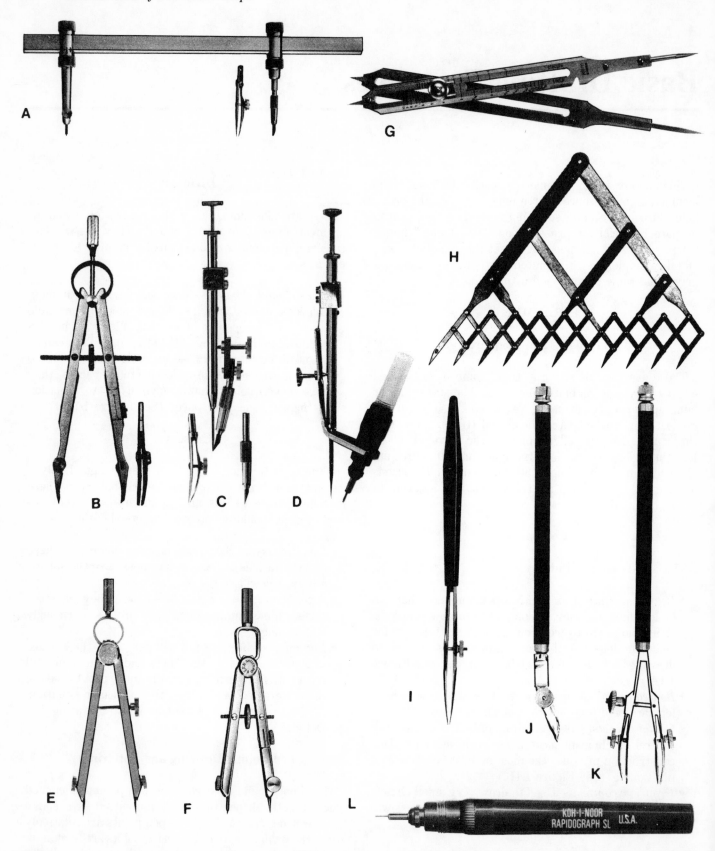

Figure 1-1. Drawing instruments. Pictured here are just a few of the instruments, the use, care and limitations of which are described in this chapter.

transfer ink to the surface. Usually this is caused by a coating of preservative added when the points are made, which sometimes causes the ink to bead. To remove this film, moisten the nib in your mouth first or if you prefer, dip the point into ammonia. Water will not remove the coating. It the point has been used and refuses to write, ammonia will dissolve the ink residue. If the nib spatters, it usually means you are applying too much pressure or the drawing surface is too rough.

Standard Ruling Pen

This was probably the most used of all drawing instruments in the past. (See Figure 1-1I.) Spacing of the blades is adjustable so that different widths of lines can be made with the same pen. It must be kept clean and the angle and adjustment carefully checked. When the points get dull, they need sharpening on an oil stone, but this is best left to a professional.

Contour and Railroad Pens

Both of these are modifications of standard ruling pens. In each the blade assembly is on a swivel. A contour pen (Figure 1-1J) is used for drawing curved lines freehand. Railroad pens are designed to draw parallel double lines (Figure 1-1K).

Note: As with all ruling pens heavy pressure or holding the pen in one spot too long will cause blotting. Use with constant speed and pressure. This takes practice.

Technical Pens

Examples of this type of pen are Leroy, Kohinoor Rapidograph, Castell, etc. (See Figure 1-1L.) They can be used as ruling pens, lettering pens, etc. Each has a hollow point with a steel plunger inside which controls the flow of ink to the surface. They are made in a number of styles and sizes. Some can be used with mechanical lettering devices such as a Leroy Lettering Set (Figure 1-2).

Replacement Points

There are several different sizes of replacement points, and they are available in three materials: stainless steel, jewel, and tungsten carbide. The stainless steel point is the least expensive to buy and is acceptable for limited use. However, the jewel point is self-polishing on the abrasive surface of coated drafting film. Though the initial cost is more, it is far more economical than the stainless point if it is to be used on film. In that case, the jewel point will last up to 500 times longer than the steel one. Tungsten carbide points are intended exclusively for use with programmed automated digital plotters. They tend to give a rough feeling on film surfaces when used in hand drafting.

Mechanical Lettering Devices

Although there are several kinds of these devices made by K&E (Leroy), Kohinoor, Wrico, etc., the most common kinds consist of a scriber which holds the pen point and a tail pin which fits into a groove on a template. (See Figure 1-2.) The templates come in various sizes and styles of lettering. With a little practice a beginner can make professional-looking lettering.

Pencils

Drawing pencils come in degrees of hardness from 9H (very hard) to 6B (very soft). In general, use 3H or 4H for guide lines or sketching for ink work; use 2H or HB for pencil lines on work maps, etc. "Non-print" or "non-repro" pencils are great for preliminary work to be inked later. "Non-repro" pencils will print on a photocopy, but

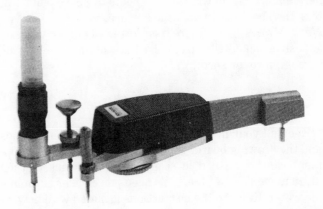

Figure 1-2. Mechanical lettering scribers and template.

not in a diazo machine. Color pencils will be discussed in detail on page 42.

Protractor

This is used to measure angles and to plot bearings, as in "metes and bounds" descriptions. Detailed use is described on pages 11 and 12.

Scales

There are many different kinds. Especially useful in dealing with petroleum maps is an Allen Engineering Scale, which is really a set of scales with inches per mile, arpents, varas, chains, etc.
Note: Accurate maps require accurate measurements.

Inks

India ink is the basic drawing medium for almost all artwork and maps which are to be reproduced. This is discussed in detail in the section "Ink Drafting on Film."

Templates

These are patterns or stencils, usually made of plastic, containing many different common shapes in several sizes. These are very useful when certain shapes must be drawn frequently. Use with care to ensure that ink will not run under or that the template will not slip. Some cheaper kinds are not cut out smoothly, and thus may turn out to be more costly in the long run.

Burnishers

These are tools, usually made of plastic or bone, used to supply rubbing pressure to a transfer material or to adhere material from wax-coated sheets. A sharp point will tear the sheet or damage the surface.
Note: Always burnish press-on letters, contour tape, or adhesive-backed film from the back of the drawing or through a cover sheet.

Final Note

Keep all your instruments clean, including your hands and the drawing board. Triangles and other plastic equipment can be washed in soapy water and rinsed, then dried immediately. Steel tools need pen cleaner or ammonia water. Refer to the instructions included with new instruments.

TECHNICAL PEN CARE

Care of your technical pen is essential for good performance. The quality of the finished product is directly related to the care given to the tools required to do the job. Care should be taken when filling as well as when cleaning as shown in Figure 1-3.

Filling

Unscrew cap (1), holder (2), and clamp ring (3) from the pen body. Pull ink cartridge from the pen body using a slight twist (4). Fill ink cartridge only to the "fill line" at $1/4$-in. from the top (5). Slowly press pen body down into filled ink cartridge using a slight twist (6), and replace clamp ring. You should refill when the cartridge becomes half full.

Starting

Start ink flow with a gentle horizontal shaking motion (7). *Do not shake over a drawing.* Holding the pen in a vertical position, draw on scratch pad until good ink flow appears (8). The pen should be recapped after each use to prevent ink from drying out in the point and in the air-breathing channel (9).

Cleaning

Disassemble pen as in Steps 1–4, and gently tap rear of pen body to remove residual ink (10). Using nib key, unscrew nib from pen body (11). Disassemble nib only if it is absolutely necessary. *Do not disassemble nib size 00 or smaller.* Rinse before placing point in cleaning solution (12). Soak in pen cleaner until dried ink dissolves (overnight if necessary) (13). Then rinse with water. Dry thoroughly with paper wipe (14).

Syringe Cleaning

If you use a pressure-bulb pen cleaning kit, disassemble the pen, and thread pen body/nib assembly into pressure-bulb coupler, body first (15). Immerse pen body completely in pen cleaning solution (16). Flush solution through pen body/nib assembly using slow squeeze-release pressure action. Repeat until nib is clean. Rinse nib assembly under lukewarm running water and dry thoroughly with paper wipe before refilling with ink.

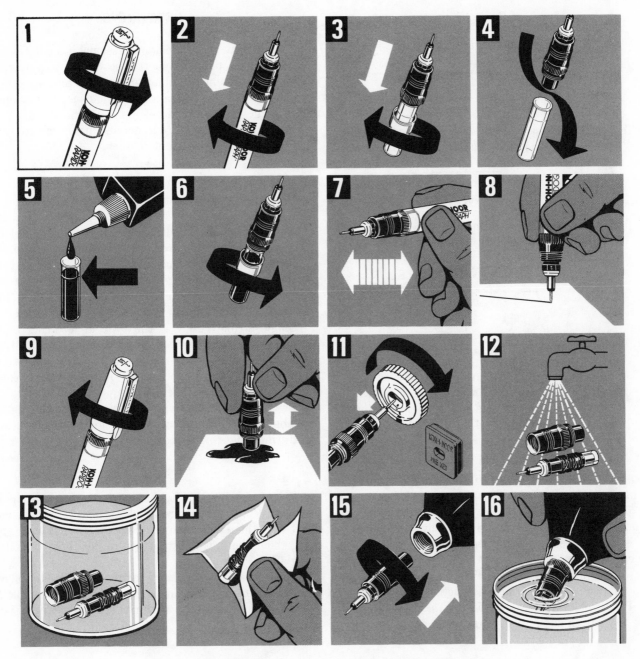

Figure 1-3. Technical pen care. (Courtesy of Koh-I-Noor Rapidograph, Inc.)

Ultrasonic Cleaning

This is designed for "on the spot" cleaning in drafting areas. It takes only seconds to clean a pen and the pen does not need to be taken apart. Just immerse the pen up to the cap threads on the barrel. Millions of energized microscopic bubbles, generated by 50,000 cycle ultrasonic action, carry cleaning solution into the smallest openings of the drawing point. The bubbles scrub the point tube inside and out.

Note: After one cleaning the solution is likely to be completely black, but it remains effective for long periods.

HINTS FOR DRAWING

Basic principles of geometry are used daily in mapping. It is especially helpful to review how to figure areas of certain figures. This is important in figuring acreage within a tract of land or the area involved in net pay maps.

Areas of Basic Figures

- To figure the area of a parallelogram (square, rectangle, etc.):

  Area = base × height
  A = bh

- To figure the area of a trapezoid:

  Area = ½ product of altitude × sum of bases
  $A = \frac{1}{2}h(b_1 + b_2)$

- To figure the area of a triangle:

  Area = ½ base × height
  $A = \frac{1}{2}bh$

Drawing Parallel Lines Using Triangles

Place one side of a triangle in the direction of desired lines. Support it on a second triangle or other straightedge. Slide the original triangle on the support in the desired sequence. (See Figure 1-4.)

Dividing a Line

Sometimes it is necessary to divide a line into equal segments even when it is difficult to divide it by measuring. (See Figure 1-5.) To do this draw a construction line through one end of the base line (X-Y) any length and any acute angle. Use a scale to measure equal segments on the construction line. Connect the last point (P) with the end of the base line (Y). With triangles draw a line through each point on the construction line parallel to line P-Y through the base line. In this manner you can divide any length line into any number of equal segments.

LETTERING

A good drawing will look professional if the lettering is of top quality, but sloppy lettering will destroy an otherwise fine drawing. Good lettering takes practice and patience. Even mechanical lettering devices require practice to get professional results. Machine lettering and transfer lettering require a certain amount of care to get the spacing and alignment correct.

Freehand Lettering

Good freehand lettering is almost a lost art these days, but having a "good freehand" is a valuable asset. It is fast and direct. Especially helpful is the ability to letter in small sizes such as those used for well names and lease information on petroleum maps. A good freehand is not stylized, just good "single stroke gothic." A little pressure at the beginning and end of each line will help to show a definite start and stop and be easier to read.

Single stroke gothic is the type of lettering recommended by The American National Standards Institute because it can be drawn rapidly and is easily legible. Contrary to the name, most letters require several strokes to complete. The recommended sequence for making this type of lettering is shown in Figure 1-6. The complete alphabet and numerals in vertical (Figure 1-7) and inclined lettering (Figure 1-8) are shown.

Spacing

Proper spacing is just as important as making the letters correctly. The letters should be placed so that spaces between them appear to be about the same. Letter spacing should be judged by the eye rather than by measuring. (See Figure 1-9.)

Sometimes it is necessary for the lettering to follow a curved feature. In this instance make guide lines that follow the curve and letter within these guides. (See Figure 1-10.)

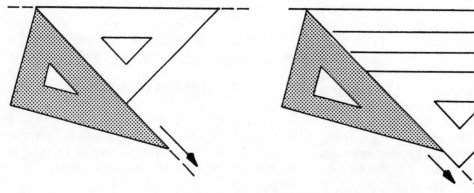

Figure 1-4. Using triangles to draw parallel lines.

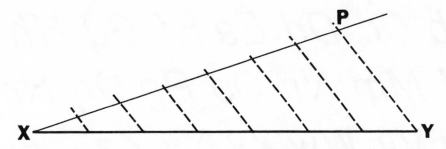

Figure 1-5. One way to divide a line into equal segments when it is difficult to do so by measuring.

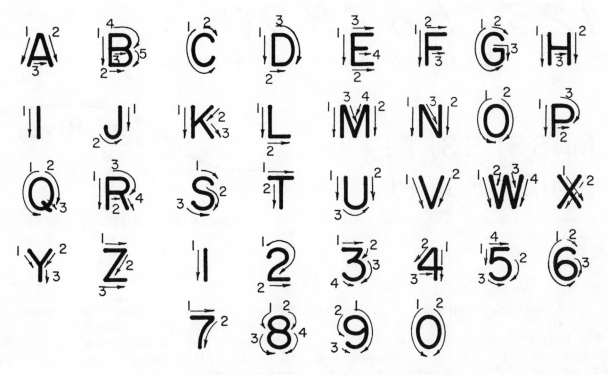

Figure 1-6. Recommended sequence for single stroke gothic letters.

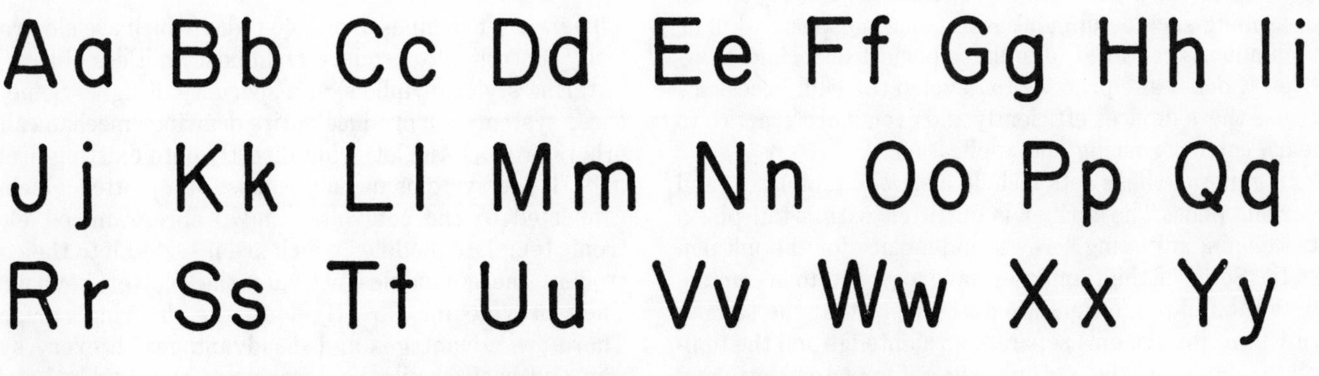

Aa Bb Cc Dd Ee Ff Gg Hh Ii

Jj Kk Ll Mm Nn Oo Pp Qq

Rr Ss Tt Uu Vv Ww Xx Yy

Zz 1234567890

Figure 1-7. Vertical single stroke gothic alphabet and numerals.

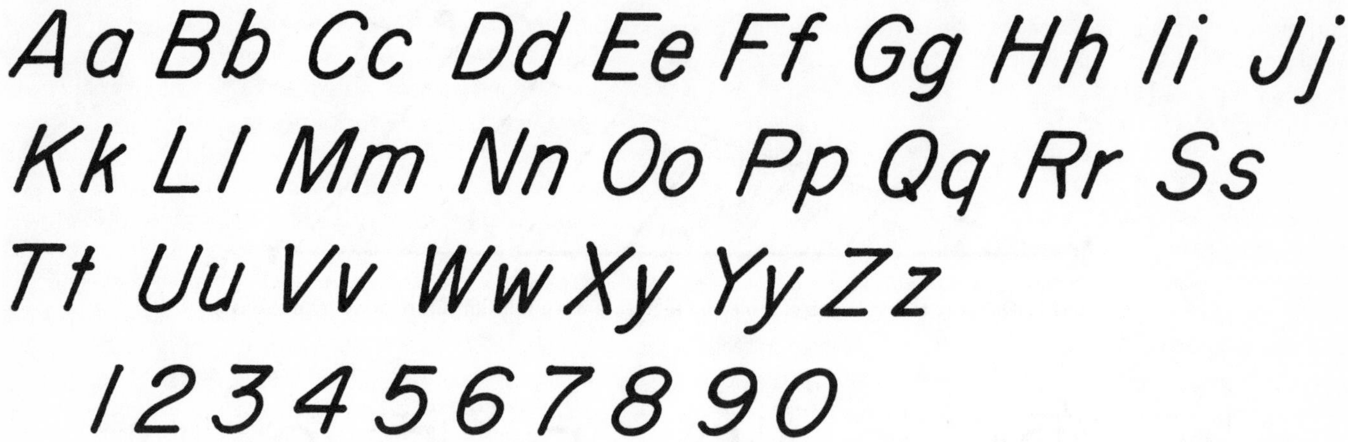

Aa Bb Cc Dd Ee Ff Gg Hh Ii Jj
Kk Ll Mm Nn Oo Pp Qq Rr Ss
Tt Uu Vv Ww Xy Yy Zz
1234567890

Figure 1-8. Inclined single stroke gothic alphabet and numerals.

MI SSI SSI PPI
MISSISSIPPI

Figure 1-9. Proper spacing should be by eye rather than measurement.

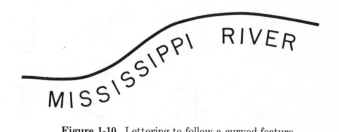

Figure 1-10. Lettering to follow a curved feature.

Mechanical Lettering

One of the draftsman's most useful tools is the lettering set, with which perfect lettering can be made easily and rapidly. (See Figure 1-2.) Of several brands available, the most familiar is probably the "Leroy," made by K&E. A great variety of lettering styles, alphabets, and symbols is available in a wide range of sizes. All the brochures describing such equipment assert that no special skill or technique is required to produce perfect lettering. However, it does take practice to develop the skill necessary to use these devices efficiently and even more practice to learn correct spacing and application.

In general, these sets include a *scriber*, templates, and various pens. The scriber is outfitted with a tail pin, a tracer pin, adjusting screws, and a place for the ink pen to fit. Some of the templates have a groove to accommodate the tail pin; others are designed so that the tail pin fits into a groove on a separate straightedge and the template glides on the straightedge. Templates (lettering guides) are usually numbered to indicate the height of letters in thousandths of an inch, and the recommended pen size to provide well-proportioned letters. The tail pin fits into the groove; the ink pen fits into the scriber, and the tracer pin follows the letter on the template. Smaller letters require a fine groove tracer pin. The ink pen must be adjusted to just clear the drawing surface so that the ink flows smoothly. Detailed instructions are included in the various sets.

Machine Lettering

There are machines available today which are electronically controlled to produce an almost limitless library of lettering styles, symbols, and specialty designs. Some of these systems can produce entire drawings mechanically; others produce the lettering directly onto existing drawings. These systems usually consist of a plotter which is connected to the controller and preprogrammed electronic template modules which are inserted into the controller. These modules activate the plotter keyboard. They provide ink directly onto the drawing surface. There are advantages and disadvantages to every system and each should be researched thoroughly before purchase as it represents a significant investment.

Other types of lettering systems include some which produce the letters directly onto a transparent tape which is then secured to the drawing. This kind of system requires less skill to operate, but there are distinct disadvantages, including less durability and a tendency to "ghost" during printing.

Transfer Lettering

There are two basic forms of transfer lettering, and the form affects their method of application. In one case, the characters are printed on the front of the sheet; the back of the characters is coated with an adhesive. In this form the characters are either cut or lifted from the front of the sheet and adhered to the artwork. Gentle, firm pressure will cause the backing to stick to most surfaces.

In the other form, the characters are printed on the back of the sheet and the waxy adhesive is coated over both the type and the sheet. In this type, pressure is applied by rubbing the front of the sheet directly over the character which is to be transferred. The rubbing adheres the wax coating so that when the sheet is removed the character comes away from the sheet and remains on the artwork. A burnisher is recommended for using this type of transfer letter. Care must be taken to not flake part of the image, and also to align the letters properly. After these sheets have been sitting around a while they lose some of the adhesive so it is best to start with a fresh sheet.

As with any type of transfer lettering or symbols, the image is not as permanent as ink. Common difficulties include torn letters, poor adhesion, flaking, and waxy residue around the character.

Ink Drafting on Film

Drafting film is usually made of polyester and especially formulated for direct ink drafting. To set up for drafting on film, the film surface should first be cleaned. A dry industrial wipe is best to clean minor surface soil. More serious soils might require the use of a liquid film cleaner. Under no circumstances should the film surface be cleaned with "pounce" or powder of any kind. The fine

particles of these materials are trapped in the "tooth" of the film surface coating. Ink will then lie on the surface of the particles without adhering to the film surface. As the powder particles eventually fall away, the ink line will flake away with it. These particles also tend to clog the openings of technical pens. (See Figure 1-11.)

The ink is retained on the film by a chemical bond to the film coating and not by penetration of the surface, as is the case with ink on paper or other porous materials. It is possible to make totally clean erasures without leaving ghosts. The drawing surface remains unaffected even after repeated erasures (assuming you use the correct erasing method). Optimum dimensional stability, retention of the original translucency and flexibility of the film, the permanence of the ink line, and the ability to withstand the rigors of repeated handling make film the best medium for permanent drawings.

Experimentation is the best approach to determine the choice of inks.

For example, Pelikan "T" Waterproof Drawing Ink 9085 has been a longtime favorite for film drafting. It is fast-drying and completely waterproof within a few minutes. Pelikan 9065 has a longer "open pen" time. It is good for use in the smaller point sizes, but doesn't dry as rapidly. Other companies make equally good inks for this purpose. See the "Drawing Ink Selection Chart," Figure 1-12. For more detailed information about films, inks, and erasure methods ask your supply dealer for a copy of Koh-I-Noor Rapidograph, Inc.'s booklet entitled *The Rapid-draw System*.

Erasing Ink Details

To protect the surface of the drafting film it is important to know the best erasure method for the type of ink. Most inks respond well to the vinyl eraser used in combination with a liquid eraser. The liquid releases the chemical bond of the ink line while the friction of the vinyl eraser results in the formation of fine eraser chips which absorb the ink. The eraser chips can be easily brushed off

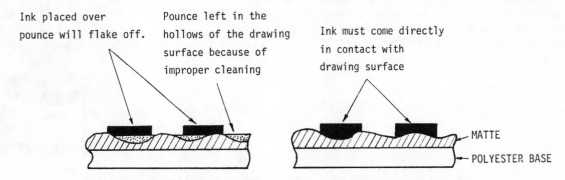

Figure 1-11. Good and poor ink adhesion. (Courtesy of Koh-I-Noor Rapidograph, Inc.)

Ink Item No.	Drawing Media	Black India-Pigmented Black	Dye Based	% Blackness of Ink Line	Ink Drying Time	Waterproof	Erasability	Opaque*	Transparent**	Scarlet	Carmine	Red	Vermilion	Orange	Yellow	Light Green	Green	Deep Green	Blue	Cobalt Blue	Ultramarine	Prussian Blue	Violet	Red Violet	Blue Violet	Sienna	Burnt Sienna	Sepia	Brown	Gray	White*
3071 Black Only	Overhead Projection Films	●		90%	Fast	Yes	Excellent																								
3073 ACETATE	Overhead Projection Films				Fast	Yes	Good	●			●		●	●		●		●				●							●		
3074 RAPIDOMAT Black Only	Film. On Flatbed Plotters	●		90%	Slow	Yes	Excellent																								
3080 UNIVERSAL	Film and Paper	●		92%	Fast	Yes	Good	●		●	●		●	●		●		●				●							●	●
3081 PLOTTER INK	Paper		●	88%	Medium	No	None	●			●			●		●		●											●	
3082 OPAQUING INK Black Only	Photo Mechanical Films	●		90%	Medium	Yes	Good																							
3083 ARTPEN INK	Paper	●		88%	Medium	Yes	Excellent	●			●			●		●		●											●	
3084 RAPIDRAW INK Black Only	Film and Paper	●		98%	Fast	Yes	Good																							
9065 PELIKAN DRAWING INK	Paper	●		88%	Medium	Yes	Good	●	●	●		●	●	●	●		●			●	●	●	●		●	●	●	●	●	●	●
9066 PELIKAN "Special"	Film and Paper	●		90%	Fast	Yes	Excellent	●			●			●		●		●			●							●	
9085 PELIKAN "T" Black Only	Film and Paper	●		90%	Fast	Yes	Excellent																							
9150 PELIKAN FOUNT INDIA	Paper	●		84%	Medium	No	None																							

Colors †

* Opaque inks are compounded from finely milled materials: Carbon for black india inks and solid pigments for color and white.

** Transparent inks are formulated with dyes.

† Colored inks are manufactured with components that are different than black inks and will not, therefore, have exactly the same characteristics as described in the above chart for black india inks.

NOTE:
Various characteristics mentioned above for black inks were determined under constant testing conditions, such as humidity, temperature and media. Some slight variations for the results indicated above may occur if your own testing is conducted under different atmospheric conditions, or when using drafting media with different absorbencies and surface textures. The results shown above are to be considered only as reference points from which initial choices can be made. For additional data regarding ink characteristics, please contact Koh-I-Noor's Customer Service Department.

Dropper Stopper Design
On all Koh-I-Noor & Pelikan 1 fl. oz. bottles.

Figure 1-12. Drawing ink selection chart. (Courtesy of Koh-I-Noor Rapidograph, Inc.)

the film surface. Vinyl strip erasers and kits are available.

One-Step Method Imbibed Eraser

The newest development in erasers is the Koh-I-Noor 9600 PT/20 eraser. It is imbibed with erasing fluid that is released from pores within the eraser by friction produced when it is rubbed against the drafting film surface. *Note:* The surface of the PT/20 will oxidize, so it is advisable to cut a fresh strip off the end to get the benefit of the erasing fluid built into it.

Changing Details on Photographic Reproductions

To erase ink lines from photographic films which have a photo-emulsion drafting surface, the PT/20 imbibed eraser should be used. Photographic image silver lines can be removed with a number of special chemicals available for this purpose. If the emulsion is on the reverse side of the film, details in small areas may be removed with the flat side of a razor blade or exacto knife. Do not use this scraping method if the emulsion is on the front side of the film. Check with your reprographics consultant for any special properties of the particular brand of film used.

USING THE PROTRACTOR TO PLOT BEARINGS

In making or reading maps it is necessary to understand directions and how they are designated. Figure 1-13 shows a "compass rose," which indicates the cardinal directions. Notice that north is at the top of the compass. All maps should be oriented the same way, with north at the top. Directions are expressed by either *azimuth* or *bearing*.

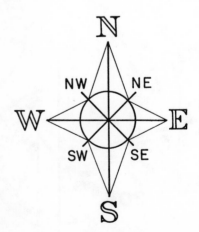

Figure 1-13. Compass rose. In dealing with maps lesson number one should be learning the cardinal directions.

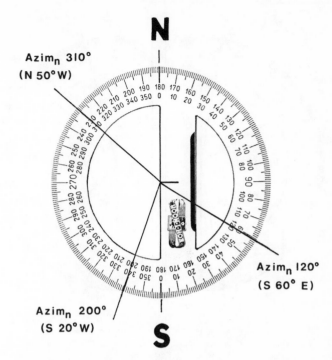

Figure 1-14. Methods of expressing direction by azimuth.

Azimuth

An azimuth is a horizontal angle measured clockwise usually from north. (South is sometimes used as a beginning for geodetic surveys that cover great areas.) A full circle encompasses 360°, so when azimuth is used, it is measured from 0° to 360°. (See Figure 1-14.)

Bearing

A bearing is the horizontal angle from the north or south, whichever is nearest, with an added designation of east or west, whichever applies. A bearing can never be more than 90°. (See Figure 1-15.) In mapmaking, horizontal angles are usually described by bearings. To plot locations by metes and bounds it is essential to understand these principles.

Plotting Bearings

To plot a bearing lay the protractor base along a north-south line with the index intersection at the point of beginning (POB). (See Figure 1-15.) If the bearing is in an easterly direction, the protractor is placed so that the curved side (showing 90°) is to the east, or right. From this position any bearing reading "north (so many) degrees east" or "south (so many) degrees east" may be measured (Figure 1-15A–D). The reverse is true for plotting a westerly bearing (Figure 1-15E–H).

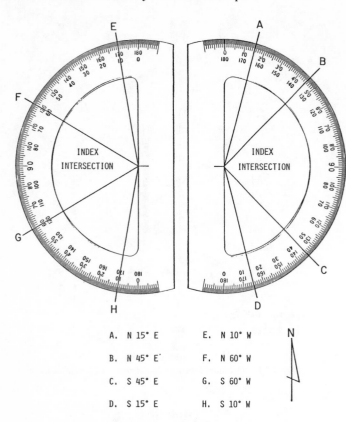

A. N 15° E	E. N 10° W
B. N 45° E	F. N 60° W
C. S 45° E	G. S 60° W
D. S 15° E	H. S 10° W

Figure 1-15. Expressing directions by bearing.

Plotting Metes and Bounds

When a tract of land is described by different bearings it is called a *metes and bounds* description. Each side is measured along a bearing line and marked at the proper distance, and a new bearing is plotted from that point. In this manner the "calls" are followed progressively around to the point of beginning. In such case it is necessary to plot each new bearing with the protractor base along a north-south line through each point of change as in Figure 1-16.

USING THE PLANIMETER

The planimeter is an instrument used for measuring the area of any plane figure by passing a tracer around the boundary line. The following text is from the first page of a set of instructions which are packed with the K & E planimeter (reprinted from the Keuffel & Esser Company, Parsippany, N.J., with permission). (See Figure 1-17A.)

The Compensating Polar Planimeter

These instructions are written on the assumption that the reader has little or no familiarity with the planimeter.

Tracer Points

Most K & E planimeters are equipped with a new crystal clear tracer lens as shown in Figure 1-17B. The lens magnifies the line being traced and permits greater accuracy. A small circle within a larger circle on the bottom of the lens is moved over the line being traced. Some K & E planimeters have a tracer point and stop, as shown in Figure 1-17C. In the text which follows, reference to the tracer point can mean either type.

How the Planimeter Works

The polar planimeter is a simple instrument for the accurate measurement of plane areas of any form. To mea-

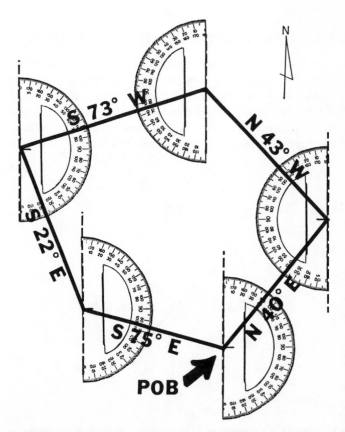

Figure 1-16. Plotting "metes and bounds" descriptions. Note the placement of the protractor at each successive point.

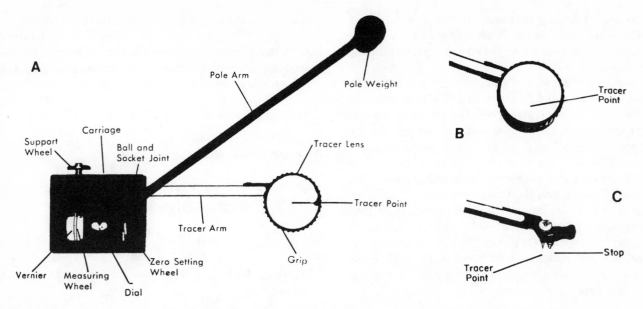

Figure 1-17. (A) The compensating polar planimeter. (Courtesy of Keuffel & Esser Company, Parsippany, N.J.) (B) Tracer lens with tracer point. (C) Tracer point and stop.

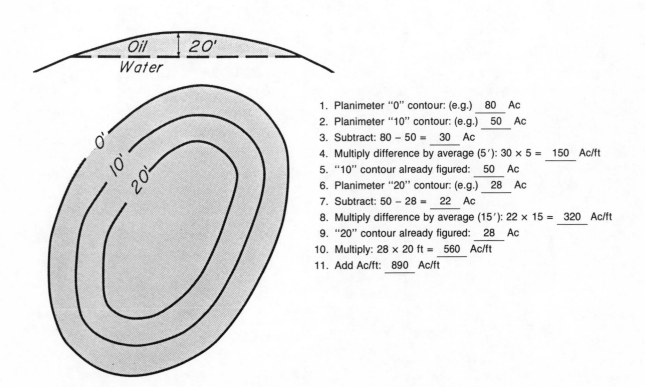

1. Planimeter "0" contour: (e.g.)   80   Ac
2. Planimeter "10" contour: (e.g.)   50   Ac
3. Subtract: 80 – 50 =   30   Ac
4. Multiply difference by average (5′): 30 × 5 =   150   Ac/ft
5. "10" contour already figured: 50   Ac
6. Planimeter "20" contour: (e.g.)   28   Ac
7. Subtract: 50 – 28 =   22   Ac
8. Multiply difference by average (15′): 22 × 15 =   320   Ac/ft
9. "20" contour already figured: 28   Ac
10. Multiply: 28 × 20 ft =   560   Ac/ft
11. Add Ac/ft: 890   Ac/ft

Figure 1-18. Figuring acre/feet with a planimeter. It is necessary to use an isopach map to figure this.

sure an area it is only necessary to run a tracer point around the periphery of the figure and read the distance shown on a measuring wheel which has revolved during the process.

The planimeter consists of two units; the pole arm unit, and the tracer arm and carriage unit. The pole arm unit is simply a bar, at one end of which is the pole, consisting of a weight with a needle point at the bottom. At the other end is a ball which fits into a socket in the carriage. Now examine the tracer arm and carriage unit. Note that it rests on three points; the measuring wheel rim, the support wheel, and the tracer point.

Swing the carriage around the tracer point. Note that the measuring wheel turns rapidly, and the dial turns slowly. When you move it parallel to the tracer arm the measuring wheel slides without turning. This characteristic sliding or turning of the measuring wheel is the key to the planimeter performance.

It is necessary to study the entire book of instructions which is supplied with the new planimeter to understand how to use it properly. However, the following is a formula for using the planimeter to figure acreage. It is based on the scale of the map.

$$(\text{scale of map})^2 \times \frac{\text{plan. reading}}{43{,}560 \text{ ft}}$$

Note: An acre is 43,560 square feet.

Example: 1 in. = 3,000 ft (scale)

$$3{,}000 \times 3{,}000 = 9{,}000{,}000 \text{ sq ft}$$

$$9{,}000{,}000 \times \frac{\text{planimeter reading}}{43{,}560}$$

See Figure 1-18 for a step-by-step example of figuring acre/feet.

2
Special Language of the Oil Patch

Because every industry has a special vernacular it is helpful to become familiar with it if you intend to understand anything else about that industry. This is especially true of the petroleum industry. For that reason this "glossary" is included within the text itself, instead of being relegated to the back of the book where it might be useful for looking up a few unfamiliar words. The following terms are not the only ones customarily used in this business, but becoming acquainted with these terms and abbreviations will help the reader to understand all that follows. Special terms used in the land department are included in the chapter entitled "Land Maps."

TERMS

Abandon—To cease efforts to produce oil or gas from a well and to plug the hole and salvage all material and equipment possible.

Accretions—The increase of land by gradual or imperceptible action of natural forces.

Acidize—To put acid in a well to dissolve limestone etc. in a producing zone so that passages are formed through which oil and gas can enter the wellbore.

Acre-foot—A unit of volume often used in oil-reservoir analysis, equivalent to the volume (as of oil or water) necessary to cover one acre to a depth of one foot.

Allowable—The amount of oil or gas that a well is permitted by authorities to produce during a given period.

Anhydrite—The common name for calcium sulfate, sometimes called gypsum.

Anomaly—A deviation from the norm. In geology the term indicates an abnormality such as a fault or dome in a sedimentary bed.

Anticline—An arched, inverted trough configuration of folded and stratified rock. Opposite of syncline.

Barrel—A measure of volume of petroleum products. One barrel equals 42 U.S. gallons.

Basin—A synclinal structure in the subsurface, formerly the bed of an ancient sea. Because it is composed of sedimentary rock and because its contours provide traps for petroleum, a basin is a good prospect for exploration.

Bit—Cutting or boring element used in drilling.

Blowout—An uncontrolled flow of gas, oil, or other well fluids into the atmosphere. A blowout or gusher occurs when formation pressure exceeds the pressure applied to it by the column of drilling fluid. A "kick" warns of an impending blowout.

Blowout Preventer—Equipment used to prevent the escape of fluids.

Borehole—The wellbore. The hole made by drilling.

Bottom hole—Pertaining to the deepest part of a well.

Bottom Hole Contract—A contract providing for the payment of money or other consideration upon the completion of a well to a specified depth.

Bottoms up—A complete trip from the bottom of the wellbore to the top.

Cap rock—Impermeable rock overlying an oil or gas reservoir. It tends to prevent migration of fluids from the reservoir.

Carbonate rock—Sedimentary rock primarily composed of limestone or dolomite.

Casing—Steel pipe placed in a drilling well to prevent the wall of the hole from caving in during drilling, and to provide a means of extracting petroleum if found.

Casing point—That depth at which a decision is made whether to run casing.

Choke—A device inserted in the flow line to regulate the rate of flow.

Christmas tree—The assembly of control valves, pressure gauges, and chokes at the top of a well to control the flow of oil and gas after the well has been drilled and completed.

Circulate—To pass from one point throughout system and back to the starting point.

Closure—The vertical distance between the top of an anticline, or dome, and the bottom, an indication of the amount of producing formation that may be expected.

Come out of hole—To pull the drill stem out of the wellbore.

Complete—To finish work on a well and put it on productive status.

Condensate—A light hydrocarbon liquid obtained by condensation of hydrocarbon vapors.

Confirmation well—The second producer in a new field.

Coning—The encroachment of reservoir water into the oil column because of uncontrolled production.

Contour map—A map with lines marked to indicate points that are at the same elevation above or below sea level.

Contract depth—The depth of the wellbore at which the drilling contract is fulfilled.

Core—(Noun) A cylindrical sample taken from a formation for geological analysis. (Verb) To obtain that sample.

Core analysis—Laboratory analysis of a core sample to determine porosity, permeability, lithology, fluid content, angle of dip, geological age, and probable productivity of the formation.

Core barrel—A tubular device from 25 to 60 feet long run at the bottom of the drill pipe in place of a bit to cut a core sample.

Correlate—To relate subsurface information obtained from one well to that of others so that formations may be charted.

Crude oil—Unrefined liquid petroleum.

Derrick—A large load-bearing structure used in drilling.

Derrick floor elevation—The elevation at the working base of the derrick.

Development well—A well drilled in proven territory in a field to complete a pattern of production (an exploitation well).

Deviation—The inclination of the wellbore from the vertical.

Dip (formation dip)—The angle at which a formation bed inclines away from the horizontal.

Discovery well—The first oil or gas well completed for a new field. Until production it is called a wildcat well. It proves the presence of a productive formation.

Disposal well—A well through which water (usually salt water) is returned to the subsurface formations.

Dolomite—A type of sedimentary rock similar to limestone but rich in magnesium carbonate, sometimes a reservoir rock for petroleum.

Driller—The employee directly in charge of a drilling rig and crew.

Drill pipe—Heavy seamless tubing used to rotate the bit and circulate the drilling fluids. Joints are usually about 30 feet long.

Drill stem—The entire length of tubular pipes, composed of the kelly, drill pipe, and drill collars, that make up the drilling assembly from the surface to the bottom of the hole.

Drill string—The column or string of drill pipe, not including the drill collars or the kelly.

Dry hole—An exploratory or development well found to be incapable of producing oil or gas in sufficient quantities to justify completion.

Dual completion—A single well that produces from two separate formations at the same time.

Electric log—A record of certain electrical characteristics of formations traversed by the borehole, made to iden-tify the formations and determine the nature and amount of fluid in them.

Elevation—Height above (+) or depth below (−) sea level.

Exploitation—Development of a reservoir.

Exploration—The search for reservoirs of oil and gas.

Fault—A break in subsurface strata where displacement occurs.

Fee—An estate of inheritance in land (also refers to the fee name or well name).

Field—An area consisting of a single reservoir or multiple reservoirs all grouped on, or related to the same geological structural feature and/or stratigraphic condition.

Field well—Well within the boundaries of a field (as opposed to a wildcat).

Fish—(Noun) Any object left in a well during drilling operations which must be removed before further operations are resumed. (Verb) To try to remove such an object.

Flowing well—A well which produces oil or gas without any means of artificial lift.

Formation—A bed or deposit composed throughout of substantially the same kinds of rocks; a lithological unit.

Formation top—The upper limit of bed or formation.

Gas

 Dry gas—Natural gas comprised primarily of light hydrocarbon vapors.

 Wet gas—Gas that carries lots of liquids with it.

 Sour gas—Gas containing hydrogen sulfide.

 Sweet gas—Gas containing little or no hydrogen sulfide.

Gas/oil contact—The point or plane in a reservoir at which the bottom of a gas sand is in contact with the top of an oil sand.

Gas-oil ratio—The number of cubic feet of gas produced with each barrel of oil.

Gas sand—A stratum of sand or porous sandstone from which natural gas is obtained.

Gusher—An oil well that has come in with such force that the oil jets out of the well like a geyser. In reality, a gusher is a blowout and extremely wasteful and dangerous.

Horizon—The geological deposit of a particular time usually identified by distinctive fossils; formation.

Hydrocarbons—Organic compounds consisting of hydrogen and carbon.

Impermeable—(Adj.) Preventing the passage of fluids. A formation may be porous yet impermeable if there is an absence of connecting passages between the voids within it.

Isopach map—A geological map of subsurface strata showing various thicknesses of certain formations or intervals covering more than one formation.

Junk—Metal debris lost in the hole.

Junk and abandon—To abandon hole because of mechanical problems (as opposed to "dry and abandoned").

Location—The place at which a well is to be or has been drilled.

Lithology—Study of rocks (to indicate type of rock).

Make a trip (tripping)—To hoist the drill stem out of the wellbore (to change bit, run a log, take a core) then return the drill stem to the wellbore.

Mud log—A record of information derived from the examination of drilling fluid and drillbit cuttings.

New pay—Refers to a new formation different from that which is already productive in the field.

Offset well—A well drilled in the next contiguous unit from an existing well.

Oil sand—A sandstone that yields oil (sometimes meaning a reservoir that yields oil whether sandstone or not).

Oil shale—A formation containing hydrocarbons that cannot be recovered by ordinary methods, but may be mined.

Open hole—Any wellbore in which casing has not been set.

Operator—Individual or company, either proprietor or lessee, operating the well or lease.

Outcrop—The exposed portion of a buried layer of rock.

Outpost—A well drilled a distance away from an existing field, producing from the same formation, by which the field is extended.

Pay sand—The productive formation (called pay, pay zone, producing zone).

Perforate—To pierce the casing wall and cement to provide holes through which the formation fluids may enter the wellbore.

Permeability—A measure of the ease with which fluids can flow through a porous rock.

PH value—(written pH) A measure of the acid or alkaline condition of a substance.

Plug and abandon—To place cement plugs into a dry hole and leave it.

Plug back—To place cement in or near the bottom of a well to exclude bottom water, to sidetrack, or produce from a formation already drilled through.

Porosity—A measure of pore space relative to mass.

Reserves—The unproduced but recoverable oil or gas in place in a formation (which has been proved by production).

Reservoir—A subsurface porous, permeable rock body in which oil or gas or both occur. Most reservoir rocks are limestones, dolomites, sandstones, or a combination of these.

Rig—The derrick, drawworks, and attendant surface equipment of a drilling or workover unit.

Rig down—To dismantle the rig and equipment.

Rig up—To prepare the drilling rig for making hole.

Run pipe—To lower a string of casing into the hole.

Scout—The representative of an oil company who gathers any data on industry development, new wells, etc.

Shot point—The place at which a charge is exploded (or vibrations otherwise produced) to create sound waves to be recorded for seismic surveys.

Show—The appearance of oil or gas in cuttings, samples, or cores, etc. from a drilling well.

Shut in—To close the valves on a well so that it stops producing. Also to close in a well in which a kick has occurred.

Sidewall cores—Samples which are collected by a coring technique especially useful in soft rock areas, a zone already drilled. Different from "diamond core" in that these are usually shot through the casing with a "bullet."

Spud—To begin drilling.

Strata—Distinct, usually parallel beds of rock. An individual bed is a "stratum."

Stripper—A well nearing depletion that produces a very small amount of oil or gas.

Subsea—Depth below sea level.

Subsurface—Below the surface of the earth.

Swab—(Noun) A hollow rubberfaced cylinder mounted on a mandrel on the upper end of a wireline. It is run into the hole to try to start the fluid flowing. If it does not get the flow started a pump is put on. (Verb) To run the swab. (Oil field jargon) To try to find out all the information you can, especially if you are not entitled to know it.

Tight formation—A petroleum- or water-bearing formation of relatively low porosity and permeability.

Tight hole—(Noun) A well about which information is restricted and passed only to those authorized for security and competitive reasons. (Verb) To withhold information from another.

Tops—The upper limit of a formation identified by logs—the log depth at this point (pick).

Trip—To pull or run a string of tubing from or into a well.

Twin—A well drilled on the same location as another well and closely offsetting it (maybe to produce from another zone).

Viscosity—A measure of the thickness of liquid or of how easily it will pour.

Wildcat—A well drilled in an area where no oil or gas production exists.

Workover—To perform one or more operations to try to increase production (examples: deepening, plugging back, resetting liner, etc.).

Zone—As applied to reservoirs, used to describe an interval which has one or more distinguishing characteristics, such as lithology, porosity, saturation, etc.

COMMONLY USED ABBREVIATIONS

abn, abnd	abandon, abandoned
ac	acre
acc.	accretions
APO	after payout
avg	average
bbl, bbls.	barrels
BCF	billion cubic feet
BFPD	barrels fluid per day
BHL	bottom hole location
BHP	bottom hole pressure
BO	barrels oil
BOP	blow-out preventer
BOPD	barrels oil per day
BPH	barrels per hour
BPO	before pay out
BSW	barrels salt water
BWPD	barrels water per day
CFGPD	cubic feet gas per day
chk	choke
circ	circulate
comp	complete, completion
CP	casing pressure, casing point
D & A	dry and abandoned
DC	drill collar
DF, df	derrick floor
dolo	dolomite
DP	drill pipe
drlg	drilling
DST	drill stem test
DTD	driller's total depth
E log	electric log
elev, el.	elevation
est	estimated
FARO	flowed at rate of
FP	flowing pressure
GIH	going in hole
GL	ground level
GOR	gas-oil ratio
inj	injection
IP	initial potential, initial production
J & A	junked and abandoned
KB	kelly bushing
lm	limestone
loc	location
lse	lease
LTD	logger's total depth
MCF, mcf*	thousand cubic feet
MI, MIR	moving in, moving in rig
MMCF, mmcf*	million cubic feet
NS	no show
O & G	oil & gas
O & SW	oil and salt water
OH	open hole, original hole
O/W	oil/water contact
OWDD	old well drilled deeper
OWWO	old well worked over
P & A	plugged and abandoned
PB, PBTD	plug back, plug back total depth
perf	perforation, perforated
perm	permeability
pkr	packer
POOH	pulled out of hole
por	porosity
proj	projected
prop loc	proposed location
psi	per square inch
rec	recovered
RU	rigging up, rigged up
sd	sand
sec	section
seis	seismic, seismograph
SG, SO	show of gas, show of oil
sh	shale
SI	shut in
s.p.	shot point
SSO	slight show of oil
STH	sidetrack hole
sur	survey
SW, sw**	salt water
SWC**	sidewall core
SWDW	salt water disposal well
SWS	sidewall samples
sx	sacks
T/	top of
TD	total depth
TP	tubing pressure
tstd, tstg	tested, testing
TVD	true vertical depth
twp	township
vis	viscosity
WC	wildcat
WO	workover, or waiting on
WOC	waiting on cement
WOO	waiting on orders
YP	yield point

---

* "M" is Roman numeral for one thousand. (One thousand thousand equals one million.)

**See "Directions" at end of abbreviation list.

Directions

C SW	center of the southwest quarter
C NE	center of the northeast quarter
C NL	center of the north line
FSL, FNL, FEL, FWL	from the south line, from the north line, etc.
SNL, WEL, etc.	south of the north line, west of the east line, etc.
NE/4, NW/4, etc.	northeast quarter, northwest quarter, etc.
NE cor, NW cor, etc.	northeast corner, northwest corner, etc.
N/2, S/2, etc.	north half, south half, etc.
NE/ly, S/ly	northeasterly, southerly, etc.
@ ra	at a right angle
alg	along (as in "along line")

Locations

When used in series, these abbreviations direct one to specific portions of sections. Examples:

SW NE	southwest quarter of northeast quarter
SW NE NW	southwest quarter of northeast quarter of northwest quarter
NE NW SE	northeast quarter of northwest quarter of southeast quarter
S/2 NE SW	south half of northeast quarter of southwest quarter

3
Maps and Surveys

The information herein is not meant as a course in cartography, but an understanding of certain fundamentals of mapmaking is essential if the reader is to get any benefit from this book.

HISTORY

The earliest maps were probably made about 4,000 years ago in Babylonia. Later the Egyptians made maps showing boundaries of property for taxing. The Romans were accurate surveyors who built almost perfectly straight roads between their cities, and they kept careful records. The Moslems made maps so that they would know what direction to face when they prayed toward the holy city of Mecca, and also to plan their trade journeys. World maps were begun in the fifteenth century when Prince Henry the Navigator, ruler of Portugal, set up a school for sea captains and gathered all available maps. Soon European sailors were discovering distant lands around the world.

It is impossible to show accurately a spherical surface on a flat map so there are many distortions on flat maps. Over the years a number of different methods have been developed to try to overcome most of these. There are different kinds of map projections: Mercator, Conic, Polyconic, Lambert's Conformal, and others. As an example, Mercator's projection is based on a cylinder with all the meridians and parallels as straight lines, and the scale is true only at the equator. It is valuable for navigators even today. Conic projections are made as if a cone were placed over the globe. On Mercator's maps parallels are straight lines; with conic projections they appear as curved lines. Lambert's maps are often used for military purposes and are the basis of U.S. aeronautical charts. This kind of map is very accurate over small areas. Regardless of the method of constructing a particular map, certain features are the same, and these are the ones we deal with every day.

LATITUDE AND LONGITUDE

Because the earth is a sphere, it has no beginning, no end and no edge. There are two reference points—the poles (Figure 3-1).

Lines of longitude are lines drawn through the poles north and south, and are called *meridians* (Figure 3-2A). They measure distance east and west of the *prime meridian* which was established near Greenwich, England. This line is universally accepted as the 0° line. Longitude measures 0° to 180° east and 0° to 180° west from the Greenwich Meridian. This is why we may refer to the "Eastern Hemisphere" and "Western Hemisphere." On the other side of the earth, 180°, we have the international date line.

Lines of latitude are lines drawn around the earth parallel to the Equator (Figure 3-2B). They are called *parallels* and measure the distance north and south of the equator. They are equally spaced in degrees, not miles. One degree of latitude equals about seventy miles. Most globes show only parallels and meridians at 15° intervals. Since the earth is flattened at the poles there is a small difference in the length of one degree.

Because a circle has 360° and a half circle 180°, from the equator to each of the poles is 90°. Latitude measures 0° to 90° north, from the equator to the North Pole; and

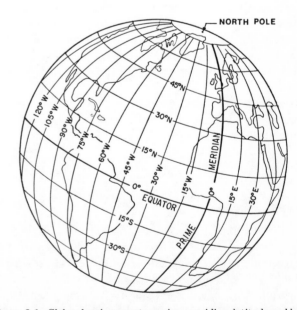

Figure 3-1. Globe showing equator, prime meridian, latitude and longitude.

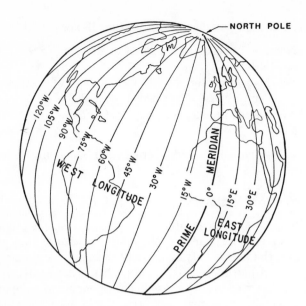

Figure 3-2. (A) Longitude. Lines of longitude measure degrees east and west of the prime meridian. (B) Latitude. Lines of latitude measure 0°– 90° north and south of the equator.

0° to 90° south, from the equator to the South Pole (Figure 3-2B).

A point on the earth's surface passes through a whole circle (360°) once every twenty-four hours. Thus all 360° of the circumference of the earth pass beneath the sun once. In one hour 1/24th of 360°, or 15°, has passed beneath the sun. One hour of time equals 15° of longitude.

Each degree of longitude is divided into sixty parts called minutes, and one minute is written (1′). Each minute is divided into 60 seconds, and one second is written (1″). (Note that these symbols are the same as we use for feet and inches.) These minutes and seconds of longitude are units of distance, not of time. But because an hour of time equals 15° on longitude, a minute or second of time equals a certain distance which can be expressed in minutes and seconds of longitude.

A quadrangle is any portion of the earth's surface bounded by the same number of degrees (or portions of degrees) such as 30° × 30°, 15° × 15°, 15′ × 15′, etc.

SURVEY SYSTEMS IN THE UNITED STATES

Colonial Survey

In 1784 Congress appointed a committee with Thomas Jefferson as chairman to decide how to go about disposing of public lands. A year or so and many reports later a survey system was adopted for most of the eastern seaboard and was called the *Colonial Survey*. It called for rectangular units six statute miles square (*statute* meaning derived by law) to be called *townships*. The interior

lots making up the township were irregular in size and shape, usually stemming from original land grants where parcels were described according to the natural condition of the land. A system in which each parcel of land is described independently is known as *metes and bounds*.

Rectangular Survey

Considerable problems arose in land identification under this Colonial system. In 1785 Congress passed the National Land Act which established the *Rectangular Survey System* and provided that all public lands must be surveyed according to the new system before they could be sold. This system used artificial boundaries based on lines of the compass rather than natural ones.

From a starting point a line is run due north to the northern boundary of the state, district or territory to be surveyed. This north-south line is called the *principal meridian*. There is also an east-west line called the *base line* running at a right angle to the meridian. Once the meridian and base line are established for a survey, then north-south lines are run parallel to the principal meridian six miles apart. The same is done with east-west lines parallel to the base line every six miles (See Figure 3-3).

Township and Range

These lines mark blocks six miles square and are the *townships*. The first tier of townships immediately north and south of the base line are called "Township One North" and "Township One South" respectively. The

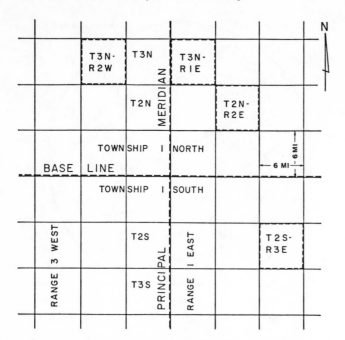

Figure 3-3. The basis for the Rectangular Survey System is a township of six miles square, beginning with a base line and principal meridian.

tiers of townships are then successively numbered as One North, Two North, Three North, etc., and One South, Two South, Three South, etc. The strips of townships lying east and west of the principal meridian are called *ranges*, "Range One East" and "Range One West," and numbered progressively in this manner. Using this system it is customary to always call township first, then range. Example: "Township 5 North, Range 3 East" or "T5N-R3E." To call it "5N-3E" is sufficient; to call it "5-3" is *not* (Figure 3-3).

By naming and numbering principal meridians, fixing base lines, and numbering townships and sections, any tract in the United States can be distinguished from every other tract. Surveying has not been continuous so there are duplications in numbering. Therefore it is necessary to know the name of the survey or of the county.

Standard Sections

After establishment of these townships it was necessary to subdivide them into sections; 36 one-mile square sections, each containing 640 acres. Sections are numbered beginning in the northeast corner (top right) across to the northwest corner (top left), then the numbering drops and runs west to east, then drops and runs east to west, as pictured in Figure 3-4A.

Each section is further divided into quarters and quarter quarters. The quarters are called by location, i.e., northeast quarter (NE/4), northwest quarter (NW/4), etc., as shown in Figure 3-4B.

The shaded portions of this section 13 are called:

A. Northeast quarter of northeast quarter, or NE/4 NE/4, or NE NE.
B. Southwest quarter of southwest quarter of northwest quarter, or SW/4 SW/4 NW/4, or SW SW NW.
C. Northwest quarter of southeast quarter, or NW/4 SE/4, or NW SE.

In this manner individual tracts can be readily identified.

Correction Sections

Because of the curvature of the earth's surface, lines extending to the poles become closer together as they approach the poles. This makes all townships narrower at the north line than at the south, about three rods narrower. In order to keep these lines as near six miles apart as possible, there are correction lines every 24 miles north of the base line and new guide meridians every 24 miles from the principal.

As this is the case, not all sections can contain exactly 640 acres, so provision was made for *correction sections* on the north and west sides of the townships. Fractional sections (correction sections) are sections 1 to 6 on the north side, and sections 7, 18, 19, 30, and 31 along the west side of the township. See shaded area in Figure 3-4A.

Subdivision of Sections

Figure 3-5 shows how sections are further subdivided from quarters. In the case of the correction sections they are subdivided much the same way except that the differences in acreage are adjusted within the north half of the north half for sections 1–6, and within the west half of the west half for the sections on the western side of the township. See Figures 3-6, 3-7, and 3-8. Notice that section 6 must be adjusted on both sides.

Sometimes sections are divided and given lot numbers which correspond to the quarter quarters. Figure 3-9 shows the typical lot numbers for a standard section. For correction sections lot numbers are assigned as shown in Figure 3-10A. For lot numbers in an irregular survey, such as that bordering on a body of water, the lot numbers vary from one survey to the next. They are consistent only within the particular survey. (See Figure 3-10B.)

Exceptions

Within the rectangular survey system some irregular tracts of land are still described by metes and bounds. In some states like California, Texas, and Louisiana, much of the land had already been divided into land grants and

(text continued on page 27)

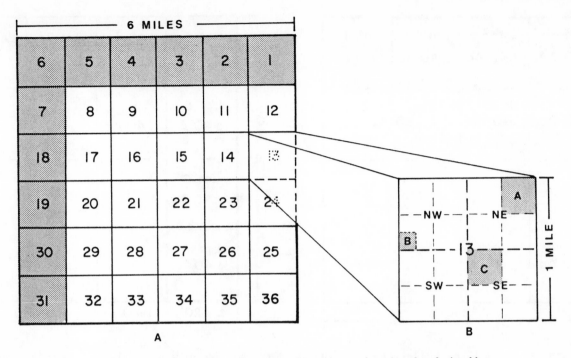

Figure 3-4. Each township is divided into 36 sections and numbered as depicted here.

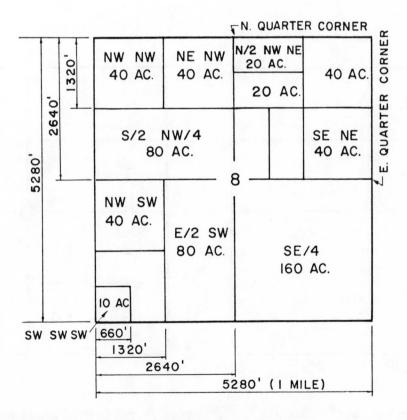

Figure 3-5. A standard section has 640 acres and is further divided into quarters and divisions of those quarters.

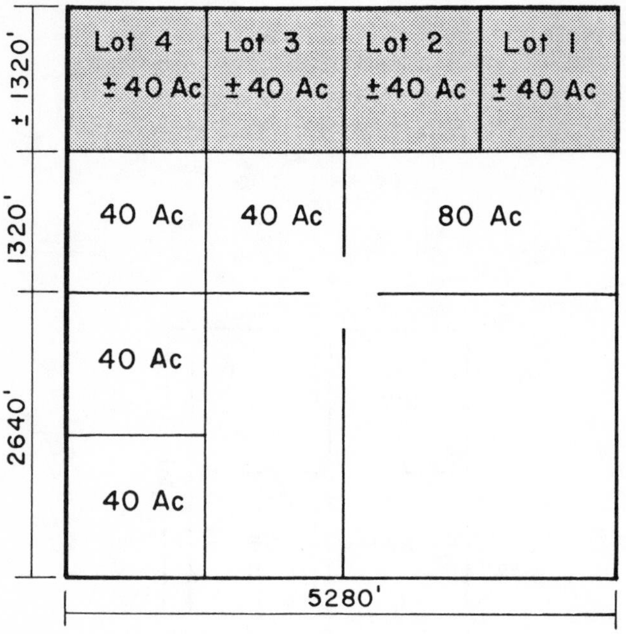

Figure 3-6. Correction sections 1–5 are adjusted in the north half of the north half.

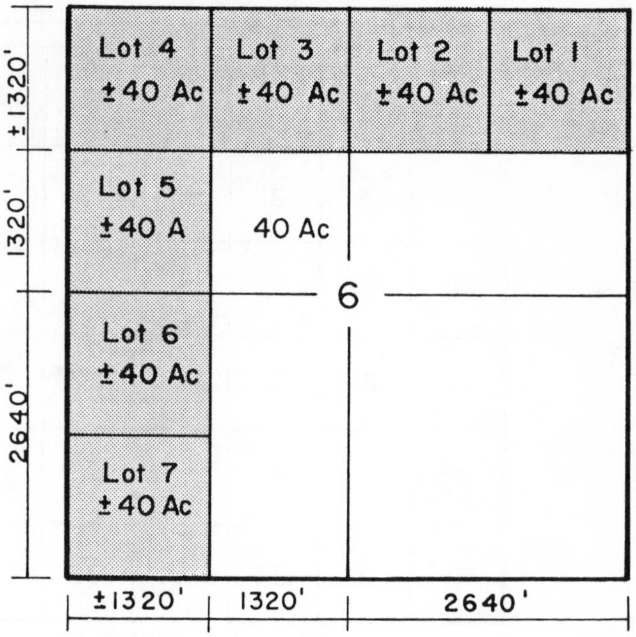

Figure 3-7. Section 6 is adjusted along both the north and west sides.

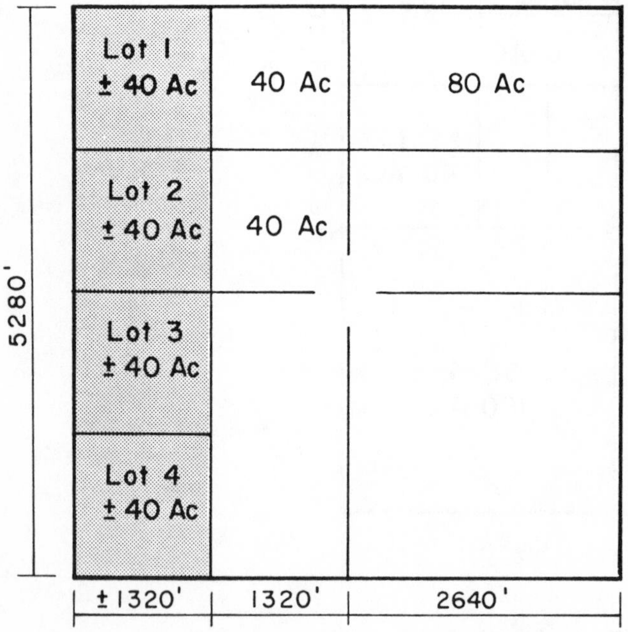

Figure 3-8. Sections along the west side of the township are adjusted along the west side. These are sections 7, 18, 19, 30, and 31.

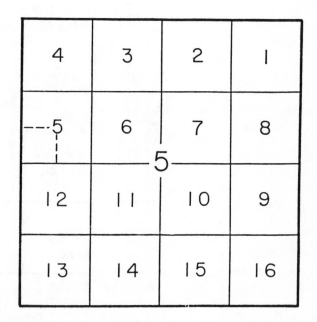

Figure 3-9. This is a typical way to number lots in a standard section.

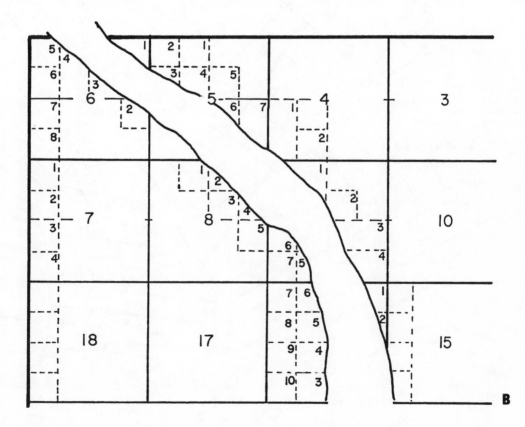

Figure 3-10. (A) Lot numbers for correction sections are indicated above. Acreage adjustments are made within northern and western lots. (B) Lot numbers for irregular surveys may vary widely.

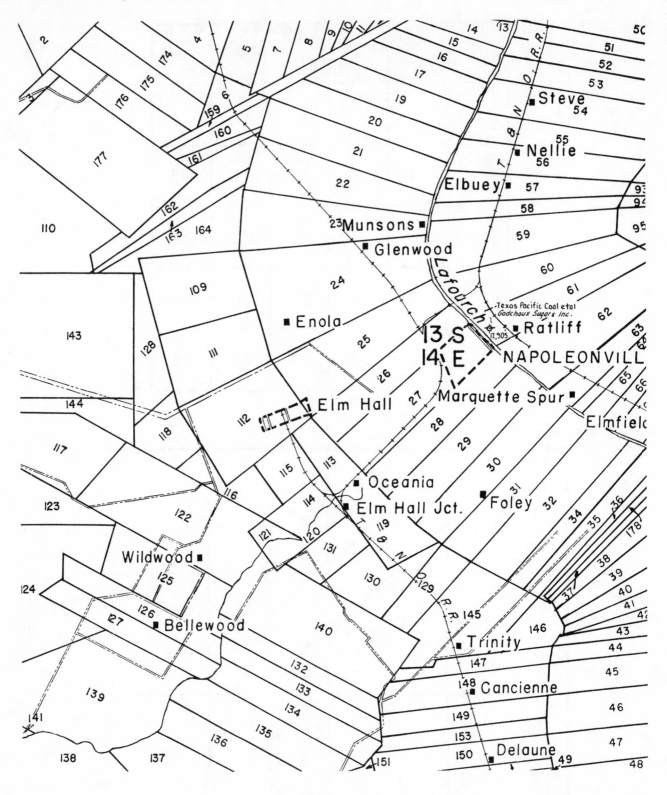

Figure 3-11. Louisiana recognizes township and range but many sections are irregular in size and shape. (Courtesy of Tobin Research.)

named accordingly by the Spanish government prior to 1850. Some of the descriptions are tied into the survey markers established under the rectangular system (Figure 3-11). In most of Texas, however, there are no townships and ranges at all. These tracts are identified by survey names and abstract numbers (Figure 3-12). It is difficult to find individual tracts on a Texas map unless you have a pretty good idea where within the county it might be located.

A few other states have different systems also. The U.S. Military Tract in central Ohio is subdivided into townships of five miles square instead of six. Georgia has military districts and a portion of Kentucky was subdivided into townships by a state survey. (See Figure 3-13.)

Offshore Surveys

Ownership of submerged lands has been contested for many years. Generally, states can claim about three geo-graphical miles from the coast line for states bordering the Atlantic and Pacific Oceans and along the Gulf of Mexico. Louisiana and Texas are exceptions and are allowed to claim nine miles.

The Bureau of Land Management has prepared leasing maps for the Outer Continental Shelf. (See Figure 3-14.) The Texas (Lambert) Plane Coordinate System is used for offshore Texas; The Louisiana Plane Coordinate System is used for offshore Louisiana. The Universal Transverse Mercator Grid System is used for the remainder of Louisiana and OCS lands of Mississippi, Alabama, and Florida.

For these offshore leasing maps, the areas are named and numbered, then further subdivided into numbered blocks of three miles square (15,840 feet square) and contain 5,760 acres. Some earlier surveys contained blocks of only 5,000 acres. Smaller blocks within the three-mile limit contain 640 acres and are handled by the respective states. A typical leasing map from the BLM is shown in Figure 3-15.

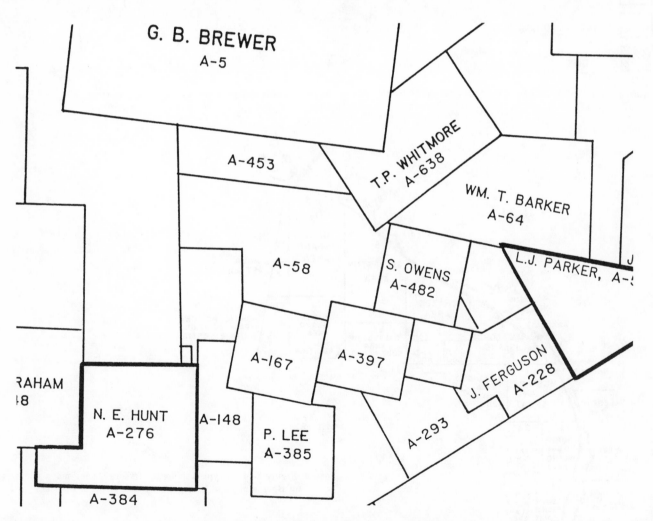

Figure 3-12. Texas surveys and abstracts are sometimes difficult to locate.

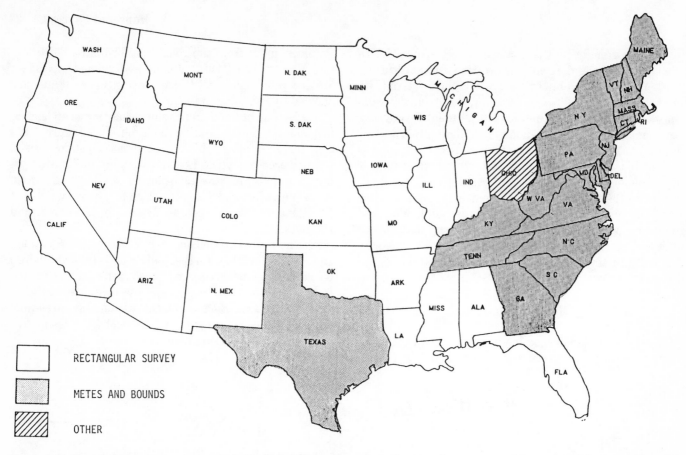

Figure 3-13. Two distinct survey systems exist in the United States: the system of rectangular surveys, and the system of "metes and bounds."

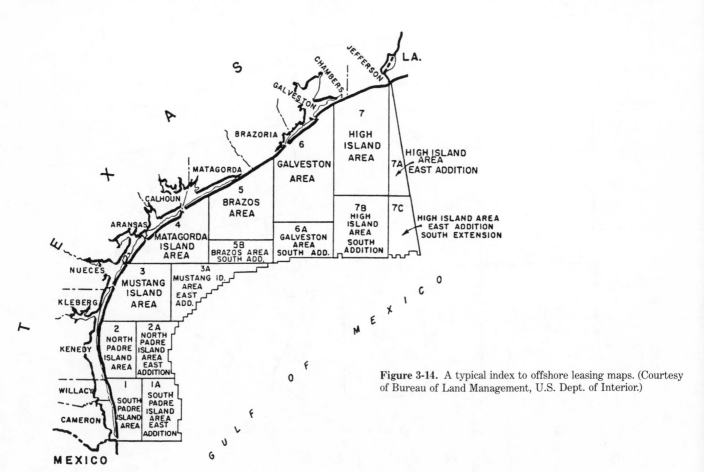

Figure 3-14. A typical index to offshore leasing maps. (Courtesy of Bureau of Land Management, U.S. Dept. of Interior.)

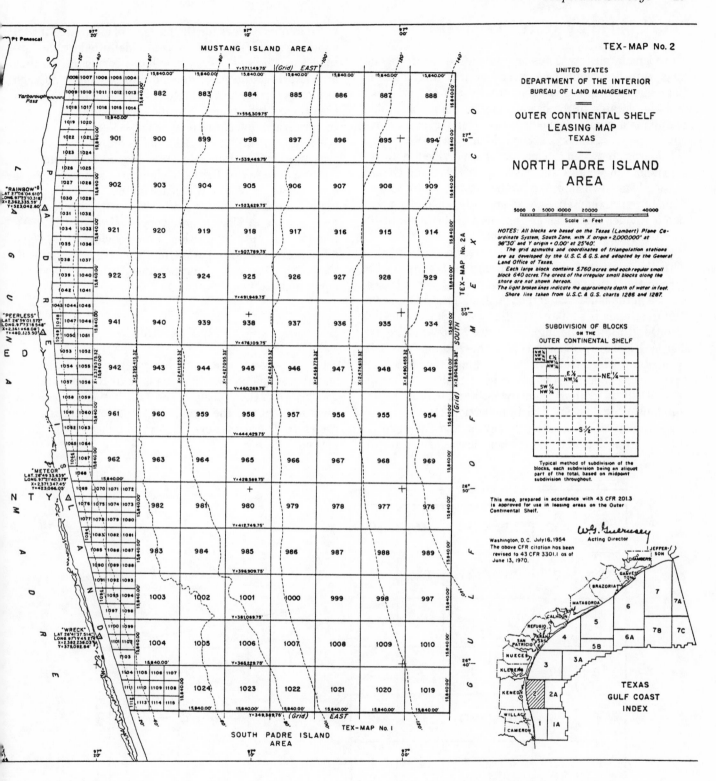

Figure 3-15. Typical offshore leasing map. (Courtesy of Bureau of Land Management, U.S. Dept. of Interior.)

SURVEY SYSTEM IN CANADA

In Canada all townships are numbered north, beginning with Township One North at the International Boundary. All ranges are east and west of one principal meridian located in the eastern part of Manitoba. Guide meridians are spaced about 30 townships apart and are numbered 1st, 2nd, 3rd, etc. meridians west.

The areas between the meridians are divided by township and range lines six miles apart, like the United States. The townships are further divided into 36 sections of approximately one square mile each. Each section is divided into quarter sections and further into 40-acre units called *Legal Subdivisions*.

The sections are numbered 1 through 36 beginning with the southeast corner, then west to the southwest corner, then up and back to the east and so forth to section 36 in the northeast corner. Although the survey system in Canada is similar to that of the U.S. note the difference in the numbering sequence as shown in Figure 3-16A. Figure 3-16B shows how the sections are subdivided into "legal subdivisions" and how they are numbered. The shaded portion of the section pictured in Figure 3-16B is called "southwest quarter of Legal Subdivision 12," or SW Lsd 12 of section 24.

In the federal lands of the Northwest and Yukon Territories, Arctic Islands, and offshore areas, lands are divided into grid areas for the purpose of administering oil and gas rights. The grid areas are identified by the latitude and longitude of the northeast corner of the grid area. Each grid area is divided into sections, and each section is further divided into sixteen units. In a certain area the grid is divided into 100 sections; in other areas the grids are divided into 80 or 60 sections.

A large part of British Columbia is unsurveyed, so this area was divided into grid areas by the Petroleum and Natural Gas Act of British Columbia. Each grid area is divided into six blocks, which are further divided into 100 units. The size of the grid area varies with its location. For example, a block might vary in size from 21,000+ acres in the southern portion of the province, to 16,000+ acres in the northern part. Units vary from 212 acres at the south boundary of the province to 160 acres at the north boundary.

MAP SCALES

For obvious reasons maps have to be smaller than the actual area mapped so that requires us to use a ratio or proportion to the real area. The ratio between the actual measurement and the comparison measurement is called the *scale*. There are several ways to indicate what scale is used.

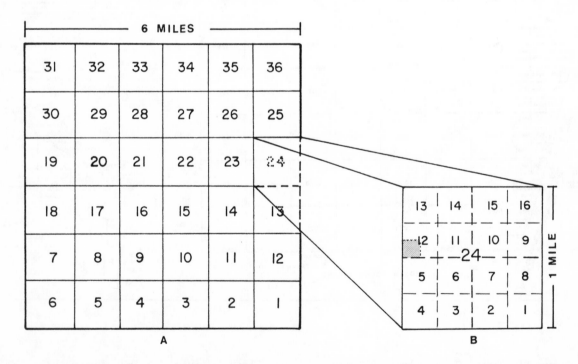

Figure 3-16. (A) A township in Canada has 36 sections, but they are numbered in a different manner than U.S. townships. (B) Canadian sections are divided into legal subdivisions instead of quarter quarters.

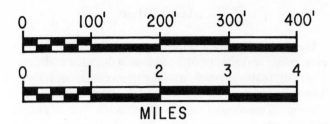

Figure 3-17. Graphic scales.

Representative fraction or proportion: 1/100 or 1:100 means that along particular lines, 1 inch = 100 inches, or 1 foot = 100 feet, or 1 mile = 100 miles, etc. It is independent of the unit of measure employed. If the denominator is larger, the scale is smaller: i.e., 1/1000 is smaller scale than 1/100.

Graphic scale: Sometimes called a *bar scale*. It is a line drawn on a map and subdivided to show different distances on that map. One end of the bar scale is usually further divided to make measuring more accurate. (See Figure 3-17.)

Some scales are stated on the map, such as: 1″ = 1,000′, or 1″ = 1 mile, etc. These scales are readily understood by most readers. However, this kind of scale presents problems if the map is reduced or enlarged.

All maps or portions of maps should show the scale. There are several scales which are common to maps used in the oil business. Although the scales listed here are not all the scales you will encounter nor will they always be used for the purpose mentioned, these scales are very common in the industry.

1″ = 4000′	regional maps, example: Tobin quads
1″ = 8000′	regional maps which cover large areas
1″ = 1 mile	some commercial maps, example: GCS bases
1″ = 2000′	prospect maps, field maps
1″ = 3000′	commercial ownership maps, lease maps
1″ = 1000′	detailed land maps, some field study maps

UNITS OF MEASURE

In working with maps it is essential to remember certain equivalent measurements and areas. The following list covers a few of these which are important to the understanding of petroleum maps.

1 mile = 5280 feet = 80 chains = 320 rods
1 square mile = 640 acres
1 rod = 16.5 feet (1 pole)
1 chain = 4 rods = 66 feet = 100 links
1 acre = 43,560 square feet
1 acre (square) = 208.71 feet square
Township (standard) = 6 miles square or 36 sections
Section (standard) = 1 square mile = 640 acres
1 nautical mile = 6080.2 feet
1 arpent = 191.83 feet
1 vara = 33⅓ inches = 2.777 feet
1 meter = 3.2808 feet
1 kilometer = 3280.83 feet = .62 mile

KINDS OF MAPS

There are many different kinds of maps, each of which serves a particular purpose. The maps included in this section are those we are most likely to need in the oil industry. We do not have to be cartographers at this time in history; that work has been done for us, in most parts of the world anyway. We have government agencies and commercial map companies to compile the information necessary to construct all kinds of maps. Some examples of relevant maps follow:

Planimetric Maps

Planimetric maps (Figure 3-18) are surveyed maps which show physical features such as rivers, lakes, forested areas and swamps, man-made formations such as roads, towns, etc., but without any representation of relief. These maps indicate survey corners and township, range and section where applicable.

Topographic Maps

Planimetric maps to which relief representation has been added are called topographic maps (Figure 3-19). Relief is shown by contour lines with elevations relative to sea level. The U.S. Geological Survey has been making "topo" maps of the entire United States and a few other places for many years.

Under the plan the Survey adopted, the unit of survey is a quadrangle bounded by parallels of latitude and meridians of longitude. Quadrangles covering 7½ minutes of latitude and longitude are published at the scale of 1 inch = 2,000 feet. The 15 minute quadrangles are published at the scale of 1:62,500 or 1 inch = approximately 1 mile. Each quad is designated by the name of a city or prominent natural feature within it. The Survey furnishes at no charge an index map of each state, and individual quadrangle maps may be ordered from the U.S.G.S. for a nominal fee.

Cadastral Maps

Cadastral maps show property and political boundaries, roads and shapes of buildings in detail in addition to physical features such as lakes, streams, and rivers. They may or may not indicate such features as woods or swamps. These maps may be obtained from local governmental sources, usually by individual counties.

Outline Maps

Outline maps show only the basic configuration of an area, with features such as a coast line, and maybe state or county boundaries indicated in simple outline form. Some may include lakes and major rivers or streams. These are usually small-scale maps which cover large areas and have a limited use. (See Figure 3-20.)

Base Maps

Base maps are merely "basic" maps upon which special data can be plotted. A good base map should include all reference information necessary for the reader to be able to describe any point on it, i.e., county lines, township and range lines with designations, and if applicable, section numbers, etc. These are the kinds of maps we most frequently work with in the oil industry. There are many commercial map companies from which these may be obtained.

Geological Base Maps

Geological base maps (Figure 3-21) are base maps on which well locations have been spotted and certain pertinent data included. These maps may be ordered commercially, or built from available data such as scout tickets, well information reports, etc. The usual practice is to order a reproducible base map from a map company and keep it up to date from company resources. Some companies solve the updating problem by subscribing to a service which provides new monthly or quarterly prints with all new well information added. The data furnished usually includes operator, well name and number, permit number, and total depth of each well.

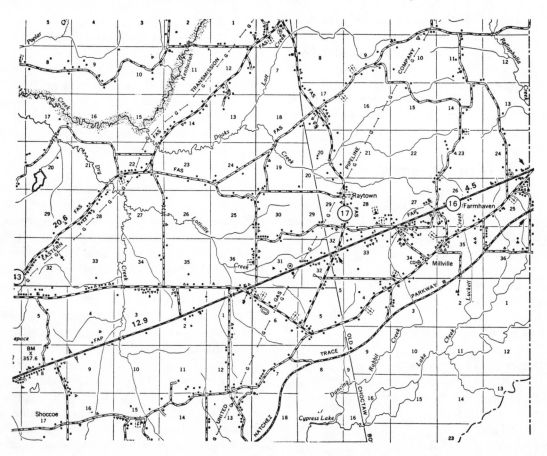

Figure 3-18. Planimetric map. (Courtesy of Mississippi State Highway Dept.)

Figure 3-19. Topographic map. Topo maps of the entire United States are available from the U.S.G.S. (Courtesy of U.S. Geological Survey.)

Seismic Base Maps

A seismic base map (Figure 3-22) usually differs from a geological base map in one way only. In addition to well locations it has locations of seismic lines, line numbers, and shot point numbers. Sometimes seismic base maps are little more than a few section corners or block corners spotted on a blank map with seismic lines and shot point numbers plotted on it.

Land Base Maps

A company land base map might be prepared from a blank base map with tracts outlined such as the one shown in Figure 3-23. This is usually made from a commercial base map but without all the excess information. Specific lease information, dates, net acres, etc. can be added as required.

Land maps will be covered in detail in Chapter 6.

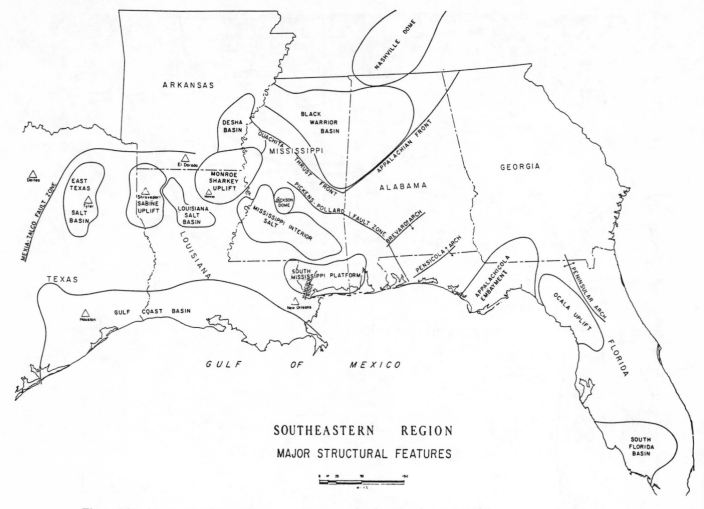

SOUTHEASTERN REGION
MAJOR STRUCTURAL FEATURES

Figure 3-20. An example of an outline map is this one used to locate major structural features in the southeast.

Ownership and Lease Maps

These ownership maps are sometimes called *land maps* (Figure 3-24). General ownership and lease information is indicated on commercial maps. They are updated at certain intervals and available usually on a subscription basis.

Contour Maps

Contours are lines that connect points of equal value. A contour map (Figures 3-25 and 3-26) is one way to portray a three-dimensional form on a two-dimensional exhibit. The third dimension, for example the height and shape of a hill, is shown by the contour values. Various types of data can be contoured: topography, geologic structure, thickness of a rock interval, and seismic times, to name a few.

Contour maps are invaluable to the petroleum explorationist in expressing geologic ideas and concepts where three-dimensional visualization is necessary.

Structural Contour Maps

Structural contour maps (Figure 3-25) depict the shape of a particular subsurface (below the surface of the ground) stratum or horizon. To be meaningful the contours must be related to a common datum—usually mean sea level (MSL). Contour values are expressed in feet or meters above or below the common datum. Seismic structure maps are contoured in *time* which can be converted to depth.

Isopach Maps

Isopach contours (Figure 3-26) are lines of equal thickness. The petroleum geologist constructs isopach or thickness maps of various data including stratigraphic intervals, thickness of oil or gas "pays," and seismic time intervals. Seismic isopach maps are usually called *isotime* or *isochron* maps.

Note: More on the various types of geologic contour maps is covered in Chapter 4.

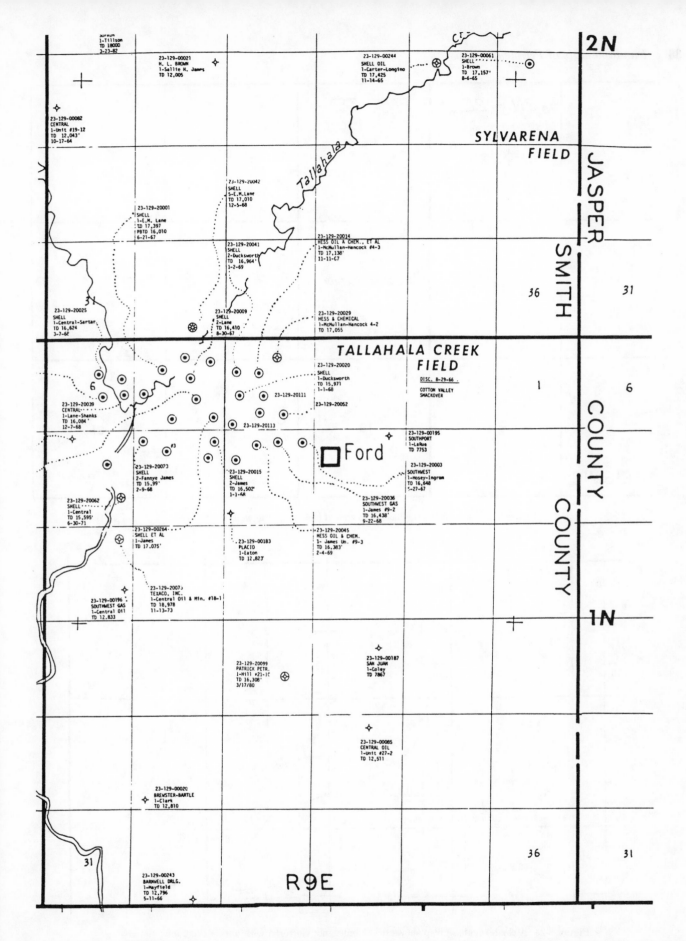

Figure 3-21. A good geological base usually includes well names and pertinent information and may be used as the basis for contoured maps. Pictured here is a portion of a commercial geological base map. (Courtesy of Geological Consulting Services.)

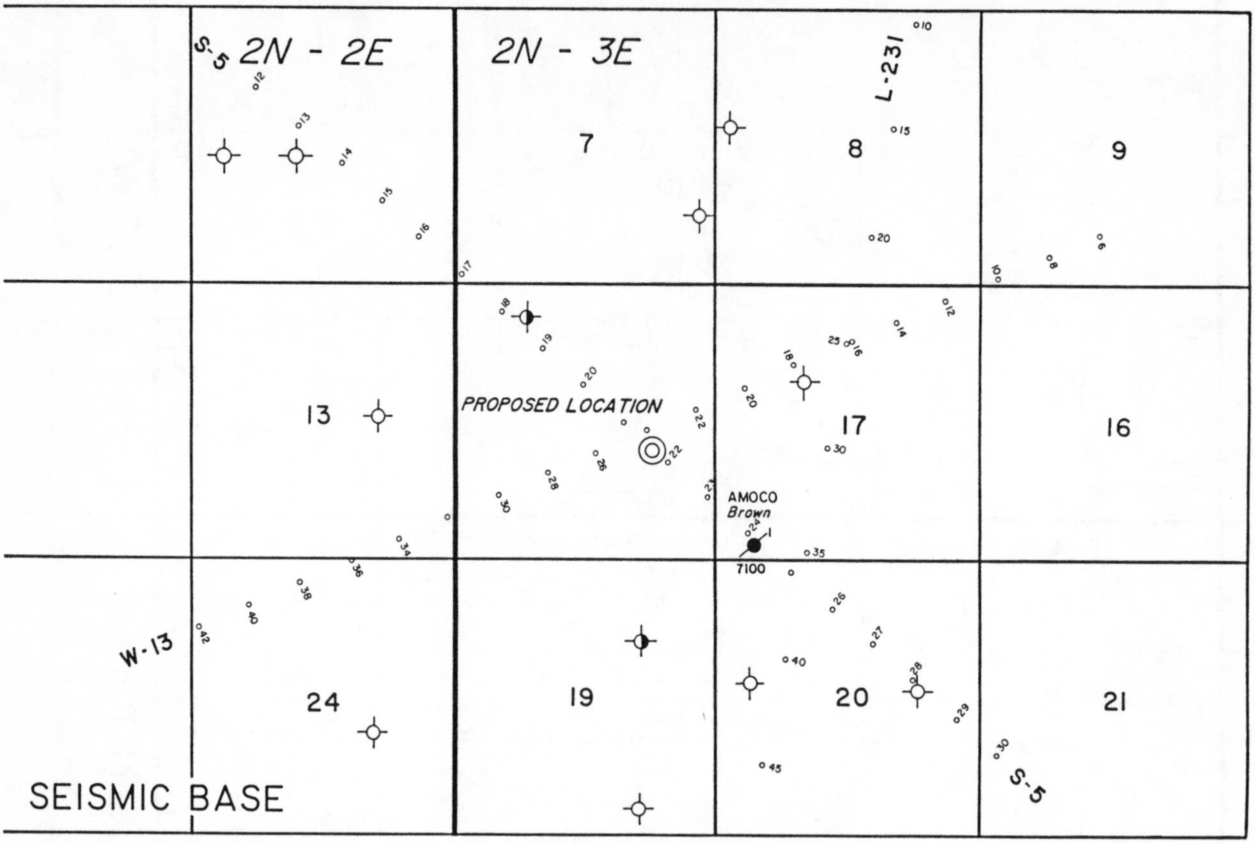

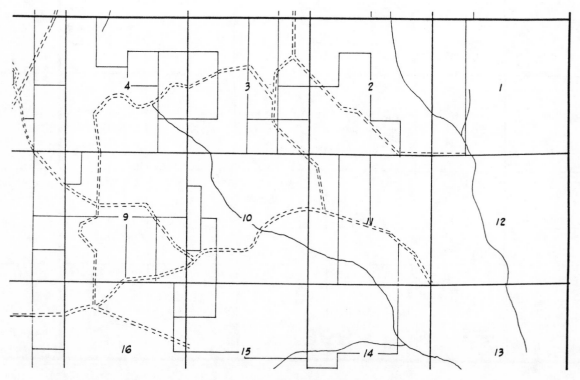

Figure 3-22. A good seismic base map should include all the wells in the area.

Figure 3-23. A clean land base map shows tracts but is not cluttered with unnecessary information.

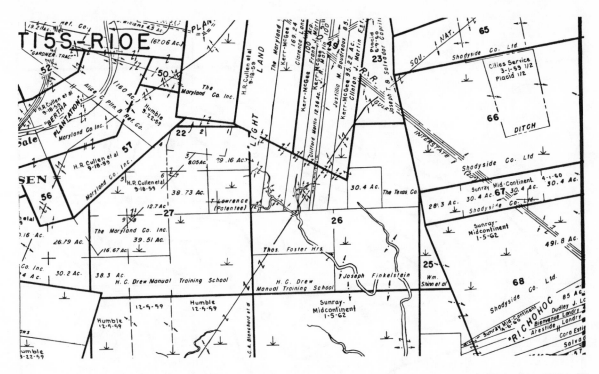

Figure 3-24. Ownership and lease map. General lease information is shown on commercial maps like this one. (Courtesy of Tobin Map Co.)

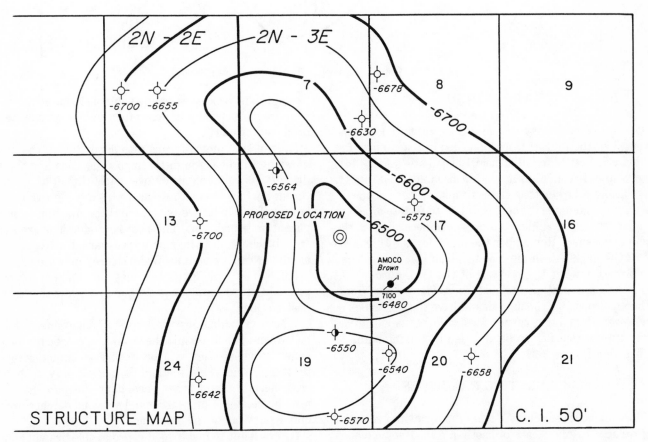

Figure 3-25. The contours of a structural contour map shows the shape of a particular "horizon" as related to mean sea level.

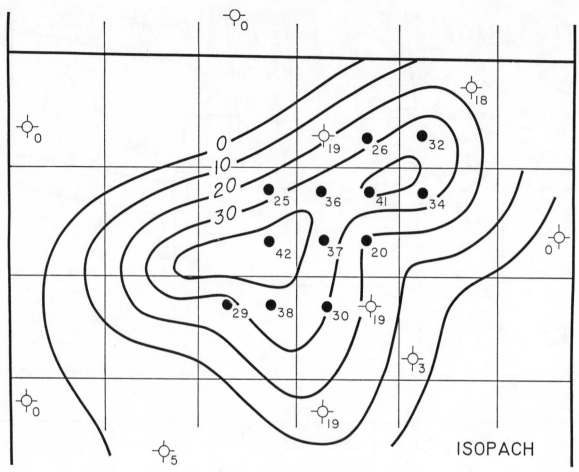

Figure 3-26. Isopach maps depict thickness of a given interval.

MAP FOLDING

When it is necessary to fold a map, first find out the purpose of the fold. If it is to be filed in a legal size file folder, it is best to fold it as near to legal size (8½″ × 14″) as possible. If your files are letter size fold it 8½″ × 11″. Do not fold it larger than those standard sizes because it may cover the name of the file. If it is to fit into a pocket of a report, for example, you must fold according to the size permissible. Remember the allow for the thickness of *all* the maps which must be included.

No matter what the purpose of the fold, *always fold right side out with the title block visible on the front.* Whenever possible the map should have the title block in the lower right hand corner. It should be folded accordian-style so that it may be unfolded with a minimum of effort. See Figure 3-27.

MAP DRAFTING PRACTICES

Most maps, cross sections, and other drawings must be reproduced by one means or another. A draftsman who is familiar with the qualities and limitations of the common reprographic processes can be valuable to his company. A well-drawn map may be less effective if it cannot be reproduced properly.

Most of the common processes depend upon the transmission of light through the map. The lines and figures drawn on the map interfere with the light passing through which keeps these areas from being exposed. It is best if the lines are opaque and the medium is transparent or translucent. The best reproductions are made from black ink drawings on a transparent material, such as film or tracing vellum. When colored inks are used the original may look great but may not make very good prints. These inks are not opaque and allow the light to pass through.

When very thin lines are necessary sometimes it might be advantageous to ink these on the back side of the drawing where they will be in direct contact with the printing paper. This method is a good way to handle cross-hachures and other secondary lines so that they may be removed or rearranged without damage to the major portions of the drawing.

It is difficult to make good reproducible drawings with penciled lines. If it is necessary to print a penciled one, it

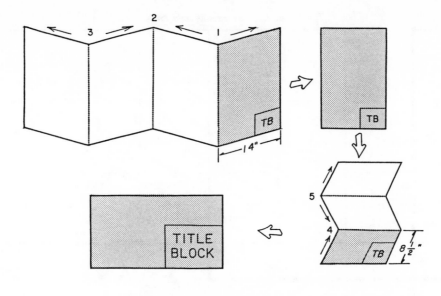

MAP FOLDING

Figure 3-27. Method of folding maps.

works better if it has been drawn on very thin paper with a very black pencil.

Maps and drawings which are to be published should be drawn slightly larger than desired so that slight irregularities in lines, lettering, etc. may be less noticeable in the final reduction. This also might be a good idea for maps meant for company brochures. One important point to remember: when a drawing is reduced, the dimensions are changed, but the ratio remains the same. This will be covered in more detail under the heading of "Reduction of Maps."

Plain black and white drawings are the most economical to reproduce. Shaded drawings can be halftone reproductions or they may be shaded with ready-made screens or shading films and then printed as any regular black and white original. Reproductions in color are expensive and should be avoided when black and white methods will suffice.

It is not necessary to have an art staff for very good maps to be produced. Several factors related to good drafting practices are just plain common sense. It is always easier to begin right than to have to redraw the project.

There are certain symbols which are standard so they are readily understood. Using these standard symbols throughout the project will make the exhibits easier to read. The U.S. Geological Survey has published sheets of standard symbols.

Different line weights make certain features instantly recognizable. State boundary lines should be heavier (wider) than county boundaries, and county lines heavier than township lines, etc. (Figure 3-28). In addition to different weights, some of these lines are also distinguished by dashes. State lines are dashed in a pattern of one long line and two short ones; county lines are shown by one long and one short. The boundaries between countries are distinguished by a series of one long line and three short ones (Figure 3-29).

Lettering on most maps is done mechanically now, with instruments which produce a variety of sizes and styles. The choice of lettering styles and sizes can make a big difference in the final presentation appearance. For this reason the entire process should be given careful consideration before any lettering is done.

Lettering should never be even slightly upside down. Lettering on a vertical line should read from bottom to top, and should be read from the right side of the map. (See Figure 3-28.) Be consistent with the style of lettering, i.e., if you choose one style of lettering for county names, letter all county names in the same style and same size.

Many maps require a "legend" which is the key to information depicted on them. For the legend to be useful it should be simple and noticeable. Any symbol whose meaning might be misunderstood should be fully explained in the legend. The best location for this is near the title block. It is distracting to find portions of the legend in several different places. Providing a legend on the map also allows the map to remain uncluttered with extra notes.

By the same token, if a feature appearing only once or twice can be identified with a short note on the body of

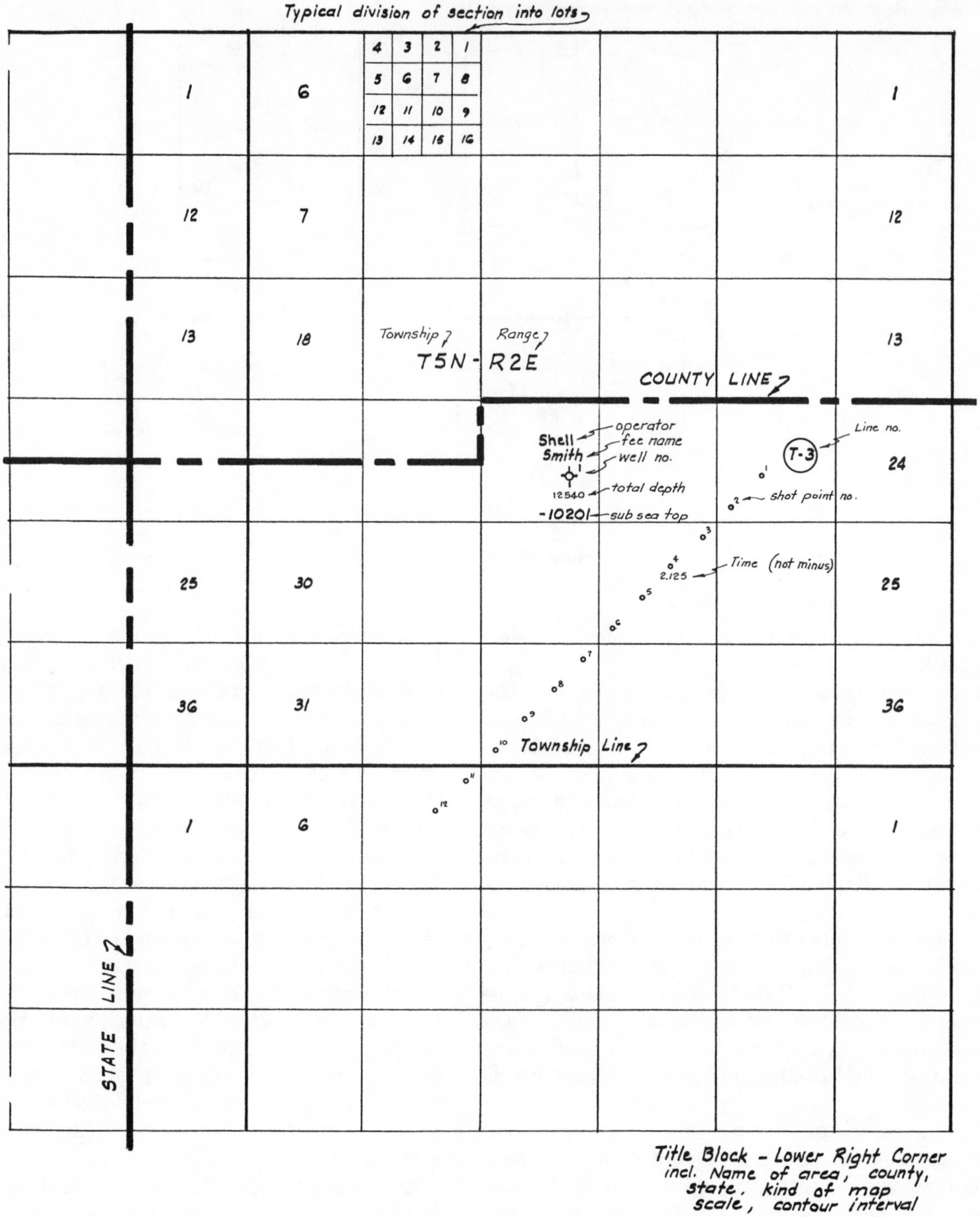

Typical division of section into lots

		4	3	2	1			
		5	6	7	8			
		12	11	10	9			
		13	14	15	16			

1   *6*   *1*

12   *7*   *12*

13   *18*   Township   Range   *13*
             T5N - R2E   COUNTY LINE

Shell —— operator   Line no.
Smith —— fee name
      —— well no.   (T-3)   24
12540 —— total depth   ₀₁
-10201 —— sub sea top   ₀₂ —— shot point no.
                          ₀₃
                     ₀₄   —— Time (not minus)
25   *30*   2.125   *25*
                  ₀₅
               ₀₆

            ₀₇
36   *31*   ₀₈   *36*
          ₀₉
       ₀₁₀ Township Line
         ₀₁₁
1   *6*   ₀₁₂   *1*

STATE LINE

Title Block - Lower Right Corner
incl. Name of area, county,
state, kind of map
scale, contour interval

Figure 3-28. A portion of a map should show enough information to be able to describe specific locations.

COUNTRY BOUNDARY

STATE BOUNDARY

COUNTY BOUNDARY

Figure 3-29. Different patterns of dashes mean specific boundaries.

the map, it is better than having to add another symbol to the legend. If the explanation is close to the feature, it can hardly be misunderstood.

On a map which is well planned and correctly drafted, it is not difficult to describe the location of any information shown or to plot new information. The base map should contain all the reference lines necessary for this. Almost all descriptions of well locations refer to township and range, sometimes sections. If these are not adequately shown on the map, it is impossible to locate wells or leases accurately. If the base map does not show sufficient information, it is worthless. Sometimes when a portion of a map is used instead of the entire map, the names of counties or the township and range designations do not appear on the portion itself. In this case, all references should be added so that the portion stands on its own.

Note: All maps should be oriented with north up. When you look at a map, the top of the map should be north. (There can be exceptions to this rule, but they are rare.)

Title Blocks

One of the most important things on a map is the title block, and the most important feature of a title block is the *area* of the map. When you know where it is, then you know if you are interested. The second most important feature is the *kind of exhibit*. Is it a structure map? Is it an isopach? Is it a cross section? By spelling it out conspicuously you can tell at a glance whether you need to unfold it and proceed. As previously mentioned, it is advisable to always place the title block in a corner, preferably the lower right corner, and to always fold the map in such a way that the title block shows on the outside after it has been folded.

Most companies have standard title blocks which are always used on their maps. If there is no set standard for your company, two examples which may be used are shown in Figure 3-30. It is also a good idea to use a graphic scale so that reduction is not a problem.

REDUCTION OF MAPS

In Figure 3-31 you will notice what happens as an exhibit is reduced. The lettering may be exactly right at actual size, but as it is reduced some of the letters become illegible. If it is known in the beginning that a certain drawing is likely to be reduced, then some provision must be made for that. Usually it is best to overemphasize the lettering. Many times lettering that is slightly enlarged on the original is hardly noticed there, but that slight enlargement can be vital to a reduction.

Another problem with reduction is in communication. It is necessary for the person who will do the reduction to understand what is expected of him. For example, when one man says he wants a map "reduced 75%," he means just that. The new map will be 75% smaller than the original—only 25% of the original. Another man may say the same and intend that his map be reduced "*to 75% of the* original size." It does make quite a difference. (See Figure 3-31.) One special problem with communicating your needs is in reference to "scale" versus "size." If you intend to get a drawing reduced "½ scale," the finished product will appear to be only one-fourth as large. When

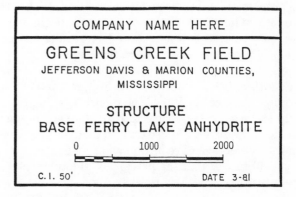

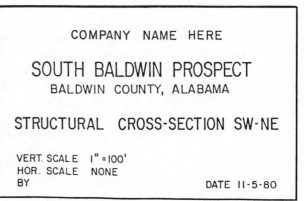

Figure 3-30. Examples of acceptable title blocks.

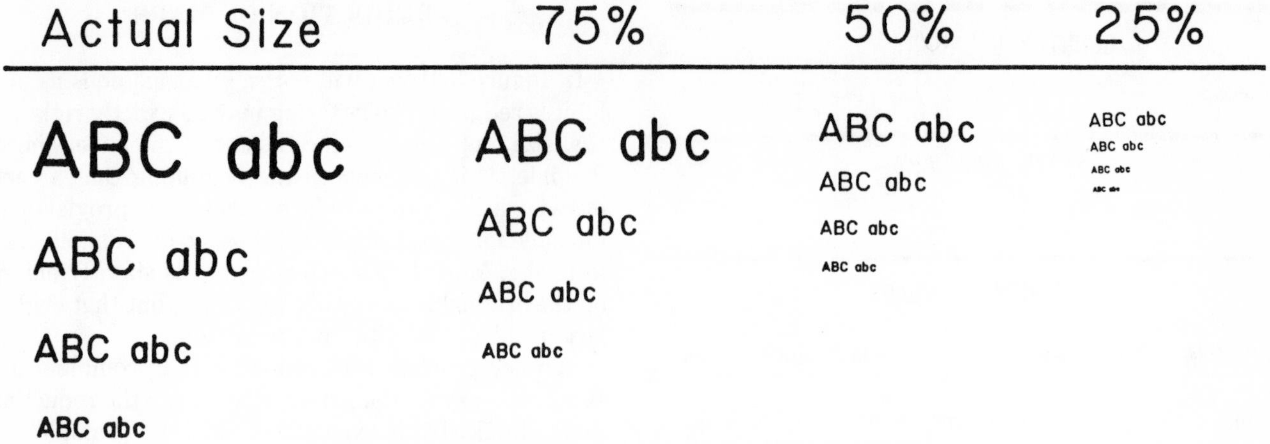

Actual Size	75%	50%	25%

ABC abc   ABC abc   ABC abc   ABC abc

ABC abc   ABC abc   ABC abc   ABC abc

ABC abc   ABC abc   ABC abc   ABC abc

ABC abc   ABC abc   ABC abc   ABC abc

ABC abc

Figure 3-31. Examples of reductions: 75%, 50%, and 25% of actual size.

a map drawn to a scale of $1'' = 1000'$ is reduced "½ scale," that means the final product will be to a scale of $1'' = 2000'$. An entire section would then be the same size as one quarter section was on the original. (See Figure 3-32.)

A person unfamiliar with reproduction methods or reductions in general may have trouble visualizing the final product. In many cases the problem is not with size but with proportion. A drawing which is reduced still has the same ratio of length to width as it had in the beginning. A large *square* map will, when reduced, be smaller for sure, but it will remain forever *square*. See Figure 3-33.

There is a product on the market now called a *proportional scale* which is a wheel on a wheel, marked for size of original and size you intend the reduction to be. By lining up the sizes it is possible to read the percentage of reduction. The reverse is also true, in that you may begin with the percentage of reduction and find out the actual size it will be. To find the percent of enlargement you merely read the wheels in reverse.

Map Coloring

Sometimes maps must be colored and often this must be done by hand. When many copies are needed, the coloring can be quite time consuming. For this reason it is best to be familiar with several different methods in order to select the best method for your project.

Color tends to increase the legibility and understanding of the exhibits so that certain features are accented and can be noticed at a glance. High color contrasts are better than low contrasts and clashing colors should be avoided when possible. The U.S. Geological Survey has set standards for colors and patterns to represent types of rocks, but they are not always used. An effort should be made to stick with one system throughout your company or certainly throughout your exhibit.

It is imperative to know how the maps are to be colored before the prints are made. The best prints to color conventionally are blue or black line diazo prints. Even these vary with different brands of paper. Papers with a gloss or hard finish should be avoided as they do not take color very well.

Color Pencils

There are many varieties of colored pencils with many different properties. No matter the brand it is best if they are applied with even strokes in the same direction and with as nearly consistent pressure as possible. Care must be taken to have a clean surface beneath the sheet to be colored as any irregularities in the surface will show up in the color.

Wax-base colored pencils require an even pressure throughout the area to be colored. Repeated stroking with too much pressure may cause a build-up and produce a shine. This kind of color may be blended with a stomp dipped in lighter fluid and rubbed over the colored area with light, fast circular motions. The solvent dissolves the wax and carries the pigment into the paper. Once the pigment is absorbed into the paper, it is almost impossible to remove without damaging the print.

Water color pencils are soluble in water but remain unaffected by solvents. They are applied in the same manner as wax pencils except a dry stomp or a wad of tissue is used to blend. For temporary maps, watercolor pencil is best since it can be revised. However, it also rubs off onto hands and smears onto other colors or uncolored areas. To avoid smearing it is sometimes helpful to place a clean piece of paper under your hand as you color. The color may be "set" by using a fixative spray available at art stores. Use of this spray requires adequate ventilation.

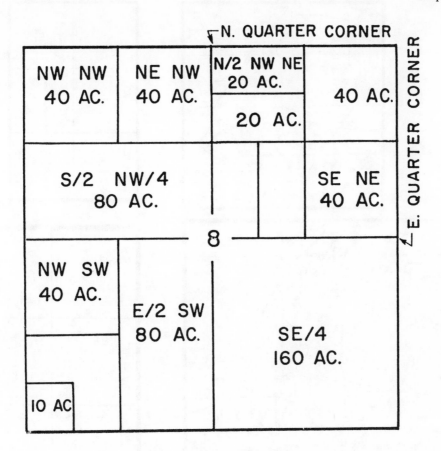

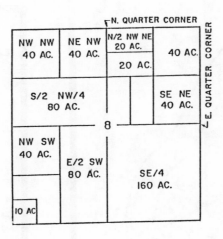

Figure 3-32. The reduced section is one-half scale, but covers only one-fourth the area.

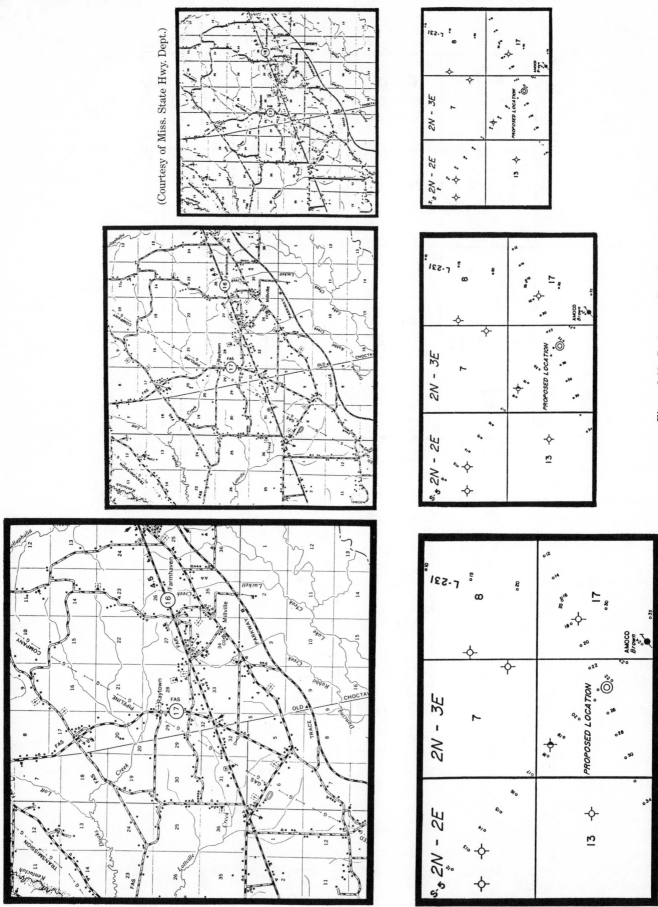

(Courtesy of Miss. State Hwy. Dept.)

Figure 3-33. Ratio, as well as size, must be considered in reductions.

Stomps

Stomps are made of rolled paper, usually soft and coarse, and are sharpened to a point. Stomps are used to spread and smooth charcoal, chalk, or colored pencils. As the ends of the stomp become shiny and no longer spread evenly, they may be rubbed against a sandpaper pad to provide a coarse surface again. It is a good idea to keep a separate sheet of sandpaper and a separate stomp for each color used.

Water Colors

Transparent water colors may be applied to some prints but they are difficult to use and cause shrinkage and distortion of scale. It is hard to color with water colors without having the overlap areas show. Use of a white blotter will help to reduce the wrinkling effect.

Using an airbrush is an effective method for coloring maps. It may cause some shrinkage but less than brush-applied watercolors. This requires much practice, cutting stencils, and a well-ventilated area in which to work. It is difficult to justify all the cutting, stenciling, and time for application for just a few prints. There are books available in art supply stores which describe airbrush methods and techniques.

Special Applications

If the maps are to be used for view graphs or 35 mm slides they may require different coloring methods. There are many kinds of graphic products for these purposes, including acetate films, pressure sensitive films, colored papers, and many different kinds of markers. Each product has a recommended use and much can be learned from the supplier catalogs. It's a good idea to read the information instead of just looking at the pictures, as human nature usually suggests. A visit to the art supply store and a little time reading catalogs and asking questions will pay dividends in the long run so you may know the product uses and limitations.

There are also a number of die cut symbols readily available for use in exhibits of all kinds. They are great time savers and allow people other than professional artists to make professional presentations.

Graphic Products

There are many products available for use in presentations. Some brands of color films are best for illustration board and some are projectable. Art supply stores carry different types and can supply you with several catalogs showing brands, types, uses, colors, and limitations. These catalogs are quite informative if you take the time to read about each type of material. When in doubt about a particular product or its use, the personnel at the supply store may be able to advise.

Transfer Lettering

Transfer lettering is just that: lettering which can be transferred to another base. Different brands are available. Some are heat resistant, others are not. All types must be burnished to ensure stability, and spraying with a fixative is added insurance. Transfer lettering is not permanent but is useful for exhibits which do not require repeated handling.

Symbols

There are many standard symbols available today, and they are applied much the same as the transfer lettering. There are also symbols which may be bought in rolls, pulled off and placed on the drawing, and held by their own adhesive. Custom symbols also may be ordered.

Graphic Tapes

Graphic tapes can eliminate hours of repetitive hand work. Hundreds of styles are available, including colors, designs, borders, broken lines and other patterns. Some are transparent, some glossy, some matte; some will project, some are flexible, others are not. These also can be custom printed. Learn which tapes work best for which jobs.

Pressure Sensitive Films

It is possible to buy almost any pattern or color in a pressure-sensitive film. Some brands work better when large areas must be covered. With some films it is possible to cut a larger section than the area to be colored and the excess trimmed, but sometimes the film adheres so quickly it is difficult to get the extra removed without damaging the print. The use of glossy prints, such as KP-5, can lessen this problem. With other matte surface prints when the damage from the excess proves to be a problem, the film can be cut to exact size first. Experiment before investing much time and money.

It is possible to get a title block or other information which is used frequently printed onto pressure sensitive film. This process allows for certain standard information to be transferred to a new base quickly, and the new information can be drafted directly onto the preprinted part.

Note: You may also make your own title block transfer film with certain products which can be run through the office copy machine. This is less expensive and immediately available. Check with the copier company for the correct product.

EXERCISE 3-1: MAPS AND SURVEYS
(Answers on pages 124–126)

Find these places on the index map (Figure 3-34).

1. Where the survey originated
2. Township 1 North, Range 1 East
3. Township 1 North, Range 1 West
4. Township 2 North, Range 3 West
5. T3N-R5W
6. T4N-R3E
7. T5N-R1E
8. T5N-R6E
9. Sec. 16-5N-6E
10. NW/4 Sec. 24-5N-6E
11. NE/4 Sec. 24
12. SW SE Sec. 24
13. NW NW Sec. 24
14. T1S-R4W
15. T1S-R7E
16. T3S-R4E

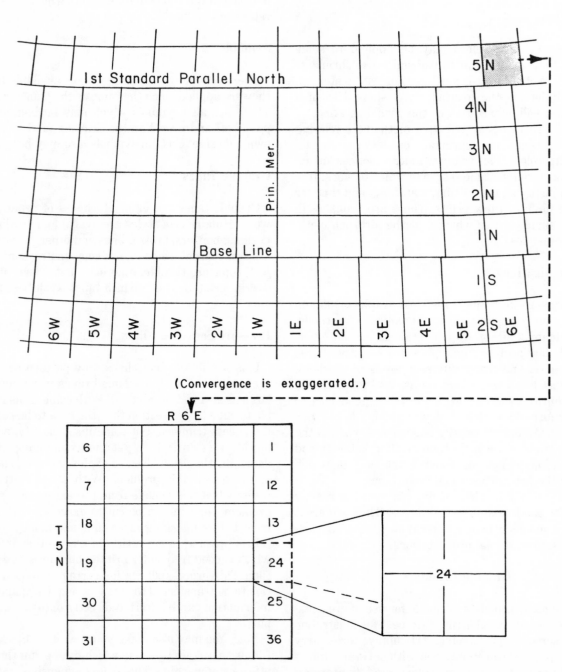

Figure 3-34. General township and range worksheet.

EXERCISE 3-2: INDEX MAPS

Index maps cover large areas on a reduced scale so that sometimes it is difficult to read all the information. Even so it is necessary to learn to use them. The index map in Figure 3-35 shows the area covered by the Southeastern States Base Maps furnished by Geological Consulting Services. The heavier lines outline each area covered by individual base maps and numbered accordingly. In the following exercise find the township and range in the appropriate county and note the base map number for each. (All are in Mississippi.)

A.	T2N-R7E	Pike County
B.	T1N-R1W	Copiah County
C.	T10N-R7E	Copiah County
D.	T11N-R5E	Copiah County
E.	1N-4W	Copiah County
F.	1N-7E	Smith County
G.	1N-17W	Marion County
H.	2N-18W	Marion County
I.	2N-14E	Marion County
J.	5N-19W	Jeff Davis County
K.	2N-12E	Walthall County

(text continued on page 48)

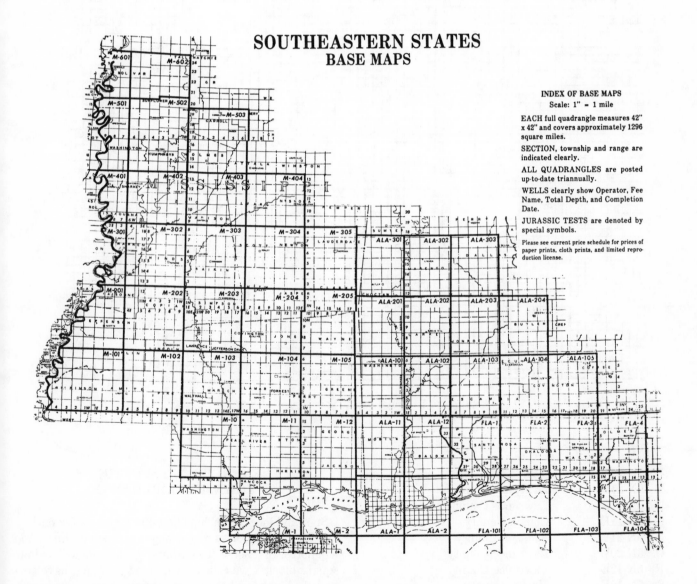

Figure 3-35. Typical index map showing available base maps in the area. (Courtesy of George Kelly Map Co., Geological Consulting Services.)

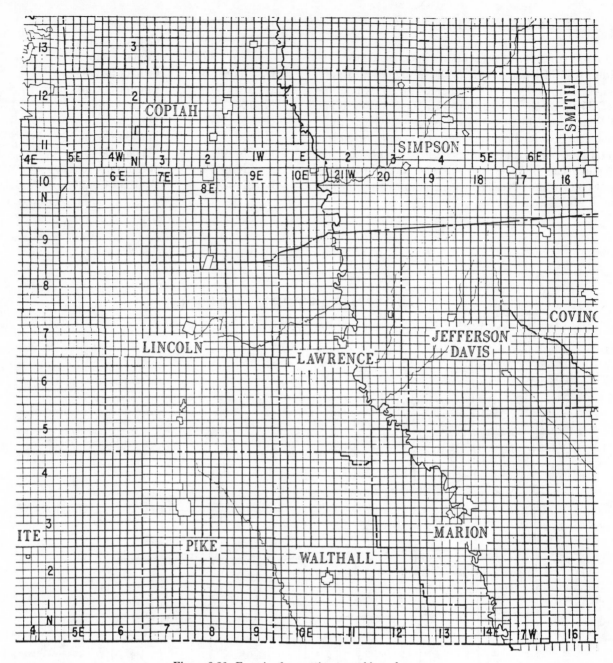

Figure 3-36. Exercise for spotting township and range.

L.	1N-13E	Marion County
M.	9N-21W	Lawrence County
N.	9N-11E	Lawrence County
O.	9N-11E	Copiah County
P.	9N-21W	Simpson County
Q.	5N-20W	Lawrence County
R.	5N-12E	Lawrence County
S.	5N-12E	Marion County
T.	5N-19W	Marion County

EXERCISE 3-3: SPOTTING TOWNSHIP AND RANGE

Spot and label townships listed in Exercise 3-2 on Figure 3-36. Watch for survey changes and county lines. You will notice that some "townships," that is, some "six-mile square blocks" we call townships may, in fact, have several designations because of survey changes or county changes.

Chapter 4
Geological Maps

GEOLOGICAL BACKGROUND

Geology is the science of the earth; it enlists all of the other natural sciences—astronomy, biology, chemistry and physics—in examining the various aspects of the earth and its history. It is the conclusion of modern geologists that "the present is the key to the past," i.e., that geologic processes that are active today on and within the earth have operated in the same manner throughout the history of the earth. The bulk of the evidence indicates that the great mountain ranges, deep canyons, and other major features of the earth's surface came into existence, not through great catastrophes, but as the cumulative result of ordinary processes still active, operating through enormously long intervals of time.

Geology is so essential to the petroleum industry that a knowledge of the basic principles of geology is useful for anyone associated with the oil business.

Geologists recognize three general rock types: igneous, sedimentary, and metamorphic. *Igneous* rock is formed when molten material, such as lava, flows to the surface to cool and solidify. This type of rock is also formed from magma that never reaches the surface. *Metamorphic* rock is formed when either igneous or sedimentary rock is buried again very deep and exposed to extremes of temperature and pressure. *Sedimentary* rocks are formed in two principal ways. Some, such as shale, siltstone, and sandstone, result from the accumulation of fragments of older rocks which have been transported by water, wind, or ice, and eventually deposited and hardened into rock. The second class is composed of material formerly dissolved in the sea. Limestone and dolomite comprise this type. Sedimentary rocks are generally deposited in layers called beds or strata.

Sedimentary rocks have generated and presently contain virtually all of the known deposits of oil and gas. Moreover, nearly all petroleum is found in sedimentary rocks of marine origin. These rocks were formed in ancient seas which covered various parts of the continents during different periods of time throughout the past 500 million years of earth history.

There are two theories used to explain the origin of petroleum: *organic* and *inorganic*. The inorganic theory assumes that hydrogen and carbon were brought together under great pressure and temperature deep in the earth to form oil and gas.

The organic theory, accepted by most scientists, presumes that the hydrogen and carbon, which constitute crude oil and natural gas, come mainly from marine animals and plants which abound in the seas. All plants and animals are composed mainly of hydrogen and carbon. Much evidence exists to support the organic theory, both in crude oil and in the rocks containing the oil.

The phrase "oil and gas reservoir" brings to mind a picture of a huge underground pool. A petroleum reservoir is actually rock with small amounts of oil trapped in the spaces or pores of the rock. This situation has been compared to water in a bucket of sand. The water does not remain in a puddle; it disperses and fills all the space between the grains of sand. That is exactly what oil and gas do in rock.

There are four conditions that must be fulfilled for oil to accumulate in rocks. There must be a *source* rock from which the oil and gas was formed, a *reservoir* rock where it is stored, a *seal* to keep it in the reservoir, and a *trap* where the oil and gas can accumulate. All four must be present, and the only place this combination occurs is in sedimentary basins.

A source rock contains the necessary carbonaceous matter from which the oil can be formed. Bituminous marine shales are the most common source rocks. Shale is formed from buried mud which has become hardened and usually layered due to pressure from overlying rocks. These marine muds are high in organic content.

The reservoir rock, usually a sandstone or limestone, must have porosity (pore space) and permeability (meaning that the pores must be connected) (See Figure 4-1), and the reservoir must be in contact with the source. Without porosity and permeability the oil could not move into the reservoir from the source.

A seal, or cap rock, is a nonporous, impermeable layer of rock overlying the reservoir so that the oil and gas will be contained in the reservoir or *carrier bed*.

Finally, a trap must exist for the oil and gas to accumulate in producible quantities. A trap is any barrier that stops the migration of petroleum, without which the petroleum would never collect into finite deposits.

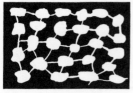

POROSITY   PERMEABILITY

Figure 4-1. Porosity, or pore space, is indicated by the white area. The dark area indicates the rock mass. If the pore spaces are connected so that fluid can flow through the rock, it is said to have permeability.

Structural traps may be formed by deformation of rock layers, i.e., folding (Figure 4-2) and faulting (Figure 4-3). Stratigraphic traps form where the reservoir becomes surrounded by impermeable rock (Figures 4-4 and 4-5). One type of strat trap is called an angular unconformity, which occurs when older inclined petroleum-bearing beds are covered by younger nonporous formations (Figure 4-6). Some traps are combinations of the two types.

Sedimentary rocks were originally deposited in essentially horizontal layers in subsiding basins, so that over long periods of time thousands of feet of these strata can accumulate. When rocks are deeply buried and subjected to the increased pressure and temperatures, they become plastic in varying degrees and can be deformed by various forces active in the earth's crust. In this manner, upfolds or anticlines, and downfolds or synclines, are formed, as well as many variations of the two.

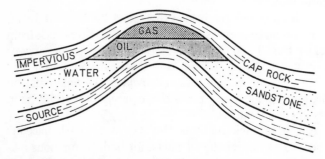

Figure 4-2. An anticline is an upfold. If all conditions are just right, oil and gas may be trapped there.

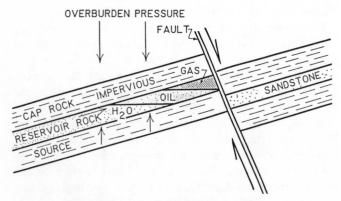

Figure 4-3. A "normal" fault is shown here.

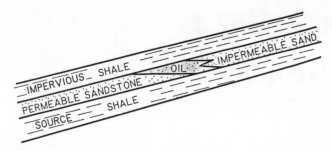

Figure 4-4. This shows a "permeability pinchout." In this case, the trap is formed where the rock is tight and the fluid cannot flow any further.

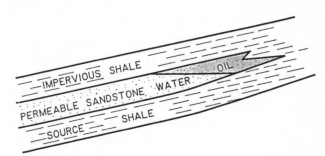

Figure 4-5. A sand pinchout, shown here, surrounded by impermeable rock, is one kind of stratigraphic trap.

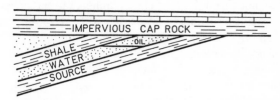

Figure 4-6. An angular unconformity, shown here, is one example of a strat trap.

If the rock layers break due to intense folding, and one side is displaced, a fault is created (Figures 4-7 and 4-8). When petroleum is trapped, it is segregated by specific gravity; that is, the gas will collect in the highest position, the heavier oil next, and still heavier saltwater on the bottom (see Figures 4-2 and 4-3).

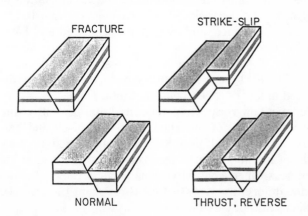

Figure 4-7. These block diagrams depict some different kinds of faults.

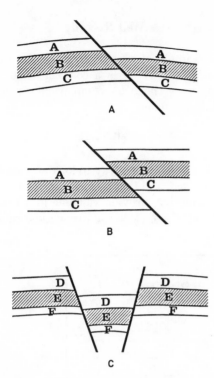

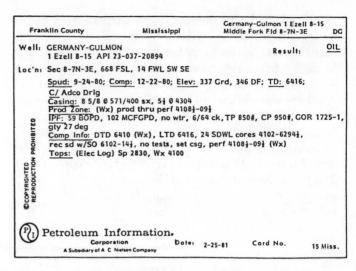

Figure 4-9. A completion card. (Reprinted with permission of Petroleum Information Corporation.)

Figure 4-8. (A) In a *normal* fault a downward movement of the overhanging side occurs, probably caused by gravity. (B) A *thrust* or *reverse* fault occurs when the overhanging side moves up, probably because of horizontal stress. (C) A *graben* is a downthrown block between two upthrown blocks.

The main objective of petroleum geologists and geophysicists is to locate these traps, which are only briefly discussed here. The tools of the trade include well logs, seismic data, aerial photos, and gravity and magnetic data, all of which eventually lead to the construction of many maps and cross sections. It has been said, with little argument, that most problems in petroleum geology are solved, in part or entirely, on the drafting table. Vague concepts become clear when developed into pictures. In this day and time computers are becoming increasingly important in developing these concepts into pictures.

SOURCES OF INFORMATION

There are many sources of information for the oil industry. Learn where to find them and how to read them. Some examples are included in this unit.

Completion Cards

Figure 4-9 is a copy of a Petroleum Information completion card, sometimes called a *scout ticket*. The information on this card includes operator, well name and number, exact location, permit number, when it was spudded

and completed, ground and derrick floor elevations, and many particulars. We see from this card that the well produced from perforations in the Wilcox formation, that it initially flowed 59 barrels of oil per day and 102 thousand cubic feet of gas per day with no water, through a $^6/_{64}$″ choke. It even tells us about sidewall cores, casing, and other formation tops. A complete set of this type of card, when filed by location, is an invaluable research asset.

Figure 4-10 shows the same type of information for an offshore well that the previous example covers for a well onshore, and reading it requires some special knowledge. For example, the location is not related to county, but to area and block. The location mentioned is the surface location only and further reading is necessary to get to the location of the bottom hole. Most offshore wells are direc-

```
SHIP SHOAL              208 FLD              API 1771140761
   KERR MCGEE           OCS 0828     WELL L-8
----------------------------------------------------------
LOC. 3671 FSL. 7655 FWL OF BLK 214
X=  2,148,055   Y=-   64,199   PTD.009000TVD   ATD DH: 007459
ATD 1ST 009071 ATD 2ST      ATD 3ST      ATD 4ST
SPUD 02/23/84 COMP 04/19/84 PBTD      TYPE GAS
OH. PBHL. 6359 FSL. 9155 FWL OF BLK 214(CORR)

OH. ABHL. MD      =TVD
STH ABHL. MD  9071=TVD  8448, N. 2481 @ E. 1424 OF SURF
OH. CSG=24 @ 367, 16 @ 815, 103/4 @ 4178, 7 5/8 @ 8255
CMP DTA IP/PF 6792-6814, CS-6 SD, 20BCPD, 2100MCF, 12/64 CK, TP 2395
  . SITP 2625, GOR 105,000, GTY 46.0
WD=00114 KB=0000118 RIG TW 54           TRANSWORLD
DATE REACHED TD 04/07/84

 02/22/84  LOC.
 02/22/84               MUD
 02/29/84 DRLG  03088   MUD 09.0 24CSG @ 367W/ 135'P. 16CSG @ 815W/
           1675
 03/07/84 DRLG  06196   MUD 09.8 10 3/4CSG @ 4178W/1900
 03/14/84 TD    07459   MUD 11.5 STK DP @ 7174, TF @ 6549, FSG
 03/21/84 DRLG  06645 STH MUD 11.0 TF @ 6650, ST @ 5012
 03/28/84 DRLG  07897 STH MUD 12.0 ISFS, FDC, CNL, GR @ 7865, NO SWC
 04/04/84 TD    08266 STH MUD 13.0 ISFS, FDC, CNL, GR @ 8256, NO SWC.
        7 5/8CSG @ 8255W/1250, TSTG CSG
 04/11/84 TD    09071 STH MUD 16.0 DISF, FDC, CNL @ 9071, SWC, 1(DH)
        PLG @ 7500-8500, WOC
```

Figure 4-10. An offshore completion card.

tionally drilled, sometimes a dozen or more from a common platform. The records for these wells would all indicate the same surface location, just different bottom hole locations. Offshore locations are also given as X and Y coordinates. This is a good practice as some of the block numbers are difficult to find on some maps. These offshore wells usually show a different actual bottom hole location (ABHL) from the one proposed (PBHL), and different total depths, such as proposed total depth (PTD), actual total depth (ATD) and true vertical depth (TVD). Many are also sidetracked and indicated by "1ST," "2ST," etc. As you can see, it is necessary to read the entire card before spotting offshore locations.

Well Record

Another example of a *scout ticket* is the well record shown in Figure 4-11. It is a compilation of the same types of data as those on completion cards but in a slightly different form.

Well Logs

There is really only one way to look at rock layers beneath the surface, and that is with a borehole. All wells, whether productive, provide valuable information. Records of drilling time, electrical properties, radioactivity,

Geol. 61 26M Rev. 6-64

WELL RECORD API #23-095-20174

Quad No. ____

Wildcat WC Area ____

Discovery ____ Pool ____

Company R. L. Burns Corp. Well # 2-1 Farm Altherr

Location 783' FNL & 660' FWL of Section

Sec. 2 T. 16S R. 6E Co. Monroe State Mississippi

Elev. Ser. ____ D. F. ____ Gr. ____ K. B. ____

I. P. P & A T. P. ____

Pay Zones ____ C. P. ____

Perfs. ____

Top Pay ____ Gravity ____ G. O. R. ____

Frac. ____ Acid ____ T. D. 5950' Drlr. & Log P. B. T. D. ____

Comm. 4/22/76 Comp. 5/28/76 Contractor Lohman & Johnson
5900' Paleoz.

CASING RECORD:
8-5/8" @927'
1200? w/500

SURVEYS
EL ____
Porosity ____
Radio Activity ____
Core Anal. ____
Mud Log ____
Others ____
Log Analysis By ____

C. S. OIL TOPS
4/21/76 M.I.
4/28/76 ¢1497'
5/ 5/76 ¢3390'
5/12/76 ¢3882'
5/19/76 ¢5382'
5/26/76 @5754 Logging Ran D.S.T.
6/ 2/76 @5950 Logging
6/ 9/76 TD 5950 Drlr. & Log D.S.T. 3090-3219 open 150 mins, rec 1744' GCSW. IFP 106-761# SIP 1401# D.S.T. 3918-41 open 150 mins, rec 10' GCM IFP 54-54# SIP 784# D.S.T. 5630-70 open 150 mins, rec 2910' GCSW IFP 288-1380# SIP 2363# D.S.T. 5702-23 open 150 mins. rec 3083' GCSW IFP 26-1460# SIP 2409#
5/28/76 P & A

SCOUT TOPS

Schlumberger Tops

Mill.	5342
U. Carter	5480
L. Carter	5634

71

Figure 4-11. One kind of well record, typically called a *scout ticket*.

and various other information are provided by well logs. These logs are important tools for the explorationist.

Drill Time Logs

A record of the time it takes to drill every foot of the hole from spudding to total depth is usually kept, and the rate is plotted on a strip log. This record, called a *drill time log*, can be recorded in minutes per foot or feet per hour.

A sudden increase in the rate of penetration by the bit is called a *drilling break*. Usually this shows a change in lithology, from shale to sandstone, gypsum to shale, etc. Sometimes it shows a difference in porosity, as very porous zones normally drill faster than tighter sections.

Some other factors which affect the rate of drilling include type of drilling fluid, rate of circulation of fluid, weight on the bit, and the kind of bit. When a new bit is in the hole, the rate of drilling usually increases, but the *relative* rates in various lithologic units are not changed much.

Wireline Logs

Subsurface conditions can be measured and recorded by means of downhole electrical, sonic, and radioactivity measuring devices. These instruments are lowered to the bottom of the borehole on a cable (wireline). As the instruments are slowly withdrawn the various measured data are recorded at the surface in the logging truck. These data are plotted against depth as a series of continuous curves on a strip log. Proper interpretation of the curves allows the geologist to know the lithology, porosity, and fluid content at any given depth in the well. To the trained eye the various logs provide a continuous "picture" of the geologic section penetrated.

Wireline logs include the various electric logs (induction logs, micrologs), radioactive logs (gamma ray, density, neutron), and sonic (acoustic) logs. Figure 4-12A is an example of an induction electric log. If sidewall cores are taken, they are usually described at the end of the electric log (Figure 14B). Sidewall cores are small rock samples taken with a sidewall gun at any desired depth. The gun is lowered into the hole on a wireline in the same manner as the logging tools already described.

Sample Logs

As a well is drilled, the material ground up by the bit is brought to the surface along with the drilling mud. These bits of rock are called *cuttings*, and these are studied and plotted on sample logs. These *sample logs* provide a rec-

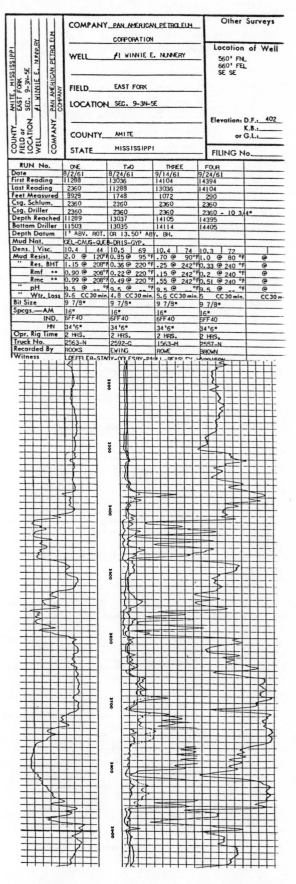

Figure 4-12A. A portion of an electric log.

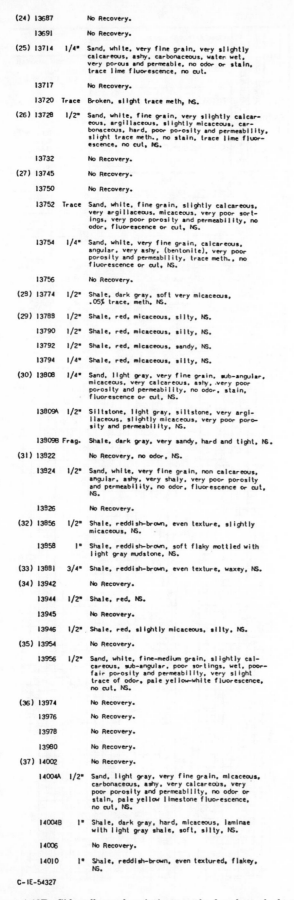

(24) 13687		No Recovery.
13691		No Recovery.
(25) 13714	1/4"	Sand, white, very fine grain, very slightly calcareous, ashy, carbonaceous, water wet, very porous and permeable, no odor or stain, trace lime fluorescence, no cut.
13717		No Recovery.
13720	Trace	Broken, slight trace meth, NS.
(26) 13728	1/2"	Sand, white, fine grain, very slightly calcareous, argillaceous, slightly micaceous, carbonaceous, hard, poor porosity and permeability, slight trace meth., no stain, trace lime fluorescence, no cut, NS.
13732		No Recovery.
(27) 13745		No Recovery.
13750		No Recovery.
13752	Trace	Sand, white, fine grain, slightly calcareous, very argillaceous, micaceous, very poor sortings, very poor porosity and permeability, no odor, fluorescence or cut, NS.
13754	1/4"	Sand, white, very fine grain, calcareous, angular, very ashy, (bentonite), very poor porosity and permeability, trace meth., no fluorescence or cut, NS.
13756		No Recovery.
(29) 13774	1/2"	Shale, dark gray, soft very micaceous, .05% trace, meth, NS.
(29) 13789	1/2"	Shale, red, micaceous, silty, NS.
13790	1/2"	Shale, red, micaceous, silty, NS.
13792	1/2"	Shale, red, micaceous, sandy, NS.
13794	1/4"	Shale, red, micaceous, silty, NS.
(30) 13808	1/4"	Sand, light gray, very fine grain, sub-angular, micaceous, very calcareous, ashy, very poor porosity and permeability, no odor, stain, fluorescence or cut, NS.
13809A	1/2"	Siltstone, light gray, siltstone, very argillaceous, slightly micaceous, very poor porosity and permeability, NS.
13809B	Frag.	Shale, dark gray, very sandy, hard and tight, NS.
(31) 13922		No Recovery, no odor, NS.
13924	1/2"	Sand, white, very fine grain, non calcareous, angular, ashy, very shaly, very poor porosity and permeability, no odor, fluorescence or cut, NS.
13926		No Recovery.
(32) 13956	1/2"	Shale, reddish-brown, even texture, slightly micaceous, NS.
13958	1"	Shale, reddish-brown, soft flaky mottled with light gray mudstone, NS.
(33) 13981	3/4"	Shale, reddish-brown, even texture, waxey, NS.
(34) 13942		No Recovery.
13944	1/2"	Shale, red, NS.
13945		No Recovery.
13946	1/2"	Shale, red, slightly micaceous, silty, NS.
(35) 13954		No Recovery.
13956	1/2"	Sand, white, fine-medium grain, slightly calcareous, sub-angular, poor sortings, wet, poor-fair porosity and permeability, very slight trace of odor, pale yellow-white fluorescence, no cut, NS.
(36) 13974		No Recovery.
13976		No Recovery.
13978		No Recovery.
13980		No Recovery.
(37) 14002		No Recovery.
14004A	1/2"	Sand, light gray, very fine grain, micaceous, carbonaceous, ashy, very calcareous, very poor porosity and permeability, no odor or stain, pale yellow limestone fluorescence, no cut, NS.
14004B	1"	Shale, dark gray, hard, micaceous, laminae with light gray shale, soft, silty, NS.
14006		No Recovery.
14010	1"	Shale, reddish-brown, even textured, flakey, NS.

C-IE-54327

Figure 4-12B. Sidewall core descriptions may be found attached to the end of the electric log.

SAMPLE LOG Sample Log

Tulsa

STATE _Arkansas_

PH. - CO. _La Fayette_

OPERATOR _BRILEY_

LEASE _MOORE_ #1

SEC. _16_ T _16S_ R _24W_

C/ NW SW

West Lewisville Field

DATE COM. _1-16-47_

DATE COMP. _____

CSG. 10 3/4 @ 125 7" @ 4062'

T. D. _4080'_

ELEV. _276 LBS_ PROD. _Testing_

First sample examined, 1750-60; in Midway.

G. sh.

Do. & ltg. cal. sh.

TOP ARKADELPHIA: 1780-90

Do. Tr. g. cryst.ll. & ltg. sdy. ck.

G. sh. Tr. ltg. shly. ck.

G. sh. G. ll. & ltg. sdy. ll.

G. sh. Ltg. cal. sh. Tr. g. ll.

TOP NACATOCH: 1900-20

G. sh. Wh. mg. np. cky. ss.

Do. (Abun. pyr.)

Wh. mg. np. cky. ss. & wh. sdy. ck.

G. sh. Ltg. mfg. sli.-np. cky. ss.

G. sh. Wh. mg. np. cky. ss. Ltg. fg. np. glau. cky. ss.

G. sh. Ltg. fg. np. f. glau. cky. ss.

G. sh. Ltg. fg. np. glau. cal. ss. (Abun. gravel.-appears to be surface gravel.)

Figure 4-13. A sample log is made from examination of the "cuttings" brought to the surface with the drilling mud.

PETROLEUM INFORMATION   Section III   8-13-80   Page 2

INITIAL CLASS: WF - New Field Wildcat; WD - Deeper
Pool Wildcat; WS - Shallower Pool Wildcat; WP - New
Pool Wildcat; WO - Wildcat Outpost; D - Development Well

* * * <u>MISSISSIPPI FIRST REPORT SUMMARY</u> * * *

* * * ADAMS COUNTY * * *

5-5N-2W, Irreg
BIG JOE OIL CO
(Box 1087, Natchez, MS
39120)
1 Aventine Plantation
API 23-001-21998

WILDCAT: (8-13-80 JK) 6600 Wx Test, Fr NWC 5, go E alg/L for 1804, Th S @ RA 52 to loc, 3½ mi NW/Kingston, 3/4 mi S/S. LaGrange Fld, ** Loc   WF

29-5N-3W, Irreg
BIG JOE OIL CO, A.S.
HUDNALL & KAY LEASE
SERVICE
4 Board of Supervisors
API 23-001-22000

HUTCHINS LANDING: (8-13-80 JK) 5000 Wx Test, 1886 FNL, 2659 FEL, ** Loc   D

11-4N-3W, NW NW NW
ECHOLS & LE BLANC
(403 Franklin, Natchez,
MS 39120)
1 Breaux 11-4
API 23-001-21999

LAKE LUCILLE: (8-13-80 JK) 7000 Wx Test, 330 FNL, 330 FWL, C/Par-Co Drlg, ** Loc   D

10-4N-3W, SW SW SW
ECHOLS & LE BLANC
10-13C Breaux
API 23-001-21996

N. LAKE LUCILLE: (8-13-80 JK) 7000 Wx Test, 330 FSL, 330 FWL, C/New & Hughes Drlg Co, Spud 8-10-80, 8 5/8 @ 600/300 sx, ** Drlg 4523   D

* * * ALABAMA DRILLING PROGRESS * * *

* * * MARION COUNTY * * *

WILDCATS:
CHARLES L. CHERRY & ASSOC   15 11S 13W NW SW NW   WILDCAT: 2950 Paleozoic Test,   WF
1 ROBERT CROW 15-5   (FR 3/25/81 JK) 1890 FNL, 490 FWL,
API 01-093-20023   3½ mi SW/Pearces Mill, 4½ mi NE/ Hamilton Fld

Contr: R.E. Williams Drlg, Spud 4/8/81, 8 5/8 @ 338 w/200, TD 2900, ran logs, 4½ @ 1305, perf 1188-92, swbd, no det, no tests, ** Temp Abnd 12/15/81

* * * MOBILE COUNTY * * *

WILDCATS:
THE SUPERIOR OIL CO   39 1N 1E   WILDCAT: 19,000 Smackover Test,   WF
1 ANNIE M. HILL ET AL   Irreg   (FR 1/18/81 JK) 484 FSL, 2174 FWL,
UNIT 39   2½ mi E/Movico, 8 mi NE/Cold Creek
API 01-097-20191   Fld (BHL 135 FSL, 1200 FWL)

Contr: NA, Spud 4/29/81, Spud 4/29/81, 20 @ 825 w/1640, 13 3/8 @ 6088 w/ 5100, PB 5840 & 5867, @ 12,958 STH ran logs, 9 5/8 @ 12,958 w/1500, TD 17,200, attd to log, lost junk in hole, PB & ST @ undisclosed depth, could not rec fsh, PB & ST @ 13,318, @ 16,784 STH, unsuccessful attempt to rec logging tool, lost logging tool, set plug, ST @ 13,290, @ 17,271, 3rd STH, att'd DST, stk tool, unable to rec, ** Prep to pull out of hole & junk well

TURNER & HICKOX, INC   31-1N-1W   WILDCAT: 2500 Wilcox Test,   WFX
B-31-5 PRATT TURNER   NW SW   (FR 12/2/81 JK) 2331 FNL, 660 FWL
LAND CO   5 mi E/Gulfcrest, 1 mi N/Chunchula
API 01-097-20133   Fld, (OWWO- 16 @ 42, 9 5/8 @ 1847, 5½ @ 12,132 (old), OTD 12,140 & D&A 10/25/78)

Contr: NA, NEW WORK:, Spud 11/27/81, TD 2488, ran logs, 5½ @ 2444 w/300, ** WOCR

PRUET PROD CO-HUGHES   13-1S-1W   WILDCAT: 12,400 Paluxy Test,   WF
& HUGHES   SE SW SW   (FR 9/30/81 JK) 330 FSL, 985 FWL, 4 mi
1 JIRICKA 13-13   N/Hatters, 3 mi N/Hatters Pond Fld
API 01-097-20202   EL: 39 GR, 59 DF, 61 KB

Contr: Larco Drlg #18, Spud 10/15/81, 9 5/8 @ 2895, TD 12,520, ran logs, EL/T: Midway 4258, T/Chalk 5239, Base Chalk 6955, 1st Eutaw 7090, Lwr Tuscaloosa 8180, Paluxy 10,910, D&A 11/8/81

FIELD WELLS:
UNION OIL CO OF CALIF   11-1S-2W   CHUNCHULA: 18,600 Smackover Test   D
1 M.V. KELLY 11-16   SE SE SE   (FR 10/21/81 JK) 250 FSL, 200 FEL
API 01-097-20203

Contr: Penrod Drlg, Spud 10/19/81, 11 3/4 @ 5240 w/2500, Crd #1 18,422-452, no det, Crd #2 18,452-482, no det, Crd #3 18,482-512, no det, Crd #4 18,512-542, no det, Crd #5 18,542-563, rec 22, no details, Crd #6 18,563-570, rec 7, no details, TD 18,570, ran logs, 7 @ 18,553 w/1400, ** WOO

UNION OIL CO OF CALIF   15-1S-2W   CHUNCHULA: 18,600 Smackover Test   D
1 J.A. SMITH 15-13   SW SW SW   (FR 12/2/81 JK) 200 FSL, 400 FWL
API 01-097-20206

Contr: Penrod Drlg, ** Loc

Figure 4-14. One example of a commercial report. (Reprinted with permission of Petroleum Information Corporation.)

ord of rock characteristics in subsurface formations. (See Figure 4-13.)

Commercial Reports

There are a number of commercial reports available to provide up-to-date information about the petroleum industry. One very good source is Petroleum Information. A sample of a report is included here (Figure 4-14). The particular sheet shown is a composite made from the new location portion (first report summary) and a part of the drilling progress report. Once a new location is reported in the publication, weekly information is carried on the well until final completion or abandonment. These are available for every part of the country.

One of the best sources of industry information for the southeastern part of the country is the *Southeastern Oil Review,* a portion of which is shown in Figure 4-15.

Commercial Maps

There are several map companies which provide excellent base maps, ownership and lease maps, and even contoured maps.

Ownership and lease maps are updated periodically to provide a good overview of activity in an area. An example of one such map is from Tobin Map Company (Figure 4-16). This kind of map is usually provided on a subscrip-

tion basis, but certain areas may be ordered separately. Another example of a lease ownership map is shown in Figure 4-17. It is part of another area of the country and provided by Petroleum Information Corporation.

Geological Base Maps

The example in Figure 4-18 is a very small-scale geological base. On a map of this scale the well names are difficult to read, but it would be useful for regional mapping. Many commercial bases are provided on a scale of $1'' = 4,000'$, or $1'' = 1$ mile, either of which is useful for general geological mapping.

Monday, December 5, 1983   SOUTHEASTERN OIL REVIEW

ALABAMA Drilling & Exploration

WILDCATS

Baldwin County

Terra Resources, Inc. No. 1 Pendleton J. Slaughter, Jr. et al Unit 29-2, 450' S & 2200' W of NE/cor Sec 29-3N-3E. 17,000' Smackover test. Loc.

Tomlinson Interests, Inc. No. 1 Charles O. Oswell Unit 23-3, 736' S & 1800' E of NW/cor Sec 23-3N-2E. 16,200' Smackover test. Set 20" 90'; 13 3/8" 3242'; 9 5/8" 14,826'; drlg 15,701'.

Blount County

Blount County Gas Expl., Ltd. # 2 No. 1 L & N RR 19-16, 658' N & 1036' W of SE/cor Sec 19-13S-3W. 2000' Paleozoic test. C/Graves. Permit renewed. Loc.

Confederate Oil Prod. No. 2 Corvin-Mulberry 26-9, 460' N & 360' W of SE/cor NE SE Sec 26-13S-4W. 4000' Paleozoic test. C/R. E. Williams. Set 8 5/8" 329'; 5½" 1600'; TD 1610'; perf 802-812, 1426-36 & 1500-08'; tstd; no details; perf 626-636'; sq perfs 626-636'; reperf 802-812'; tstd; no details; unable to rec fsh; set pkr 1435'; tstg.

McGregor Oil & Gas Investments, Inc. No. 1 Mary 14-16, 370' S & 764' W of NE/cor SE SE Sec. 14-13S-4W. 2000' Paleozoic test. Loc.

C/Bay. Set 16" 117'; 10¾" 2893'; crd 12,888-940'; TD 13,080'; 7" 13,080'; perf 12,902-938'; F/648 BOPD, 1,030,000 CFGPD, 17/64" ch, TP 1365#, GOR 1594 to 1, grav 49.5 deg, SITP 2717#; F/816 BOPD, 1,500,000 CFGPD, 18/64" ch, TP 1470#; IPF: 661 BOPD, 1,060,000 CFGPD, 16/64" ch, TP 1930#, GOR 1604 to 1, grav 51.7 deg.

Fayette County

Anderman-Smith Operating Co. No. 1 Randolph 25-13, 660' N & 660' E of SW/cor Sec 25-14S-13W. 3000' Paleozoic test. C/Apollo. Set 8 5/8" 412'; TD 2870'; 4½" 2870'; perf 2780-88 & 2790-2802'; IPF: 442,000 CFGPD, ¼" ch, TP 300#; perf 2228-30, 2236-48 & 2252-64'; IPF: 6,525,000 CFGPD, ¾" ch, CP 450#.

Ronson Industries, Inc. No. 1 Hassinger Dreux 1-T 29-12, 660' S & 670' E of NW/cor NW SW Sec 29-16S-9W. 3100' Paleozoic test. C/D. R. Clary. Set 7" 311'; TD 3100'; ran logs; waiting on orders.

Swift Energy Co. No. 1 Charles W. Nolen 35-2, 660' S & 1980' W of NE/cor Sec 35-16S-13W. 4100' Paleozoic test. C/See Land. Set 8 5/8" 400'; TD 3950'; 4½" 3942'; perf 3802-10' & 3812-16'; acidized & frac'd; IPF: 327,000 CFGPD, 20 BOPD, 18/64" ch, TP 300#, grav 44 deg.

NE Sec 12-17S-6W. 2200' Paleozoic test. Set 7 5/8" 350'; TD 2026'; tstg.

Calhoun-Tutwiler No. 1 Ala. By Products 30-1, 660' N & 1800' E of SW/cor Sec 30-16S-5W. OTD 2704'. C/Graves. Will clean out & test. Cleaned out 2358'; frac'd open hole; waiting on orders.

Ridgely Pet. Corp. 81-I No. 1 Ala. By-Products Co. 17-4, 478' N & 660' E of SW/cor NW NW Sec 17-16S-5W. 3500' Paleozoic test. C/Graves. Set 7½" 300'; TD 2706'; 4½" 2700'; perf 2522-32'; frac'd; PB 2300'; perf 2054-66'; tstd; no details; perf 2030-40'; perf 2040-50'; sq; perf 1520-22'; sq; prep to run cement bond log.

Ridgely Pet. Corp. 81-I No. 1 Center Coal 20-6, 3079' N & 660' W of SE/cor W½ Sec 20-16S-5W. 3000' Paleozoic test. C/Graves. Set 7" 300'; TD 1543'; 4½" 1535'; perf 1100-1500'; frac'd; cleaned; perf 1456-66'; sq; temp abnd.

Ridgely Pet. Corp. 81-I No. 23-11 Rogers, 449' N & 514' E of SW/cor NE SW Sec 23-15S-3W. 3000' Paleozoic test. C/Graves. Set 7" 330'; TD 2067'; waiting on orders.

Ridgely Pet. Corp. 81-I No. 1 U.S. Pipe 2-12, 572' N & 493' W of SE/cor NW SW Sec 2-15S-3W. 2578' Paleozoic test. C/Graves. Set 7" 300'; TD 2578'

Figure 4-15. Portion of weekly report. (Reprinted with permission of *Southeastern Oil Review.*)

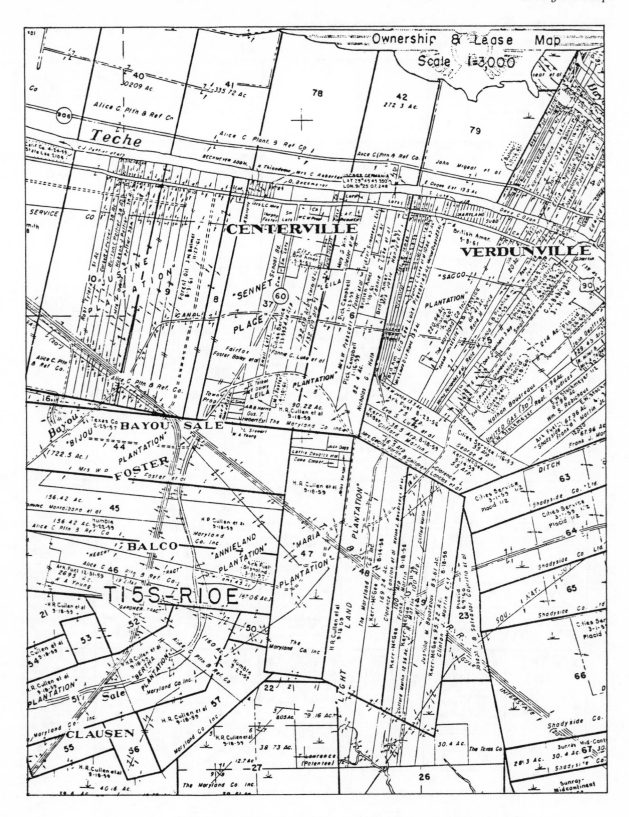

Figure 4-16. A lease ownership map. (Reprinted with permission of Tobin Map Company.)

**Rocky Mountain Area
Lease Ownership**

*Actual scale sample
Scale: 1" = 3,000'*

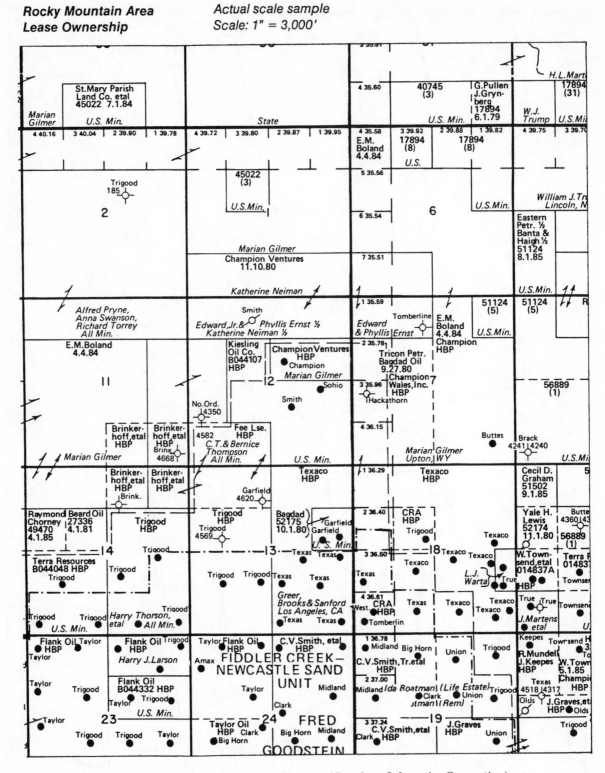

Figure 4-17. A lease ownership map. (Courtesy of Petroleum Information Corporation.)

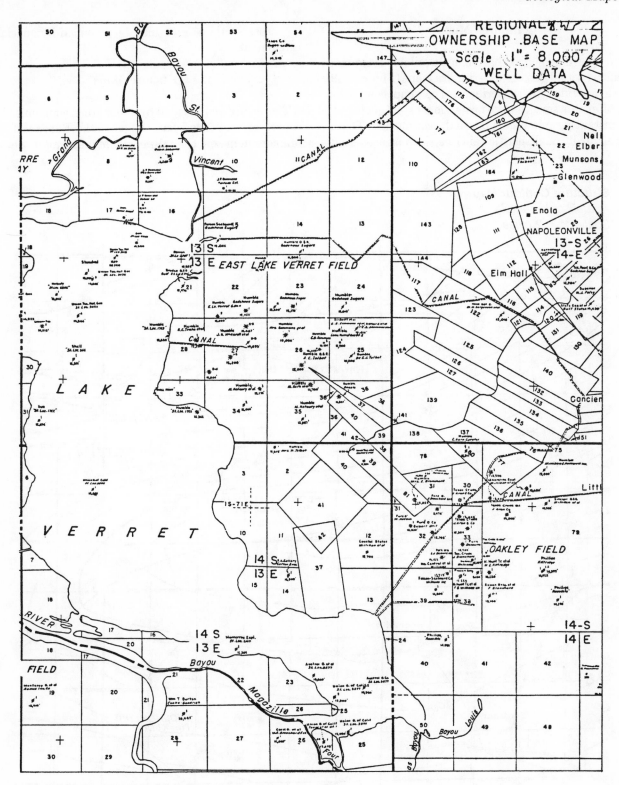

Figure 4-18. A commercial geological base map. (Courtesy of Tobin Map Corporation.)

Contoured Maps

Not only are geological base maps available from map companies, actual geological structure maps (Figure 4-19) may be provided to subscribers. The map companies which offer this service have professional staff geologists who constantly review and update the contouring. This is done regionally, and specific services, such as area stud-

ies, cross sections, etc., may be provided by special arrangement.

Offshore Maps

These may be provided by commercial companies but a source of very good base maps is the Bureau of Land Management or the Minerals Management Service.

Structure Contour Map
Actual scale sample
Scale: 1" = 2 miles

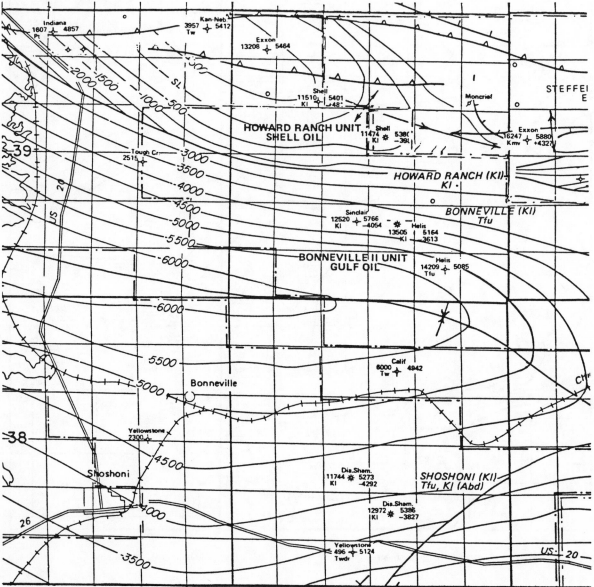

Figure 4-19. Structural contour maps are available usually by subscription. (Reprinted courtesy of Petroleum Information Corporation.)

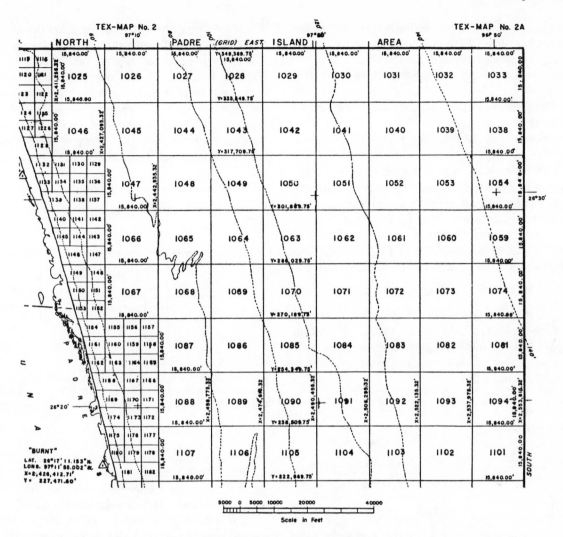

Figure 4-20. Offshore lease map. (Courtesy of Bureau of Land Management, U.S. Dept. of the Interior.)

Other examples of this type of map were included in "kinds of maps" in Chapter 3, and a larger-scale portion of an offshore lease map is shown in Figure 4-20. Notice that these maps include exact measurements of blocks, the X and Y coordinates, latitude and longitude, and the locations of U. S. C. & G. Stations. The dashed irregular lines through the area indicate sea depths. Large-scale maps for lease information, geological studies, or seismic studies may be built using only the information provided on these leasing maps. BLM maps do not show well control.

WELL SPOTTING

If there is a single most important function of the geological draftsman, or the geological technician, it is prob-

ably the spotting of well locations onto base maps. The correct location of the well is the first step in exploration geology. If the well location or the pertinent information is in error, it is impossible for anything else to be correct. The geologist interprets all the sources of data available to him in order to arrive at the best possible location for drilling. An enormous investment in time and money is at stake. There have been cases in which weeks (or months) of work have been discarded because an error went unnoticed until too late.

As a geologist maps an area and decides that it looks promising as a good prospect, leases are bought, deals are made, and contracts are signed. Precise locations are vital to the program. As you learn more about how these decisions are made it will become clear why this is so. (The same is true of lease posting, to be discussed in Chapter 5.)

Rule number one: *Read the entire description before spotting.* Check county, township and range, section number, area names, block numbers, etc.

There are several things to remember in well spotting:

1. Check the scale of the map and select the proper measuring device.
2. After measuring and marking, recheck before inking.
3. Check the county—as we have seen, some township and range numbers are repeated in several counties.
4. Check the area (offshore) as the same block numbers may appear in different areas on the same map.
5. If the location spots directly on top of another well and if it is not a recompletion, workover, etc., then check both the new location and the old. Then reconcile!

To begin: Gather all the correct maps; there may be more than one to spot. Find out how much information your company wants to include and which symbols your company uses. There are several acceptable variations. See Figures 4-21 and 4-22.

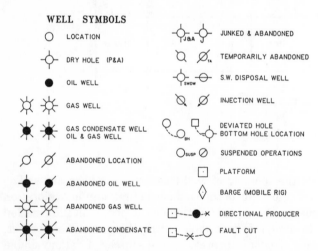

Figure 4-21. The well symbols pictured here are standard symbols, although there are other special ones used in some cases.

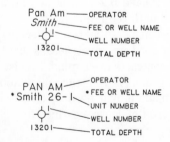

Figure 4-22. Acceptable ways to show minimum well data.

After reading the entire description through, you may find that you must begin at the end and work backwards. Example: Description reads: "500′ FNL, 30′ FEL SW NE Sec. 10-5N-9E, Scott County, Mississippi." First, it is necessary to find Scott County, then township 5N-9E, then section 10. When section 10 has been located, find the northeast quarter, then the southwest quarter of the northeast quarter. Only then do you begin measuring 500 feet from the north line and 30 feet from the east line (of the SW NE).

Figure 4-23 gives some examples of well location descriptions. An explanation of how to locate the wells follows:

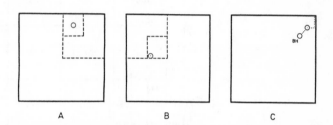

Figure 4-23. These well locations are evidence that the entire description must be read before spotting: (A) C NW NE; (B) 100′ FSL, 200′ FWL SE NW; (C) Surf. loc.: 660′ FNL, 500′ FEL of sec. BHL: S 45° W 700′ from surf. loc.

- Figure 4-23A. The description reads: C NW NE. Find the NE quarter first, then the NW quarter of that, then the center of that.
- Figure 4-23B. The description reads: 100′ FSL, 200′ FWL SE NW. Find the NW quarter first, then the SE quarter of that. Then measure 100′ from the south line and 200′ from the west line of the quarter quarter.
- Figure 4-23C. The description reads: Surf. loc: 660′ FNL, 500′ FEL of sec. BHL: S 45° W 700′ from surf. loc. Beginning at the NE corner of the section, measure 660′ south and 500′ west to find the surface location. Place a protractor with the index intersection at this point, measure south 45° west, and mark. Draw a light line from the surface location through this point and measure 700′ along this line to bottomhole.

Once the location has been established and checked you may ink it onto the base map. At this point you will need to use judgement about the size of the symbol and accompanying data. As a rule, try to match the size of the new information with the size already on the map. If it is a new base without any wells, make the symbol large enough to be seen easily, not so large as to clutter the map. If the location is in an area of seismic lines, it is wise to make the well symbol larger than the shot points to readily distinguish between them. The well symbols in Figure 4-21 are some of the standard ones used in the industry. However, some oil companies and some map companies use slightly different ones. Check with your company for the preferred ones.

It is the opinion of this writer that the dry hole symbol -◇- is preferable to ∅ which is also the symbol for an abandoned location. In this manner it is easy to distinguish between holes which have actually been drilled and locations which were never more than proposed locations. The examples (Figure 4-22) of ways to show well data are acceptable, but there are other ways. It is possible to include so much information that the map is cluttered and confusing.

When spotting well locations from different sources, you will encounter the exact location written in several different ways. Assuming standard sections, the following are two examples, each called three different ways, and these are only a few of the possibilities.

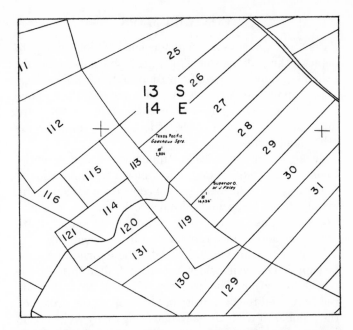

Figure 4-24. As in this example of a geological base map, no matter what attitude the sections are, the well information should be lettered in horizontal fashion, parallel with the bottom of the map. (Courtesy of Tobin Map Company.)

1. "660′ FSL, 330′ FEL SW NW"
   is the same as:
   "1,980′ FNL, 990′ FWL"
   and both are the same as:
   "1,980′ S, 990′ E of NW cor."

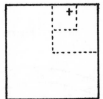

2. "330′ FNL, 330′ FEL NW NE"
   is the same as:
   "330′ FNL, 1,650 FEL"
   and both are the same as:
   "C NE NW NE"

There are times when it is necessary to work on a portion of a map which has no indication of scale. It should not happen, but it frequently does. In an area covered by the rectangular survey system, if the sections are reasonably standard the easiest way to figure the scale is to measure one section. Standard sections are one mile on a side, so in this case it does not present a problem. In an area covered by the rectangular system, but with sections which were surveyed by metes and bounds, as in Figure 4-24, you may measure the township. (This assumes that at least two corners of the township are indicated.) It should be six miles on a side. In areas like Texas, where no townships are used, you must have an indication of scale on the map to be certain. Note the horizontal attitude of the well information regardless of the shape of the section.

TYPICAL UNIT NUMBERS

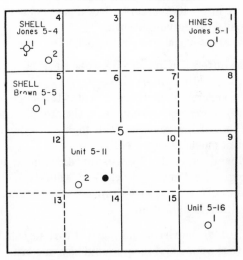

Figure 4-25. In some parts of the country, this is typical of the way units are numbered. When this system is used, it is easy to identify locations by unit number.

Figure 4-25 shows a unit numbering system which is used in some parts of the country. The unit numbers roughly correspond to lot numbers in this particular case. In the example, the well in unit 1 is called "Hines #1 Jones unit 5-1." Unit 4 has two wells within the unit: the Shell #1 Jones unit 5-4, and the Shell #2 Jones unit 5-4.

See Exercises 1 and 2 on well spotting at the end of this chapter.

CONTOUR MAPS

Contouring allows a two-dimensional exhibit (a map) to depict a three-dimensional form. A topographic map, for example, shows the configuration of the land surface. Topographic contours are lines of equal elevation above or below sea level. The contour *values* indicate the third dimension, such as valleys, ridges, hills, and various other land forms.

Geologic contour maps are fundamental and essential to oil and gas exploration. They allow the explorationist to portray geologic ideas and concepts from various data, mainly from wells and seismic surveys. The explorationist must be able to "read" contour maps and visualize the forms and shapes represented by the contours.

In order to map subsurface data, the information must be supplied by wells which have been drilled through the target formation. The accuracy of a contour map is directly related to the density of "control" in the area, i.e., the number of wells. A map containing many wells is said to have dense control, in contrast to a map with few wells or sparse control. Seismic data also provide control for geologic and seismic maps.

Many kinds of data can be contoured including: elevation of a geologic stratum above or below sea level, thickness of a formation or interval, seismic times, gravity or magnetic intensity, percentage of a particular rock type, or porosity of a given interval.

There are several principles governing contouring:

1. The difference in value between successive contours is the contour interval.
2. The spacing of contours indicates the slope or gradient. The closer the contours, the steeper the slope.
3. Where slope reverses, the highest or lowest contours must be repeated.
4. Closed contours represent extremes, such as "highs" or "lows," "thicks" or "thins."
5. Contours cannot cross (unless overhang or thrust faulting is indicated).

Figure 4-26 shows contour maps of various common solids. Both the cone and the pyramid have a constant slope. Note the difference in contour spacing for these shapes and that for the hemisphere and the ellipsoid which have both gradual and steeper slope.

Structural Contour Maps

Structure maps are probably the most common contour maps used in the oil industry. The model in Figure 4-27 indicates the shape represented by the contour map in that figure. By making structure maps, the geologist is able to see where possible traps are located. Refer to earlier description of traps (Figures 4-2 and 4-3).

These maps (Figures 4-28 and 4-29) depict the shape of a particular geologic horizon. If this horizon is entirely

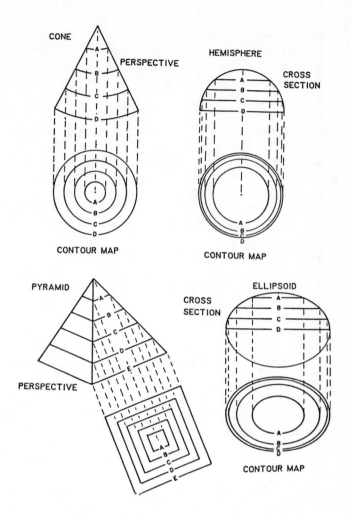

Figure 4-26. Contour map of common solids.

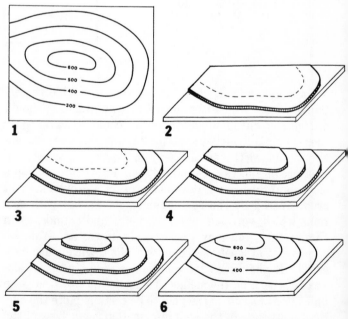

Figure 4-27. If a model were made by cutting out sections of foam board to match each contour in the map, it would be easy to see the kind of shape represented by these contours.

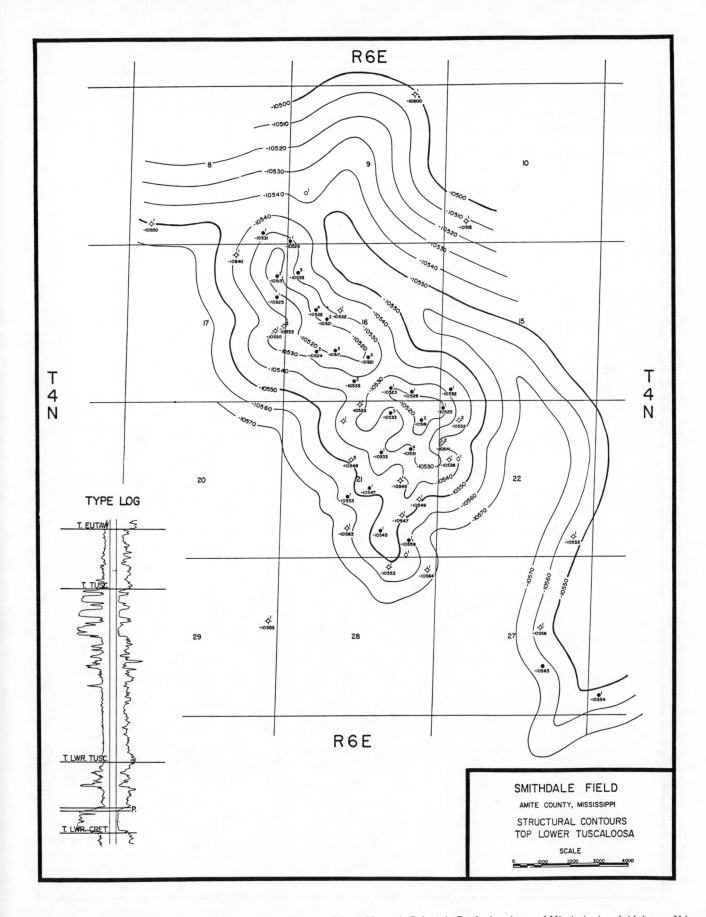

Figure 4-28. Structural contour map of Smithdale Field. (Reprinted from *Mesozoic-Paleozoic Producing Areas of Mississippi and Alabama*, Volume II, by permission of the Mississippi Geological Society.)

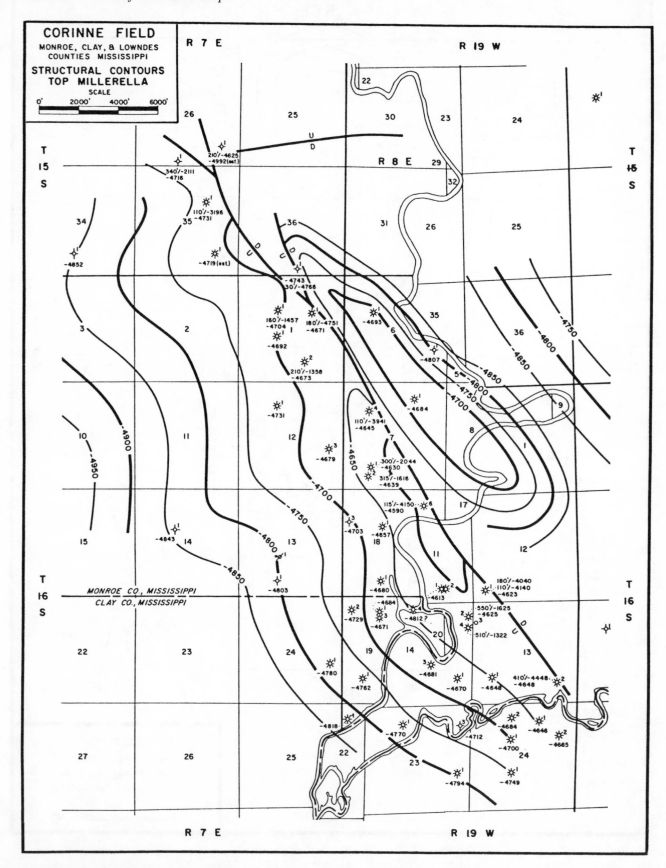

Figure 4-29. Structure map of Corinne Field. (Reprinted from *Mesozoic-Paleozoic Producing Areas of Mississippi and Alabama*, Volume II, by permission of the Mississippi Geological Society.)

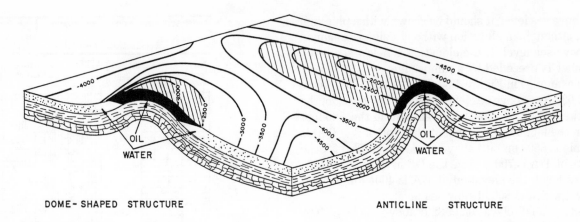

Figure 4-30. This block diagram shows how the contours of an oval shaped anticline differ from those of a dome shaped anticline.

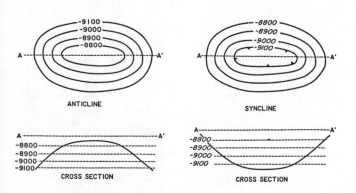

Figure 4-31. An anticline and a syncline may look the same on a map except for the values. Note the shapes in profile.

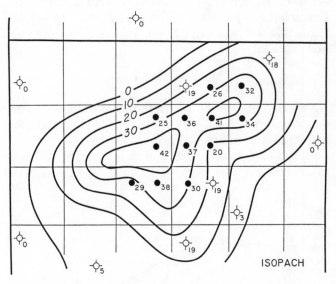

Figure 4-32. An isopach depicts areas of thick and thin deposition.

below the ground, it is a *subsurface* map. Petroleum geologists deal mainly with subsurface maps. Contour values are expressed in feet or meters above or below a common datum, usually mean sea level (MSL).

The block diagram in Figure 4-30 shows the contours for an elongated anticline and the more circular contours which indicate a dome-shaped structure, also an anticline. Both anticlines and synclines may appear the same on a contour map, but the numbers tell the story. Usually the syncline is marked by "ticks" or hachure marks. In Figure 4-31 the contours appear to be the same, but the values are reversed. As you can see by the respective cross sections or profiles, the anticline folds upward and the syncline folds downward.

Isopach Maps

Isopach means equal thickness and isopach contours show areas of thick or thin instead of "form" as in a structure map. Isopach contours may connect points of equal sand thickness (as in the isopach map in Figure 4-32), thickness of a certain geological formation, the interval between two particular horizons, the percentage

of sand or shale within a formation, feet of oil or gas pay, or porosity of a given rock unit.

Relating Log Depth to Sea Level

In order to make a meaningful structure map, the geologist must "correlate," or compare, the well logs in the area. As he matches the logs, he will pick a "key horizon," the top or bottom of an easily recognizable bed. In comparing any two things, it is necessary to find something which is common to both. In the case of well logs, the common factor is their relationship to mean sea level (MSL).

Having chosen the key horizon, its elevation relative to sea level is found by subtracting the depth from the elevation of the derrick floor (DF), because logs are measured from the working floor of the derrick. If the elevation is above sea level, it should be shown with a plus sign in front, although an elevation without a sign is assumed to be above sea level. If the elevation is below sea level, the number is preceded by a minus sign.

In the examples in Figure 4-33, Well #1 has a DF elevation of 1,000 feet above sea level, and the key horizon, the top of the "A" formation, was reached at the 860-foot depth on the log. The elevation at the "top of A" (T/A) is 1,000′ minus 860′ or 140′ above sea level. In Well #2, the log depth at T/A is 700′. Since the DF in this well is 400′ above sea level, the elevation of T/A is 400′ minus 700′ or −300′, which is 300′ below sea level.

Well #3 has a DF elevation of 320′ above sea level. T/A appears at the 1,320′ depth on the log, which is 1,000′ below sea level, or −1,000′. (320′ minus 1,320′ equals −1,000′.) In Well #4, operators had to drill only to 1,040′ to reach the key horizon at the same point, −1,000′, because that well was drilled from a derrick floor only 40′ above sea level.

Marking Log Tops

Now that we can see where the numbers used to contour maps come from, we need to be able to read the log and figure the subsea depths.

Figure 4-34 shows a portion of an electric log with certain formation tops marked. This one is called a "one

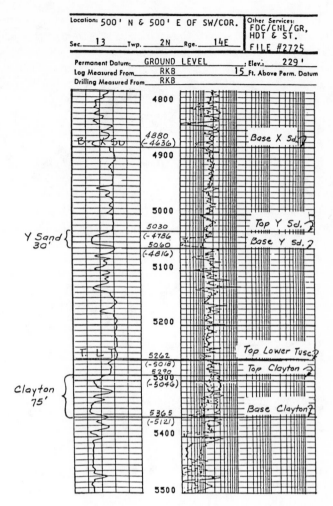

Figure 4-34. After the "tops" are picked on the log, the subsea elevations must be figured.

inch" log, meaning 1 inch equals 100 feet of vertical distance. In order to convert these marked "tops" to subsea depths, it is necessary to subtract the log depth from the derrick floor elevation. There is no derrick floor elevation shown on this particular log heading, although there is sufficient information to figure it. The "permanent datum" is ground level elevation, which is 229 feet above sea level. However, the log heading states that the log is measured from "RKB," the rotary kelly bushing, which is on the derrick floor. It also states that the RKB is 15 feet above the permanent datum. If ground elevation is 229′, and the kelly bushing is 15′ above that, then we must add 229′ plus 15′ to get the 244′ basis for figuring subsea depths in this well.

The base of the "X Sand" is marked at 4,880′ on the log, so the subsea depth at this point is 244′ minus 4,880′ or −4,636′, or 4,636′ below sea level. The top of "Y Sand" is marked at 5,030′, so the subsea elevation is −4,786′. Other tops are marked on the log, with the subsea elevations in parentheses.

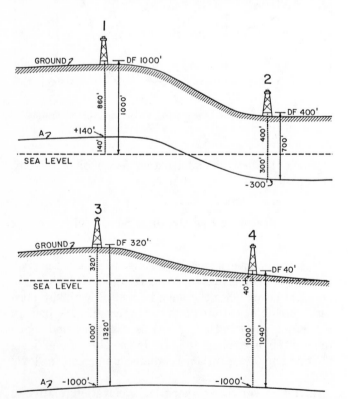

Figure 4-33. To compare well logs, it is necessary to use a common datum, which is usually mean sea level.

When figuring intervals as you would for an isopach map, it is not necessary to convert to subsea elevations. An isopach map has nothing to do with depth, only thickness. In this case, the "Y Sand" covers 30′ from 5,030′ to 5,060′. The "Clayton Sand" is 75′ thick, from 5,290′ to 5,365′.

Map Symbols for Geological and Geophysical Maps

The symbols pictured in Figure 4-35 (a–o) are some of the more common ones to be found on geological and geophysical maps. They are not the only ones encountered, but rather the usual ones. Contour values should be noted in line with the contour (a), not on top of or below it. Subsurface contour values are indicated by a minus sign. Subordinate contours (b) should not be as heavy as major contours, and many contours are broken (dashed) (a,b,c) where doubtful. Points of contact, oil to

water, gas to oil, are shown by light dashed contours and so named on the map (d,e). When a closed contour, or a "nose," represents a syncline or a "low" area, it is the usual practice to denote this by hachures, or ticks (f).

Faults are drawn to scale (using double lines) whenever possible, and the direction of throw always indicated. It is acceptable to indicate the downthrown side of a fault with a line drawn heavier than the other side (g). One way to show direction of displacement is to indicate "up" or "down" or "U" or "D" (h). Some explorationists prefer to indicate the downthrown side with a hachure as shown in (i). As with contours, a broken fault indicates a "possible" fault (j). Arrows parallel to the fault usually indicate strike-slip (with no vertical displacement) (k), unless shown on a cross section. Then it indicates direction of displacement.

The fault in (l) with "teeth" *could* indicate the *upthrown* side of a thrust, or reverse fault. (When in doubt, *ask!*) The wavy line in (m), usually means a permeability barrier on a map, but can mean an unconformity if shown on a cross section. The arrows in (n) and (o) indicate direction of dip, with (n) showing a trough, and (o) showing a ridge or high. Sometimes these symbols are accompanied by an indication of degree of dip.

Since most companies have one preferred system, it is advisable to check the individual symbols with the boss.

Mechanics of Contouring

This book is not intended to teach how to contour complicated geological features, or how to "interpret" the data. However, this portion may be used to demonstrate how to place contours on a map according to where control points indicate they should be. In the example in Figure 4-36, we see several control points with values from 5 to 53. If we connect the points along straight lines and

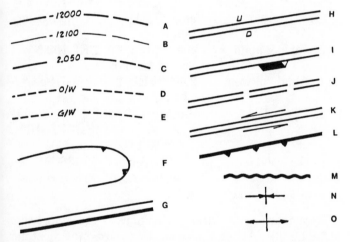

Figure 4-35. These symbols are common ones found on geological or geophysical maps.

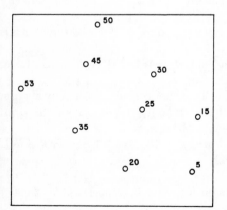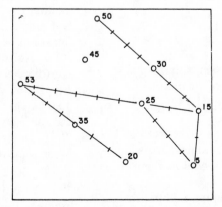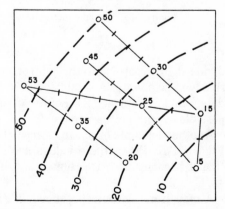

Figure 4-36. Linear interpolating of values for contouring.

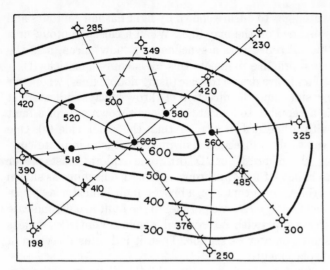

Figure 4-37. This map shows the values used for the model in Figure 4-33.

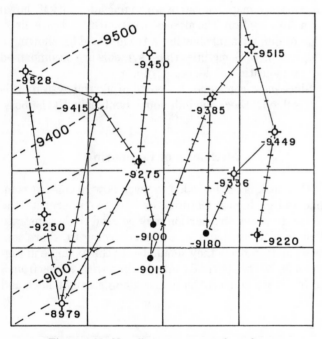

Figure 4-38. Not all structure maps show closure.

divide them according to the control values, a pattern of five-foot segments is established. If we "connect the dots," that is, connect the points of "equal value" it is possible to contour these data.

Another example of linear interpolation is depicted in Figure 4-37. When these values are contoured we see that it becomes a structure map of the model in Figure 4-29.

A map of dense control is shown in Figure 4-38 to provide the reader with contouring practice. Usually the more control points, the easier it is to contour. See Exercise 3 at the end of this chapter for practice in contouring.

EXERCISE 4-1: WELL SPOTTING
(Answers on pages 127–129)

Spot these wells on Map A (Figure 4-39). Figure scale first.

1. Gas well   1,500′ FSL, 1,200′ FEL Sec. 9-1N-9E, Smith Co.
2. Dry hole   300′ FNL, 660′ FEL Sec. 28-1N-9E, Smith Co.
3. Location   500′ FNL, 700′ FWL NW NE Sec. 3-10N-14W, Smith Co.
4. Dry hole   330′ FNL, 330′ FEL NE SW Sec. 18-1N-10E, Jasper Co.
5. Oil well   C SE SW Sec. 5-10N-13W, Jasper Co.
6. Gas cond.   1,980′ FNL, 1,720′ FWL Sec. 32-2N-10E, Jasper Co.

Spot these wells on Map B (Figure 4-40). Figure scale.

1. Temp. abdn.   Fr NW cor Sec. 139-13S-14E, go NE alg line 500′ th SE/ly @ rt angle 1,000′ to loc in Assumption Ph.
2. Junk & abnd.   400′ FSL, 1,000′ FEL N/2 NW/4 Sec. 41-14S-14E
3. Abnd. oil well 2,000′ FEL, 2,100′ FSL Sec. 12-13S-13E
4. Dry hole   Surf. loc. 2,300′ FSL, 3,000′ FEL Sec. 13-14S-13E; BHL: S 41° W 1,500′ fr surf loc.
5. Gas cond.   Fr NW cor Sec. 59-13S-14E, go E alg line 2,500′, th S @ rt angle 400′.

Spot these wells on Map C (Figure 4-41). Map scale: 1″ = 1 mile. All of these locations are in Freestone County.

1. Fr SE cor of J. Randai Survey, A-535, go N 1,300′, th E @ rt angle 900′ to loc. in G. H. Dunn Survey (drilling).
2. S. Campbell Survey, A-128, 600′ FSL, 1,000′ FEL (location).
3. R. A. Nelson Survey, A-474, 700′N, 600′ E of SW cor (dry hole).
4. Fr SE cor Wm. T. Barker Survey, A-64, W/ly alg line 1,900′, th S/ly @ rt angle, 1,100′ to loc. in L. J. Parker Survey, A-518 (gas well).
5. T. H. Davis Survey, A-188, 850′ FSL, 700′ FWL (abnd gas well).

Spot these wells on Figure 4-42 (Map D). (1″ = 2,000′).

1. *Wildcat:* Operator: Biglane Well: Bittick #1
   Location: Begin @ NW cor. sec. 87-7N-2W Adams

(text continued on page 76)

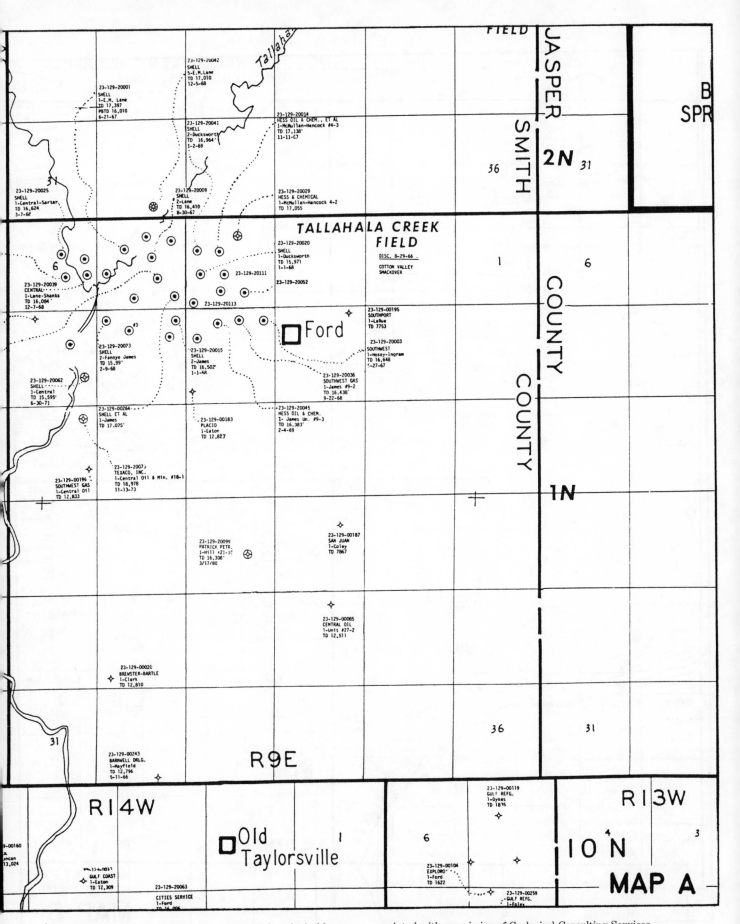

Figure 4-39. Map A is a portion of a commercial geological base map, reprinted with permission of Geological Consulting Services.

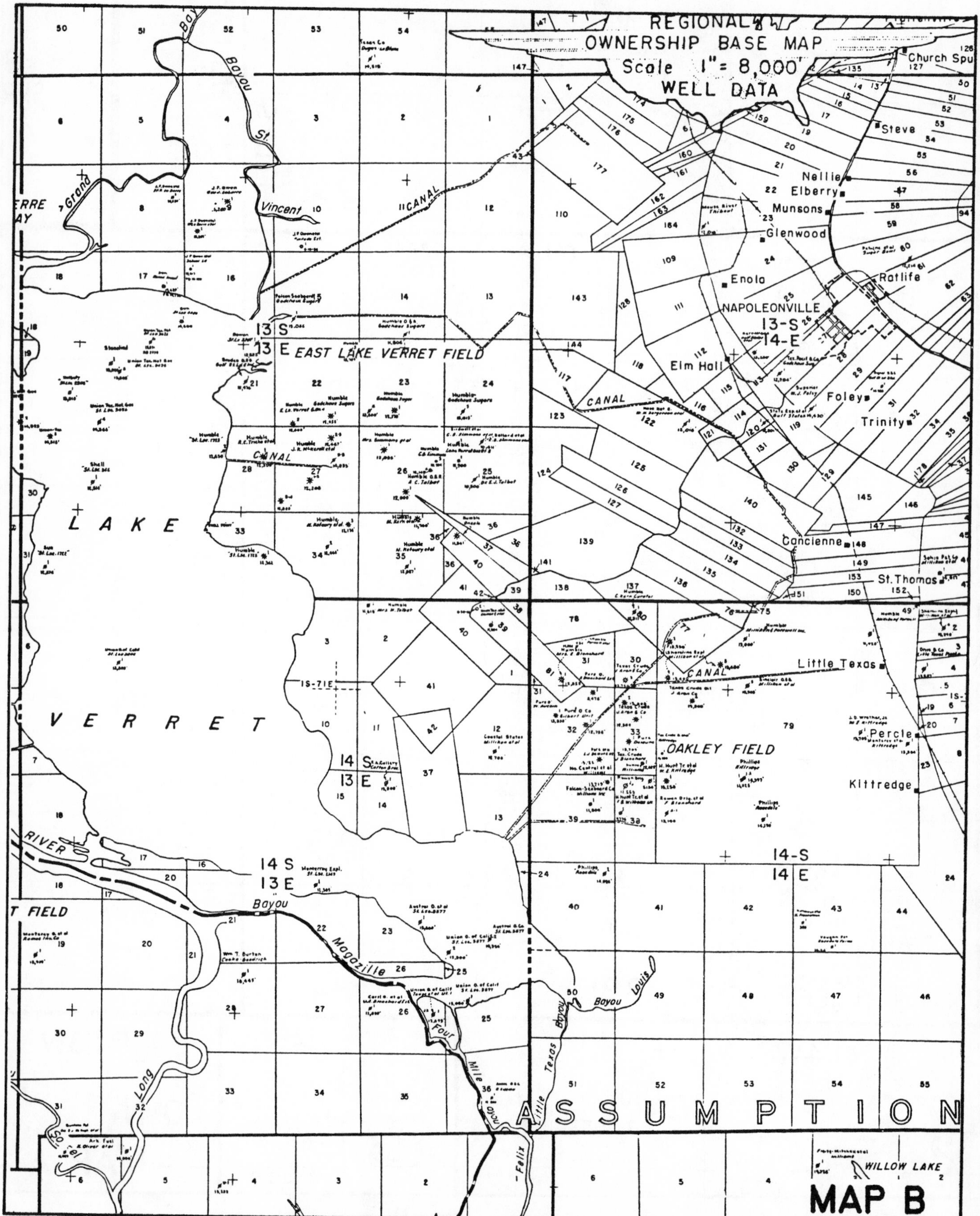

Figure 4-40. Map B shows an area of irregular sections on a small scale map, used mainly for regional mapping. (Courtesy of Tobin Map Company.)

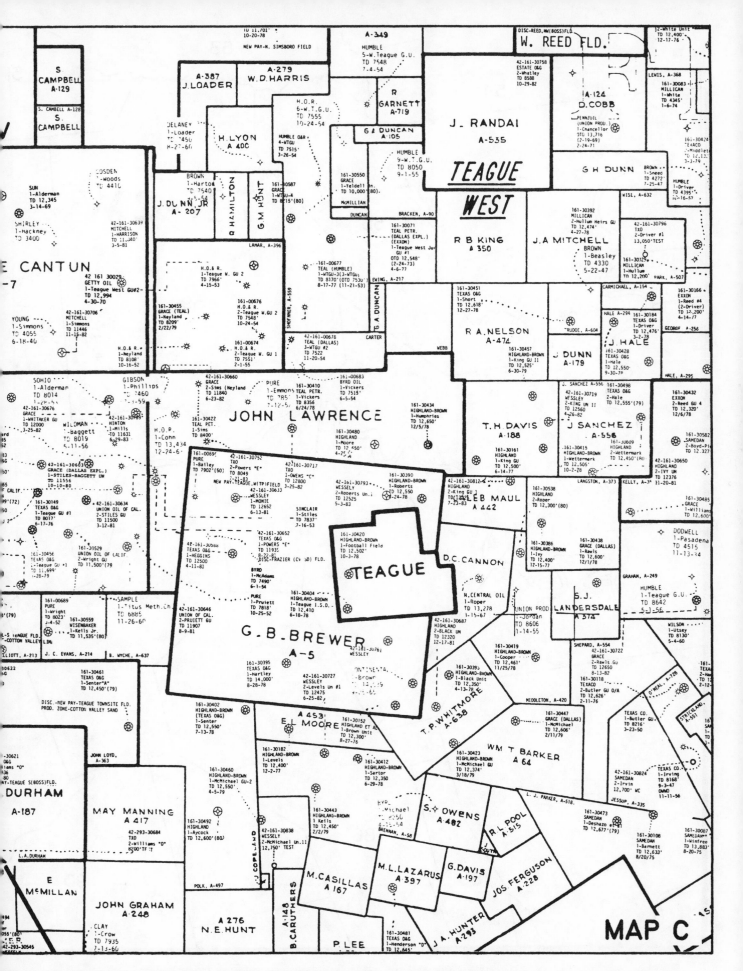

Figure 4-41. Map C is of a portion of Texas, in which the wells are located by surveys and abstracts, instead of sections, township and range.

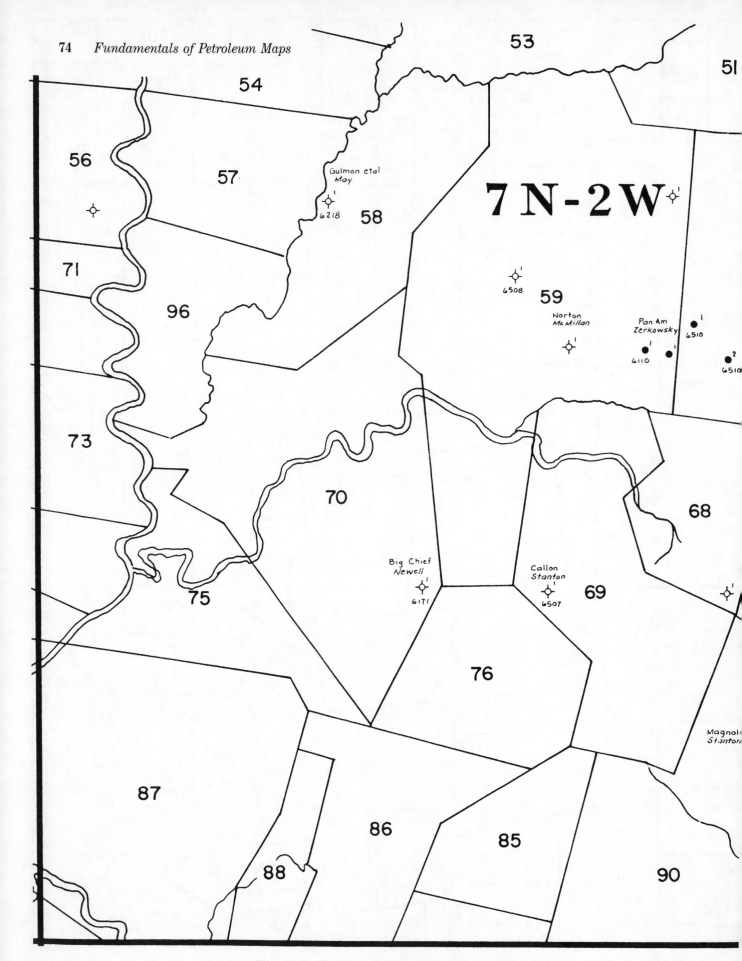

Figure 4-42. Map D is a good scale to use for prospecting.

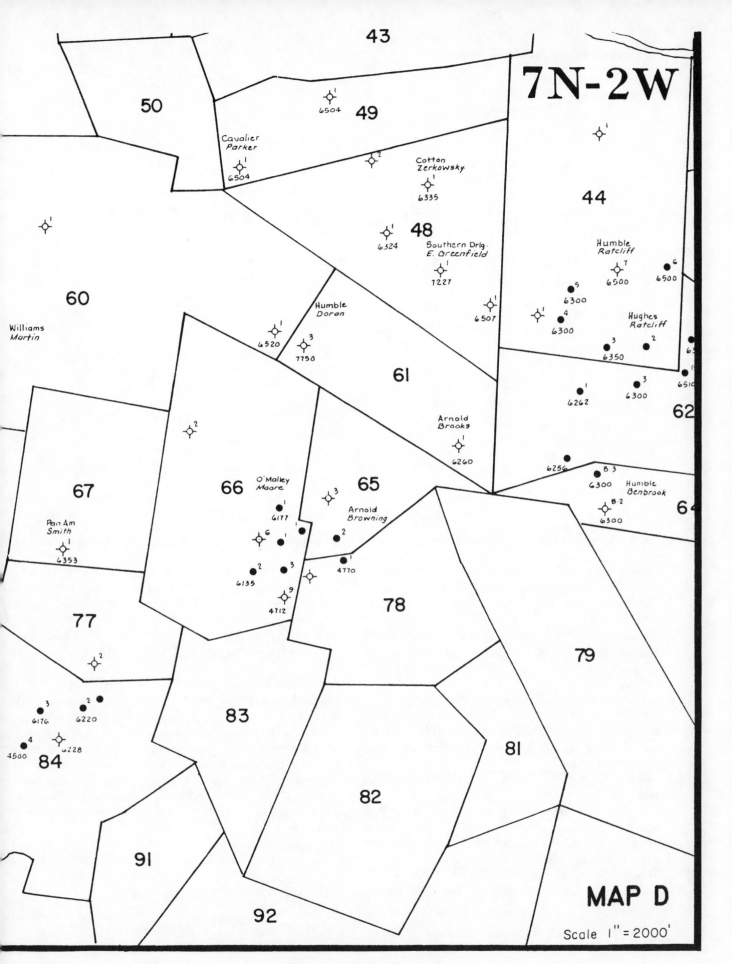

Figure 4-42 (continued).

Figure 4-43. This exercise may be used for mechanical contour practice. (The more control you have, the easier it is to contour in this manner.)

County, then SE/ly alg sec. line 3,450′, th S/ly @ rt angle 990′. Present operation: Location.

2. *Wildcat:* Operator: V. Smith, C. Conerly   Well: J. Champion #3
   Location: Fr SW cor sec. 69-7N-2W (cor. com. to 69, 76, 85) Adams Co., go N/ly alg line and ext. thereof 2,250′, th east @ rt angle 530′. Present operation: Drilling.

3. *Wildcat:* Operator: J. Donald   Well: D. Martin #1
   Location: Fr SE cor. sec. 57-7N-2W Adams Co., 2,925′ W alg line, th N/ly @ rt angle 1,000′ to surf. loc., th N 75° 30′ W 920′ to BHL. Present operation: Temp aband.

4. *Wildcat:* Operator: S. Sallis   Well: International Paper #1-A
   Location: Fr most westerly cor. sec. 50-7N-2W Adams Co., go SE alg sec. line 1,130′, th N/ly @ rt angle 2,150′ to loc. in sec. 50. Present operation: Discovery well I.P. 200 bopd TD: 6,079′.

5. *Wildcat:* Operator: Shell Oil   Well: L. Pacific #1
   Location: Fr most NE/ly cor. sec. 79-7N-2W Adams

Co., go S 34° 00° W 1,300′ to loc. in sec. 79. Present operation: Testing TD: 5,967′.

6. *Wildcat:* Operator: So. Minerals   Well: #2 Masonite
   Location: 670′ N, 930′ W of SE cor. sec. 60-7N-2W, Adams Co. (cor. com. to sec 60, 67, 66) to loc in sec. 60 Present Operation: J & A TD: 3,020′.

Note: From the time a well location is reported until it is finished, the symbol remains that of a "location" (○). Whether it is drilling, testing, tripping, coring, etc., the symbol is the same. Some companies use various means to indicate the specific operation, but this is not standard industry practice. A well is not "finished" until it is "completed" (put on stream), "junked" (and abandoned), "plugged" (dry and abandoned), or some other final disposition is made. At that time, the appropriate symbol should be used.

EXERCISE 4-2: CONTOURING

Draw in the contours on Figure 4-43.

Chapter 5
Geophysical Maps

GEOPHYSICS

Geophysics is the study of the physics of the earth. The geophysicist studies and interprets earth magnetism, gravity, and seismic data. Sensitive instruments are used to measure variations in a physical quality that may be related to subsurface conditions that point to probable oil- or gas-bearing formations. Prospecting in this way does not guarantee success, but the combination of geophysical and geological information reduces the risks.

A magnetic survey records the intensity of the earth's magnetic field. These are made from either an airplane or a boat. A gravity survey measures variations in the earth's gravitational field. It shows differences in density below the surface. A seismic survey records sound waves reflected from subsurface layers and accounts for most of the geophysical budget.

The first seismograph, a seismometer, was used in 1841 to measure the vibrations of the ground during earthquakes. During World War I, a German scientist developed a practical use for a seismograph. He recorded vibrations of the earth when enemy artillery was fired and calculated their positions. He thought some miscalculations had been caused by the variation of the sound waves as they passed through geological formations, so he applied basic geological concepts and hit the target every time.

After the war the scientist reversed the process to measure the distance from the explosion to the seismograph and to estimate the geological subsurface formations. After finding his theories practical, he formed the first seismic exploration company. Soon after that, a crew was brought to this country to explore the Gulf Coast region.

In seismic surveying, an energy source near the surface produces vibrations similar to the shock waves caused by an earthquake (Figure 5-1). This may be done by using explosives placed in holes in the ground, or by using one of several kinds of vibrator trucks. The shock waves travel down through layers of rock, which act as reflectors. When the shock waves encounter different rock layers, some of the energy bounces back to the surface to be picked up by special detectors, called *geo-*

phones. These geophones are laid out in a pattern and connected to a recording device in an instrument truck that plots the time it takes for the waves to travel to each layer and back. The time is measured in seconds and fractions of seconds. The energy is converted to digital form and stored for later computer analysis. The final record is a seismogram, or seismic record. Figure 5-2 shows a seismic record section composed of several seismograms. At the top of the record section are the shot point numbers, and the times are recorded on the left side. As the geophysicist works the section, he picks "key horizons" and notes the times, instead of depths. These times are then transferred to a map, and the data can be contoured to show structure or thickness. A thickness map made on time is called an "isotime" or "isochron" map.

SEISMIC BASE MAPS

Before any shooting began, it was necessary for the seismic company to obtain permits to go onto the property. The area was surveyed and a pattern of shot points determined. The shot point locations were then spotted onto a base map. Sometimes a seismic base map is little more than section corners with the shot points located

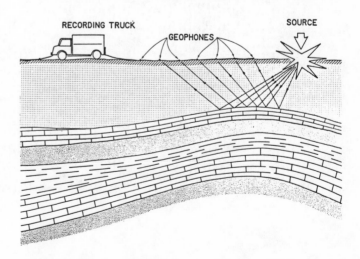

Figure 5-1. This is a simplified diagram of shooting seismic.

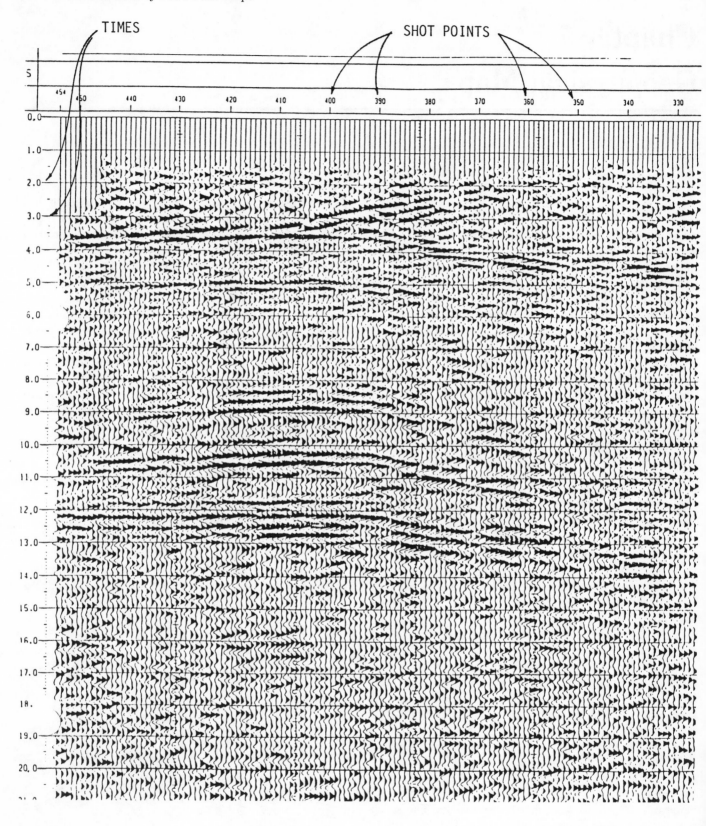

Figure 5-2. Pictured here is a portion of a seismic record section. The shot points are numbered across the top and the times down the left side.

(Figure 5-3). Other times the shot points are spotted onto a geological base map with complete well control (Figure 5-4). The shot points must be numbered and the lines numbered or named.

Different companies have different policies regarding their maps. In areas of extreme density of seismic lines, some geophysicists like to have the points connected by fine lines, making it easier to follow the course of a particular line. Some prefer to add "tags" to the shot points to indicate the direction of the remainder of the line. One uncluttered way to indicate the difference is to place shot point numbers at a right angle to the direction of the line.

In this manner, when several lines cross or converge, it is easy to distinguish between them without adding unnecessary clutter.

SEISMIC STRUCTURE MAPS

Many times seismic lines are shot in areas with little or no well control. In this case, the seismic map would show only times. Where there is well control, the subsea elevations of the wells must be considered, along with the seismic times. The times may be converted to depths, and equivalents vary from one area to another. The structure

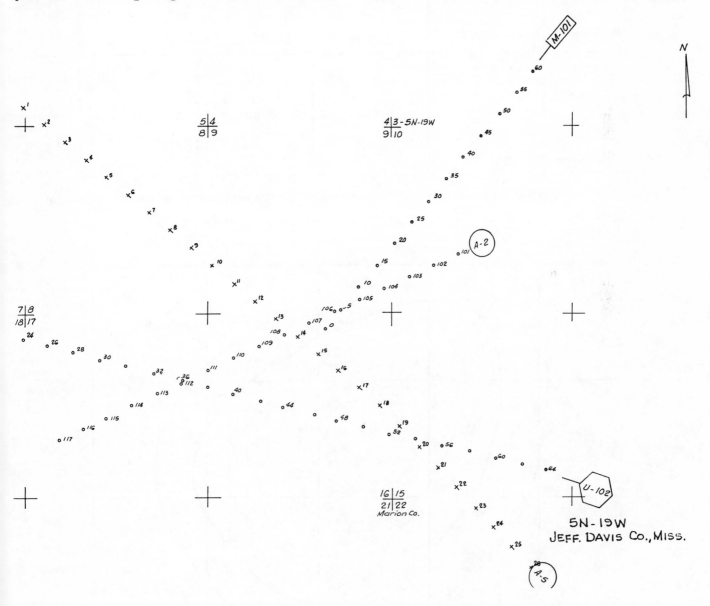

Figure 5-3. Sometimes shot points are located on maps having only section corners as a guide.

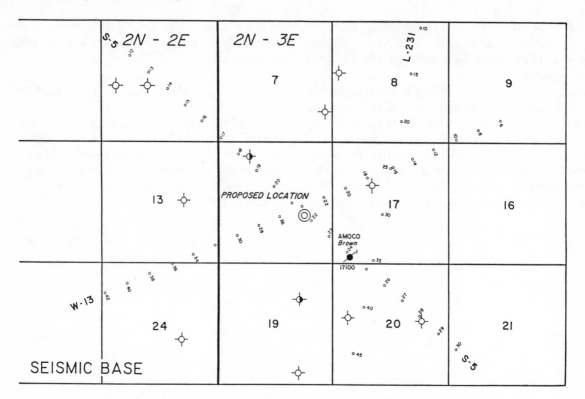

Figure 5-4. This is an example of a seismic base map, which includes well control in the area.

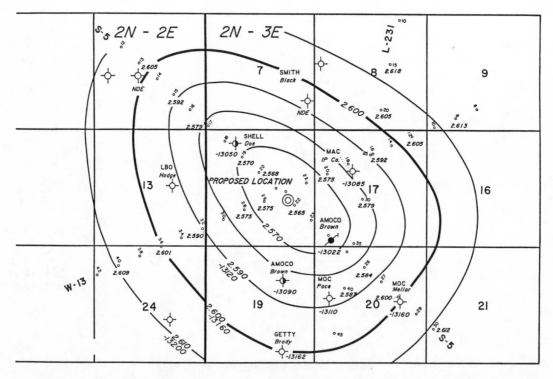

Figure 5-5. Seismic structure map. It is necessary to assess well information along with the seismic information.

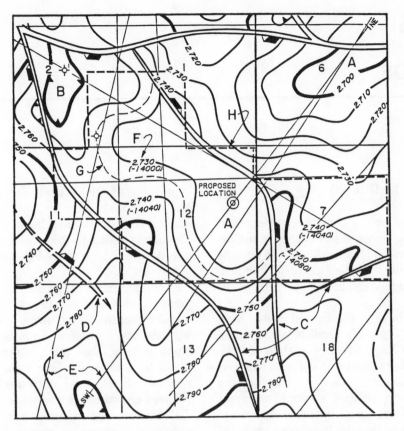

Figure 5-6. Seismic structure map shows how to indicate several features: (A) a "high"; (B) a "low"; (C) faults; (D) possible fault; (E) presence of seismic lines; (F) seismic times with subsea equivalent; (G) assumed oil/water contact; (H) acreage outline.

map in Figure 5-5 shows how geological and geophysical data are coordinated.

The map in Figure 5-6 is one of complicated geological features, including faults. In this case, the seismic lines are indicated by fine lines merely to show their presence. A preliminary map on a bigger scale with shot points and times had to be prepared before a map like this one could be made.

Seismic structure maps convey the same forms that are portrayed by geological structure maps. The difference is in the information used to construct them, and the contours are labeled in times instead of feet. Refer to structural contour maps in Chapter 4 for general information.

SEISMIC ISOTIME MAPS

Seismic isopach maps are called *isotime* or *isochron* maps. They serve the same purpose as geological isopach maps in that they portray areas of thick and thin deposition. Instead of "feet of pay" these maps show times, in seconds and milliseconds.

Chapter 6
Land Maps

BACKGROUND

It has taken centuries for the laws that govern land ownership to evolve, and they are still changing and developing. This chapter on land maps will not get into the details of the law, but will provide a little history to help toward the understanding of the land maps used every day in the oil industry.

Most of the laws we have in the United States have evolved from European, especially English, law since the Norman Conquest gave England a new system of land-holding in 1066. After that time, grants of land were rewards for services rendered to a lord or a baron or the king. Few individuals were allowed to own land free of obligation to others, as we know it today. As events changed boundaries and rulers, the laws were amended and developed.

The United States also has been influenced by the Spanish, especially in the Southwest, and the French, in Louisiana. In fact, Louisiana laws are different from those in other states because of that influence. During this country's Colonial period, Spain held much land in the West, Southeast, and Southwest. France owned almost all the land along the Mississippi River, including the Ohio Valley and areas in the South.

The British Crown granted to certain groups land grants which extended from the Atlantic to the Pacific, even though nobody knew exactly where the Pacific Ocean was. Several of the states have charters which included all this area, but some of the western land was already claimed by other countries, and much of it was claimed by the Indians. All of this led to great confusion over who owned what. After all the wars, treaties, homesteaders, and land speculators had influenced land ownership, the United States finally developed what is probably the best arrangement for individual land ownership in the world today.

Chapter 3 covers the survey systems used in this country in detail and explains how any tract in the United States can be distinguished from any other tract.

Unlike most countries in the world, private ownership of land in this country usually carried with it ownership of the *fee,* which meant that the landowner also owned everything under his land. Extensive use of these mineral resources is comparatively recent, since most of the mineral industries have been founded in this century. The laws relating to the ownership of minerals have followed, rather than preceded, the development of these industries.

Even though we in the oil industry call our ownership maps "land maps," we are more interested in mineral owners than in surface owners. In this chapter we deal with the distribution of the mineral ownership. It is not intended to go into laws, contracts, special clauses of leases, etc., but rather how to find the information necessary to make the land maps used in the industry.

Once a company has an area of interest for prospecting, the landman needs a tract map of the area. Usually a commercial ownership map can tell the landman who owns the minerals and if there is a lease in effect on a particular tract. This saves valuable time and money because these maps are usually updated monthly. Of course to be certain, it is often necessary to check the courthouse records. Checking records in the courthouse can be an entire course in itself. Public lands can be checked through the Bureau of Land Management, and state lands can be checked with the State Land Offices in individual states.

No matter how many records are available, or how many leases have been taken, it is difficult to get the big picture until all the information has been recorded on a map. Only then does the landman know if all the interests have been leased and how that information affects the company's prospect.

LAND TERMINOLOGY AND ABBREVIATIONS

Assignment—The transfer of an interest in property (or minerals) (from the *Assignor* to the *Assignee*).

Back-in—Interest which reverts to a party upon the fulfillment of certain conditions and terms.

Bonus—Money paid to the lessor by the lessee when the former signs a lease.

Deed—A legal instrument in writing in which the owner of property, (the *Grantor*) conveys to another (*Grantee*) some right, title, or interest in or to property.

Et al—Abbreviation meaning "and others."

Et ux—Abbreviation meaning "and wife."

Et vir—Abbreviation meaning "and husband."

Fee simple ownership—A situation in which one entity owns all the land, surface and minerals, surface rights, leasing rights, royalty.

Gross acres—The total number of acres in the entire tract without regard to ownership or leasehold.

HBO (held by operations)—Leases kept in force by drilling or other work.

HBP (held by production)—Leases kept in force by producing well.

Lease—A written instrument which is made by the owner of property or minerals (the *Lessor*) giving another party (the *Lessee*) the use of the premises for a particular purpose for a given length of time (the *Term*).

Leasehold—An interest or right in land held under a lease.

Life estate—An estate in which the ownership of the property by the *Life tenant* is only during that person's lifetime (or the life of another party). After the termination of the person's life, the estate goes to the *Remainderman*.

Metes and bounds—A method of describing property, "metes" meaning "measure" and "bounds" meaning "boundaries."

Mineral lease—A written agreement by the lessor giving the lessee the right to go on the land and explore for oil, gas, or other minerals, and, if found, to produce and remove these from the premises.

Mineral owner—Separate from surface—has the right to lease or remove the minerals. Mineral rights take precedence over surface rights.

Net acres—Gross acres less other interests. Example: If three parties own equal shares in a 60-acre tract, each owns 20 net acres. If a company leases two of those interests, the company has leased 40 net acres.

Open acreage—Acreage in which the minerals are not under lease.

Overriding royalty (ORRI)—Interest payable to third party out of proceeds from production. This differs from the royalty interest in that it comes out of the "working interest," or that part of the production that goes to the person who acquired the lease rather than to the landowner. This interest ends with the expiration of the lease.

Paid-up lease—Lease which does not require rentals to keep it in force.

Plat—A map of a certain tract or tracts of land.

POB—Point of beginning, where the description starts.

Primary term—The length of time a lease is valid.

Prescription—In the state of Louisiana the surface rights and minerals are not separated. The surface owner owns the mineral rights under the land unless they were reserved by the previous owner for ten years (maximum reservation). If there is no production on the property at the end of the ten-year reservation, the minerals automatically "prescribe" to the present owner of the land. This process is called prescription.

Royalty—Interest retained by the lessor in the lease and payable out of any proceeds of production before expenses are paid.

Royalty owner—Owns a portion of oil and gas produced from the land. The owner cannot lease or get any bonus money, but owns royalty at production. The person owns this royalty, even if the lease expires. This is sometimes called "perpetual royalty."

Working interest—The portion of oil production money out of which operating and development costs are paid.

READING LEASES

There are many different kinds of oil, gas, and mineral leases. Different states have preferred forms for standard leases, and landmen have different preferences. There are three examples of lease forms included here. Figure 6-1 is a special Louisiana lease form, i.e., Bath's form for a "paid up" lease. Figure 6-2 is a Form 88⅛ for use in Arkansas. The type of lease is noted in the top left corner of each. Figure 6-3 is called a "Producers 88," and this particular one is for Mississippi. In each case these examples show only a portion of the front page of the lease, the part one needs to be able to plot it. Different pertinent data have been indicated on Figure 6-3. It is nearly impossible, in most cases, to know exactly the "net" interest of the parties, just by reading the lease. There was a time when it was directly related to the amount of rentals paid. For years, rentals were fifty cents an acre; then for a time the lessors were paid a dollar an acre in rentals. The amounts have changed over the years, so this is not a reliable indication. The bonus money is never mentioned on the face of the lease. There are ways to find out the interest: by knowing the bonus per acre, by checking the lease acquisition form, or by seeing the actual check or broker's report. A check of mineral ownership or a lease take-off also shows this information. (For examples of complete lease forms and similar documents see *Landman's Encyclopedia*/Third Edition, Gulf Publishing Company, Houston, 1987.)

HOW TO SHOW LEASE DATA

One company may use a method indicating lease information which is different from the method of another. It is beneficial if the same system is used throughout one company, certainly throughout a single project. For the

(text continued on page 87)

BATH-Ⓑ-GRAM

BATH'S FORM LOUISIANA SPEC. 14-BR1-2A-PX PAID UP 2-77

OIL, GAS AND MINERAL LEASE

THIS AGREEMENT made this_____day of_____, 19____, between

lessor (whether one or more), and_____
lessee, WITNESSETH:

1. Lessor in consideration of_____Dollars ($_____),
in hand paid, of the royalties herein provided, and of the agreement of Lessee herein contained, hereby grants, leases and
lets exclusively unto Lessee for the purposes of investigating, exploring, prospecting, drilling and mining for and producing oil, gas and all other minerals, laying pipe lines, building tanks, power stations, telephone lines, and other structures
thereon to produce, save, take care of, treat, transport and own said products and for dredging and maintaining canals,
constructing roads and bridges, and building houses for its employees, and, in general, for all appliances, structures,
equipment, servitudes and privileges which may be necessary, useful or convenient to or in connection with any such

operations conducted by Lessee thereon, or on any adjacent lands, the following described land in_____
Parish, Louisiana, to-wit:

Comprising_____acres, more or less.

This lease also covers and includes battures, accretions and all other land owned by Lessor adjacent to the land
particularly described above.

2. Subject to the other provisions herein contained, this lease shall be for a period of_____years from this
date (called "primary term") and as long thereafter as (1) oil, gas, sulphur or other mineral is produced from said land
hereunder or from land pooled therewith; or (2) it is maintained in force in any other manner herein provided.

(a) It is the intention of the parties that this lease shall also extend and apply to all outstanding mineral rights
or servitudes affecting the lands herein described as the same may revert to Lessor, his heirs, or assigns, from time to
time.

3. For the consideration hereinabove recited, this lease shall remain in full force and effect during the primary
term, without any additional payment and without Lessee being required to conduct any operations on the land (either
before or after the discovery of minerals), except to drill such wells as might be necessary to protect the land from
drainage, as hereinafter provided.

4. The royalties to be paid by Lessee are: (a) on oil, and other hydrocarbons which are produced at the well in
liquid form by ordinary production methods, one-eighth of that produced and saved from said land, same to be delivered
at the wells or to the credit of Lessor in the pipe line to which the wells may be connected; Lessor's interest in either
case to bear its proportion of any expenses for treating the oil to make it marketable as crude; Lessee may from time to
time purchase any royalty oil or other liquid hydrocarbons in its possession, paying the market price therefor prevailing
for the field where produced on the date of purchase; (b) on gas, including casinghead gas, or other gaseous substance
produced from said land and sold or used off the premises or for the extraction of gasoline or other products therefrom,
the market value at the well of one-eighth of the gas so sold or used, provided that on gas sold at the wells the royalty
shall be one-eighth of the amount realized from such sale; such gas, casinghead gas, residue gas, or gas of any other
nature or description whatsoever, as may be disposed of for no consideration to Lessee, either through unavoidable
waste or leakage, or in order to recover oil or other liquid hydrocarbons, or returned to the ground, shall not be deemed
to have been sold or used either on or off the premises within the meaning of this paragraph 3 hereof; (c) on all other
minerals mined and marketed, one-eighth, either in kind or value at the well or mine, at Lessee's election, except that
on sulphur the royalty shall be one dollar ($1.00) per long ton.

5. If Lessee during or after the primary term should drill a well capable of producing gas or gaseous substances
in paying quantities, (or which although previously produced Lessee is unable to continue to produce) and should
Lessee be unable to operate said well because of lack of market or marketing facilities or governmental restrictions, then
Lessee's rights may be maintained beyond or after the primary term without production of minerals or further drilling

operations by paying Lessor as royalty_____Dollars ($_____)
per year, the first payment being due, if said well should be completed or shut-in after the primary term, within sixty (60)
days after the completion of such well or the cessation of production and such payment will extend Lessee's rights for one
year from the date of such completion or cessation. If such a well should be completed during the primary term, the first

Figure 6-1. A portion of a sample lease form used in Louisiana.

FORM 88⅛, REVISED O. FICE SUPPLY CO., EL DORADO, ARK.

Form 88⅛ OIL AND GAS LEASE (⅛ GAS)
WITH RELINQUISHMENT OF DOWER AND UNITIZATION AGREEMENT

This AGREEMENT, Made and entered into on this the_____day of_____, 19_____

by and between_____

_____

_____of_____

party of the first part, hereinafter called lessor (whether one or more), and_____

_____

of_____party of the second part, hereinafter called lessee.

WITNESSETH: That the said lessor for and in consideration of_____

_____DOLLARS, cash in hand paid, the receipt whereof is hereby acknowledged, and
of the covenants and agreements hereinafter contained on the part of the lessee to be paid, kept and performed, ha____

granted, demised, leased and let, and by these presents do_____grant, demise, lease and let unto
said lessee, for the sole and only purpose of mining and operating for oil and gas and laying of pipe lines, and of building tanks, power stations, and structures thereon to produce, save and take care of said products, all that certain tract of

land situated in the county of_____State of Arkansas, to-wit:

and containing_____acres, more or less.

It is agreed that this lease shall remain in force for a term of_____years from this date,
and as long thereafter as oil or gas, or either of them, is produced from said land by the lessee.

In consideration of the premises the said lessee covenants and agrees:

First. To deliver to the credit of lessor, free of cost in tanks or pipe line to which lessee may connect his wells, the
equal one-eighth (⅛) part of all oil produced and saved from the leased premises.

Second. To pay lessor for gas from each well where gas only is found, the equal one-eighth (⅛) of the gross proceeds

at the prevailing market rate, for all gas used off the premises, said payments to be made
and lessor to have gas free of cost from any such well for all stoves and inside lights in the principal dwelling house
on said land during the same time by making his own connections with the well at his own risk and expense.

Third. To pay lessor for gas produced from any oil well and used off the premises or for the manufacture of casinghead gas, one-eighth (⅛) of the gross proceeds at the prevailing market rate for the gas so used, for the time during which

such gas shall be used, said payments to be made_____

If no well be commenced on said land on or before the_____day of_____, 19_____,
this lease shall terminate as to both parties, unless the lessee, on or before that date, shall pay or tender to the lessor, or

to the lessor's credit in the_____Bank of_____
Arkansas, or its successors, which shall continue as the depository regardless of changes in the ownership of said land, the

sum of_____DOLLARS,
which shall operate as a rental and cover the privilege of deferring the commencement of a well for twelve months from
said date. In like manner and upon like payments or tenders the commencement of a well may be further deferred for
like periods in the same number of months successively. And it is understood and agreed that the consideration first recited herein, the down payment, covers not only the privileges granted to the date when said first rental is payable as
aforesaid, but also the lessee's option of extending that period as aforesaid, and any and all other rights conferred.

Should the first well drilled on the above described lands be a dry hole, then, in that event, if a second well is not
commenced on said land within twelve months from the expiration of the last rental period for which rental has been
paid, this lease shall terminate as to both parties, unless the lessee on or before the expiration of said twelve months
shall resume the payment of rentals in the same amount and in the same manner as hereinbefore provided. And it
is agreed that upon the resumption of the payment of rentals, as above provided, that the last preceding paragraph
hereof, governing the payment of rentals and the effect thereof, shall continue in force just as though there had been
no interruption in the rental payments.

If said lessor owns a less interest in the above described land than the entire and undivided fee simple mineral estate
therein, then the royalties and rentals herein provided shall be paid the lessor only in proportion which lessor's fee simple
mineral interests therein bears to the whole and undivided fee simple mineral estate in the lands.

Lessee shall have the right to use, free of cost, gas, oil and water produced on said land for his operation thereon
except water from wells of lessor.

When requested by lessor, lessee shall bury his pipe line below plow depth.

No well shall be drilled nearer than 200 feet to the house or barn now on said premises, without written consent of
the owners.

Lessee shall pay for damages caused by his operations to growing crops on said land.

Figure 6-2. A portion of lease form 88½, sometimes used in Arkansas.

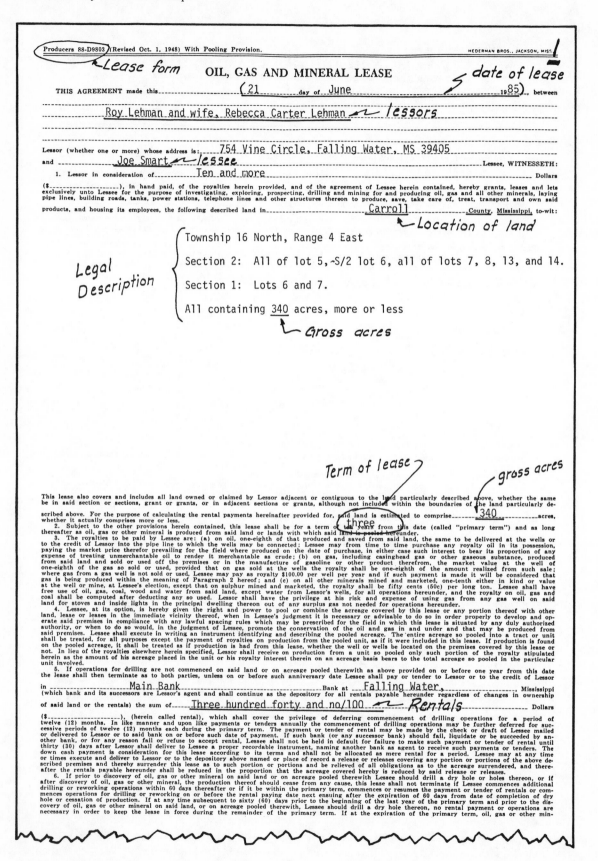

Figure 6-3. Producers 88 form used extensively in Mississippi. Note the different kinds of information and where they are found in the lease form.

benefit of those for whom no prearranged pattern exists, there are several examples of acceptable systems in Figure 6-4. The data here are illustrated in different ways within individual tracts and are for comparison of methods only. It would not be acceptable practice to include all different methods on one map. A detailed look at the different tracts follows in Figures 6-5, 6-6, and 6-7.

Certain features are easily recognizable on any land map, regardless of the particular system used. One example is the use of a *lease hook* and a *land hook*. (See Figure 6-4, tract A. & E.) The lease hook indicates that the property (minerals) on each side of the road and on each side of the railroad are all covered under the same lease. The land hook indicates that all portions connected by the hook are owned by the same entity, whether under lease or not. There are several variations of configuration for a *lease* hook, (see tract E) but the *land* hook shown here seems to be universally accepted.

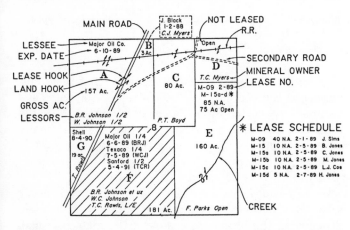

Figure 6-4. This illustrates several ways to show lease data. Do not mix the different ways on the same map.

The data indicated in tracts A, B, and C of Figure 6-5 tell many things. Tract A, for example, tells the reader that:

- Major Oil Company has leased the entire 157-acre tract.
- It is leased from B. R. Johnson and W. Johnson.
- Each lessor owns an undivided one-half interest in all 157 acres.
- The lease covers acreage on both sides of the main road and that portion north of the railroad.
- The data further indicate that the lease will expire in June 1989.

Because there is no indication otherwise, we assume that Major Oil Company owns a full interest in this tract.

Tract B is too small to include all the necessary information, so a "boxed" notation is made outside the tract with an arrow directing the reader to tract B.

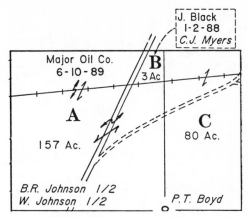

Figure 6-5. Tracts A, B, and C.

- It encompasses three acres.
- The minerals are owned by C. J. Myers.
- It is leased to J. Black.
- The lease is good until January 2, 1988.

Also in Figure 6-5 there is a secondary road shown by parallel dashes. It is unnecessary to hook portions of the tract across this type of road as it is understood that ownership is continuous unless indicated otherwise. When a secondary road forms the boundary of a tract of land, it may be indicated by making one side of the road a solid line. This effectively divides ownership of the land, yet still tells the reader that the road in question is a secondary and not a main road.

Tract C (Figure 6-5) shows that P. T. Boyd owns all of the minerals in the 80-acre tract, which includes that portion north of the railroad track and both sides of the secondary road. This tract is not leased.

In Figure 6-6 we see another unleased (open) tract (tract D) owned by T. C. Myers. There is no indication of gross acres, but we may assume this to be a standard section in which a quarter quarter contains 40 acres.

Tract E (Figure 6-6) contains 160 acres, 85 of which have been leased and 75 of which remain open. This tract is owned by a number of individuals, as evidenced by the lease schedule. In this case, we know the lease numbers and expiration dates of each. When it is difficult to include all the lease information in the tract, the data may be shown on a lease schedule. This schedule may or may not be indicated directly on the map; it may involve a separate sheet. In any case the data listed within the tract reflect that some pertinent data are detailed in some place other than in the tract itself.

Tract F (Figure 6-7) tells the reader that three companies have leases which total 100% interest in this tract. Major Oil leased B. R. Johnson's one-quarter interest until June 6, 1989. The notion "et ux" indicates Mr. Johnson's wife is co-owner of that interest. Texaco holds a

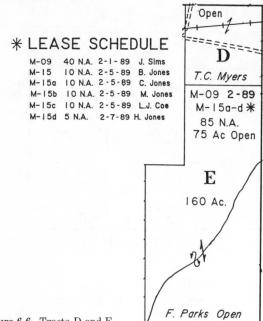

✳ LEASE SCHEDULE

M-09	40 N.A.	2-1-89	J. Sims
M-15	10 N.A.	2-5-89	B. Jones
M-15a	10 N.A.	2-5-89	C. Jones
M-15b	10 N.A.	2-5-89	M. Jones
M-15c	10 N.A.	2-5-89	L.J. Coe
M-15d	5 N.A.	2-7-89	H. Jones

Figure 6-6. Tracts D and E.

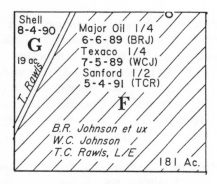

Figure 6-7. Tracts F and G.

quarter interest lease until July 5, 1989, from W. C. Johnson; and Sanford leased one-half interest from T. C. Rawls, who has a life-estate in the tract. The gross acres (181) may be indicated in a corner of the tract or may be in the center, as shown in tracts A or C. This tract has been cross hachured (or cross hatched) to indicate at a glance that the interest in this tract is divided.

Tract G follows the pattern in principle.

Figure 6-8 is a portion of a general land map. Because this is a "company" map, only lease numbers and expirations are essential on company-owned leases.

Figures 6-9 and 6-10 are examples of commercial lease and ownership maps available from various companies.

PLOTTING LEASES

Plotting leases correctly is a very important job in the petroleum industry. No matter how many files of leases and take-offs exist, or how much time and money have been spent on research and acquisition, it is nearly impossible to get the total picture until the leases have been plotted onto one map.

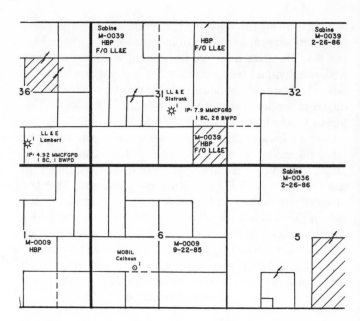

Figure 6-8. Company land maps have to show only the information needed for that particular map.

As with well spotting, it is imperative that this information be correct and complete. When all the notes and documents collected by the landman have been carefully read and the data recorded, the big picture finally emerges. Only then is it readily seen how the leases fit together, where gaps in leases occur, and how much remains to be done.

Usually land maps are of necessity drawn to a larger scale than that used for most geological maps. The scale depends on the ultimate purpose of the map. One map may show only general lease information; another may be intended to reflect everything known about the area. After a decision is made regarding the purpose and the area of interest, the scale may be chosen. Next, it is necessary to collect all the leases in the area and to make a work map of the area. It is helpful to sort the leases according to location first.

Metes and Bounds

If the lease is described by metes and bounds, begin at the point of beginning (POB) and follow the description carefully. The use of a protractor to plot bearings is covered in Chapter 1 (Figure 1-16). (See Exercise 1 at the end of the chapter for practice in plotting metes and bounds.) If the bearings and distances are carefully plotted and the description fails to arrive back at the point of beginning, it is said that the description "doesn't close." In this case, after making certain all the calls were followed correctly, it is necessary to have the leases checked against the field notes or original deeds to clear up any discrepancy. Many times it is merely a matter of

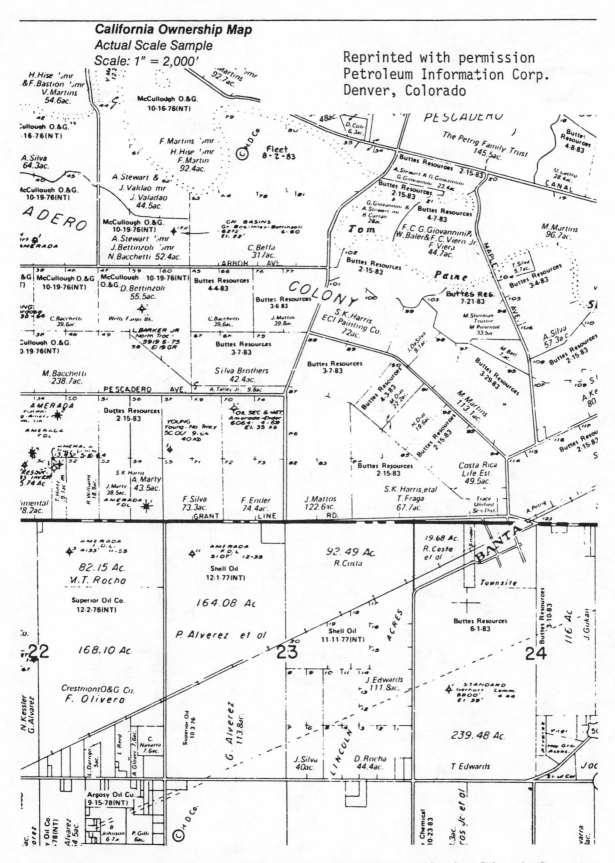

Figure 6-9. Example of a lease ownership map commercially available. (Courtesy of Petroleum Information Corporation.)

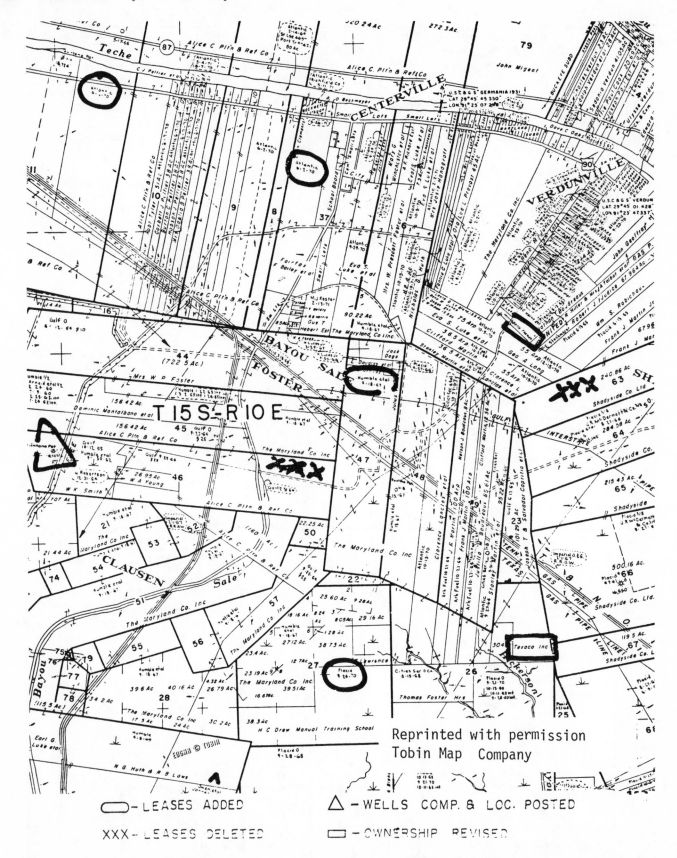

Figure 6-10. Example of lease ownership map showing how the company indicates a new lease or an expired one. (Reprinted with permission of Tobin Map Company.)

correcting a typographical error. Whatever the cause of the problem, the error should be reconciled.

Rectangular System

If the description is one of portions of sections, begin at the end and work backwards. For example, if the description reads SW SE NW, first find the northwest quarter, then the southeast quarter of that, then the southwest quarter of that. The placement of a comma is the key to the description. As you can see in Figure 6-11, it makes quite a difference. A description reading "N/2 SE SW SW NE SW" means very little without punctuation. Taken literally, this description boils down to a tract approximately $87' \times 165'$ (about ³/₁₀ths of an acre), which would hardly be described in such a manner. In Example A the description calls for the north half of the southeast quarter of the southwest quarter, *and* the southwest quarter of the northeast quarter of the southwest quarter, for a total of thirty acres. By changing the comma placement, Example B reads: the north half *and* the southeast quarter of the southwest quarter, which totals 380 acres. Example C reads: the north half of the southeast quarter *and* the southwest quarter, which totals 240 acres. (See Exercise 2 at the end of the chapter for practice in plotting leases.)

N/2 SE SW SW NE SW

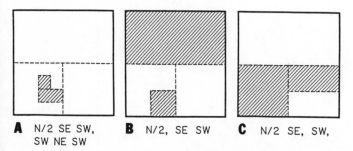

A N/2 SE SW, SW NE SW   **B** N/2, SE SW   **C** N/2 SE, SW,

Figure 6-11. It is very important to punctuate land descriptions correctly. A comma in this case actually means "and."

FIGURING NET ACRES

To figure net acres, use the following formula:

mineral interest × gross acres = net acres

Example: ¼ interest in a 40-acre tract would be 10 net acres.

$$¼ \times 40 = 10$$

When simple fractions are involved, it seems simplistic to worry about a formula for figuring net acres. In dealing with mineral interests, it is possible to get involved in very complex interests. For this reason, it is advisable to convert to decimals.

Example: ⁴⁵/₉₃₂ interest in a 40 acre tract would be 1.931 acres.

$$(45 \div 932) \times 40 = 1.931$$

Example: 30% interest in 75.45 acres = 22.635 net acres.

$$.30 \times 75.45 = 22.635$$

(See Exercise 3 at the end of the chapter for practice in figuring net acres.)

USING AN ACREAGE NOMOGRAPH

The nomograph in Figure 6-12 can be used to estimate distances if the acreage is known, or to estimate acreage

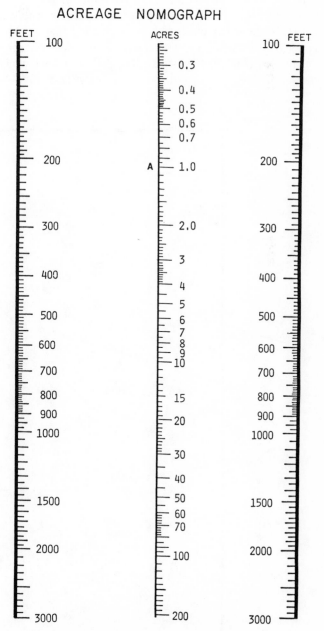

Figure 6-12. Acreage nomograph.

if the distances are known. The outside columns represent feet and the middle column represents number of acres. The "1.0" at "A" in the figure represents one acre, and every number above that point indicates tenths of an acre.

If a tract of land measures 660' by 660', you may place a straightedge at the 660 mark in the left-hand column, connect it to the 660 mark in the right-hand column, and it will cross the acreage column exactly at the 10-acre mark. So a square tract which is 660' on a side will encompass 10 acres.

Put a straightedge from 500' in one column to 1,500' in the other column, and it crosses the middle column at about 17 acres.

If, for example, you know only one dimension of the tract but you know the number of acres, it is possible to estimate the other dimension in much the same manner. A 9-acre tract which measures 450' on one side, will measure about 860'–870' on the other. A 9-acre tract which measures 450' on one side would be exactly 871.2'. As

you can see, this nomograph is handy for estimation only, but it can save a lot of time if an estimate is all you need.

EXERCISE 6-1: PLOTTING METES AND BOUNDS
(Answers on pages 129–131)

Figure 6-13 is the outline of one section drawn to a scale of 1″ = 1000′. Use a protractor to plot this metes and bounds description:

Beginning at the SE corner of section, go W along section line, 1,200', then N 500' to POB. Then N 16° E along W ROW of gravel road for 1,000', then N 12° W along old farm road 800' to fence corner, then N 73° 30' W for 1,600', then S 34°W 1,150', then S 53° E for 1,500', then S 12° E 540' to large oak tree, then N 77° E a distance of 790' to POB.

Estimate acreage involved. Note: It is possible to estimate acreage in irregular tracts by dividing them into triangles and parallelograms and calculating the areas of these figures.

Figure 6-13. Section outline. Use a protractor to plot metes and bounds description.

EXERCISE 6-2: PLOTTING LEASES

Figure 6-14, Land Map A, and Figure 6-15, Land Map B, cover the area described in the leases in Figures 6-16 through 6-21. The description of Lease 1 is found in Figure 6-3. It is already plotted for you in Figure 6-14. Plot Leases 2 (Figure 6-16) through 7 (Figure 6-21) on Land Maps A and B (Figures 6-14 and 6-15).

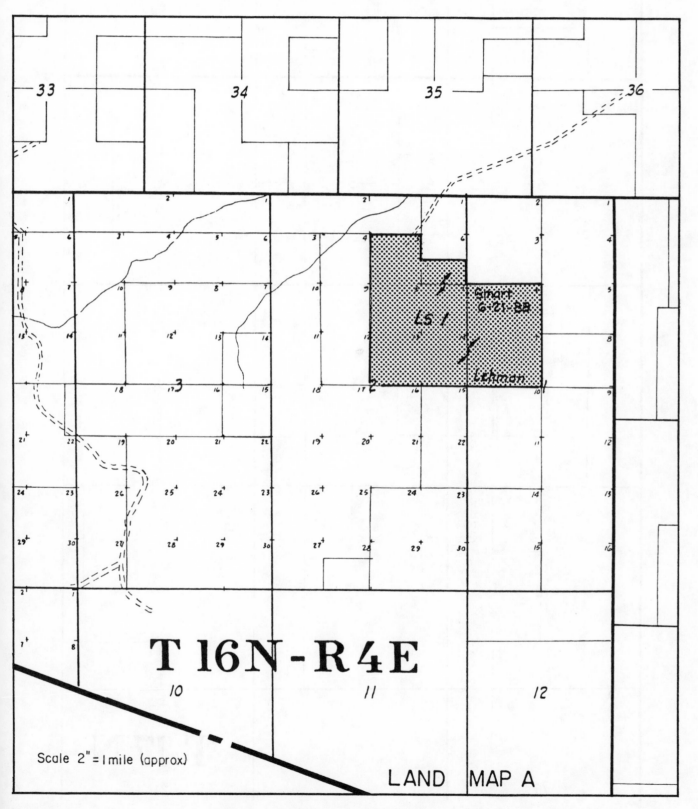

Figure 6-14. Land map A with Lease 1 already posted.

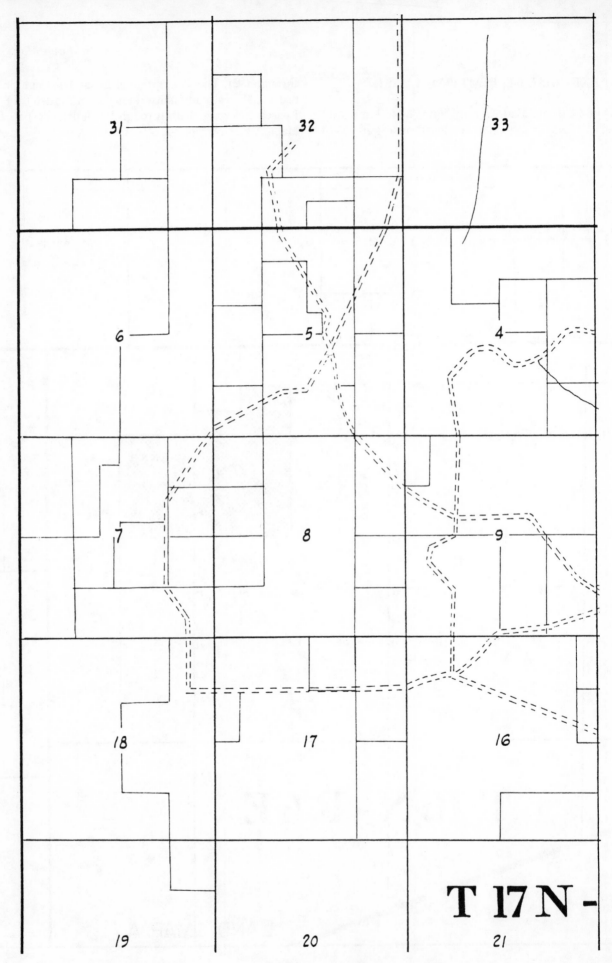

Figure 6-15. Land map B.

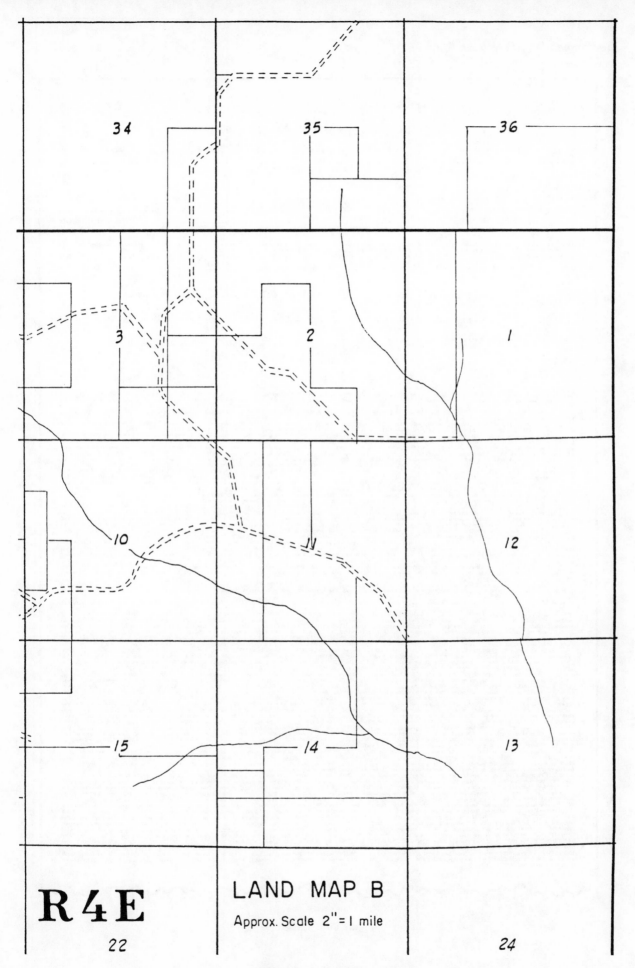

Figure 6-15. Continued

Producers 88-D9803 (Revised Oct. 1, 1948) With Pooling Provision. HEDERMAN BROS., JACKSON, MISS. 2

OIL, GAS AND MINERAL LEASE

THIS AGREEMENT made this 15 day of September 1985, between

Amos Lehman, W. G. Lehman and Mary Lehman Jones

Lessor (whether one or more) whose address is: Rt. 6, Box A, Improve, MS 39423

and Joe Smart Lessee, WITNESSETH:

1. Lessor in consideration of Ten and more Dollars ($________), in hand paid, of the royalties herein provided, and of the agreement of Lessee herein contained, hereby grants, leases and lets exclusively unto Lessee for the purpose of investigating, exploring, prospecting, drilling and mining for and producing oil, gas and all other minerals, laying pipe lines, building roads, tanks, power stations, telephone lines and other structures thereon to produce, save, take care of, treat, transport and own said products, and housing its employees, the following described land in Carroll County, Mississippi, to-wit:

All of lot 1 South of creek, all of lots 3, 4, 5, 8, 9, and all of lot 10 south and east of the creek in Section 3, T 16N- R 4E. Also in Section 2, T 16 N - R 4 E, lots 1 and 2 north and west of the creek.

This lease also covers and includes all land owned or claimed by Lessor adjacent or contiguous to the land particularly described above, whether the same be in said section or sections, grant or grants, or in adjacent sections or grants, although not included within the boundaries of the land particularly described above. For the purpose of calculating the rental payments hereinafter provided for, said land is estimated to comprise 323 acres, whether it actually comprises more or less.

2. Subject to the other provisions herein contained, this lease shall be for a term of three years from this date (called "primary term") and as long thereafter as oil, gas or other mineral is produced from said land or lands with which said land is pooled hereunder.

3. The royalties to be paid by Lessee are: (a) on oil, one-eighth of that produced and saved from said land, the same to be delivered at the wells or to the credit of Lessor into the pipe line to which the wells may be connected; Lessee may from time to time purchase any royalty oil in its possession, paying the market price therefor prevailing for the field where produced on the date of purchase, in either case such interest to bear its proportion of any expense of treating unmerchantable oil to render it merchantable as crude; (b) on gas, including casinghead gas or other gaseous substance, produced from said land and sold or used off the premises or in the manufacture of gasoline or other product therefrom, the market value at the well of one-eighth of the gas so sold or used, provided that on gas sold at the wells the royalty shall be one-eighth of the amount realized from such sale; where gas from a gas well is not sold or used, Lessee may pay as royalty $100.00 per well per year and if such payment is made it will be considered that gas is being produced within the meaning of Paragraph 2 hereof; and (c) on all other minerals mined and marketed, one-tenth either in kind or value at the well or mine, at Lessee's election, except that on sulphur mined and marketed, the royalty shall be fifty cents (50c) per long ton. Lessee shall have free use of oil, gas, coal, wood and water from said land, except water from Lessor's wells, for all operations hereunder, and the royalty on oil, gas and coal shall be computed after deducting any so used. Lessor shall have the privilege at his risk and expense of using gas from any gas well on said land for stoves and inside lights in the principal dwelling thereon out of any surplus gas not needed for operations hereunder.

4. Lessee, at its option, is hereby given the right and power to pool or combine the acreage covered by this lease or any portion thereof with other land, lease or leases in the immediate vicinity thereof, when in Lessee's judgment it is necessary or advisable to do so in order properly to develop and operate said premises in compliance with any lawful spacing rules which may be prescribed for the field in which this lease is situated by any duly authorized authority, or when to do so would, in the judgment of Lessee, promote the conservation of the oil and gas in and under and that may be produced from said premises. Lessee shall execute in writing an instrument identifying and describing the pooled acreage. The entire acreage so pooled into a tract or unit shall be treated, for all purposes except the payment of royalties on production from the pooled unit, as if it were included in this lease. If production is found on the pooled acreage, it shall be treated as if production is had from this lease, whether the well or wells be located on the premises covered by this lease or not. In lieu of the royalties elsewhere herein specified, Lessor shall receive on production from a unit so pooled only such portion of the royalty stipulated herein as the amount of his acreage placed in the unit or his royalty interest therein on an acreage basis bears to the total acreage so pooled in the particular unit involved.

5. If operations for drilling are not commenced on said land or on acreage pooled therewith as above provided on or before one year from this date the lease shall then terminate as to both parties, unless on or before such anniversary date Lessee shall pay or tender to Lessor or to the credit of Lessor in Improve Bank at Improve, Mississippi (which bank and its successors are Lessor's agent and shall continue as the depository for all rentals payable hereunder regardless of changes in ownership of said land or the rentals) the sum of Three hundred twenty-three and no/100 Dollars ($________), (herein called rental), which shall cover the privilege of deferring commencement of drilling operations for a period of twelve (12) months. In like manner and upon like payments or tenders annually the commencement of drilling operations may be further deferred for successive periods of twelve (12) months each during the primary term. The payment or tender of rental may be made by the check or draft of Lessee mailed or delivered to Lessor or to said bank on or before such date of payment. If such bank (or any successor bank) should fail, liquidate or be succeeded by another bank, or for any reason fail or refuse to accept rental, Lessee shall not be held in default for failure to make such payment or tender of rental until thirty (30) days after Lessor shall deliver to Lessee a proper recordable instrument, naming another bank as agent to receive such payments or tenders. The down cash payment is consideration for this lease according to its terms and shall not be allocated as mere rental for a period. Lessee may at any time or times execute and deliver to Lessor or to the depository above named or place of record a release or releases covering any portion or portions of the above described premises and thereby surrender this lease as to such portion or portions and be relieved of all obligations as to the acreage surrendered, and thereafter the rentals payable hereunder shall be reduced in the proportion that the acreage covered hereby is reduced by said release or releases.

6. If prior to discovery of oil, gas or other mineral on said land or on acreage pooled therewith Lessee should drill a dry hole or holes thereon, or if after discovery of oil, gas or other mineral, the production thereof should cease from any cause, this lease shall not terminate if Lessee commences additional drilling or reworking operations within 60 days thereafter or if it be within the primary term, commences or resumes the payment or tender of rentals or commences operations for drilling or reworking on or before the rental paying date next ensuing after the expiration of 60 days from date of completion of dry hole or cessation of production. If at any time subsequent to sixty (60) days prior to the beginning of the last year of the primary term and prior to the discovery of oil, gas or other mineral on said land, or on acreage pooled therewith, Lessee should drill a dry hole thereon, no rental payment or operations are necessary in order to keep the lease in force during the remainder of the primary term. If at the expiration of the primary term, oil, gas or other mineral is not being produced on said land, or on acreage pooled therewith, but Lessee is then engaged in drilling or reworking operations thereon or shall have completed a dry hole thereon within sixty (60) days prior to the end of the primary term, the lease shall remain in force so long as operations are prosecuted with no cessation of more than sixty (60) consecutive days, and if they result in the production of oil, gas or other mineral, so long thereafter as oil, gas or other mineral is produced from said land or acreage pooled therewith. In the event a well or wells producing oil or gas in paying quantities should be brought in on adjacent land and within one hundred fifty (150) feet of and draining the leased premises, or acreage pooled therewith, Lessee agrees to drill such offset wells as a reasonably prudent operator would drill under the same or similar circumstances.

7. Lessee shall have the right at any time during or after the expiration of this lease to remove all property and fixtures placed by Lessee on said land, including the right to draw and remove all casing. When required by Lessor, Lessee will bury all pipe lines below ordinary plow depth, and no well shall be drilled within two hundred (200) feet of any residence or barn now on said land without Lessor's consent. Lessee shall be responsible for all damages caused by Lessee's operations hereunder other than damages necessarily caused by the exercise of the rights herein granted.

8. The rights of either party hereunder may be assigned in whole or in part, and the provisions hereof shall extend to their heirs, successors and assigns; but no change or division in ownership of the land, rentals or royalties, however accomplished, shall operate to enlarge the obligations or diminish the rights of Lessee; and no change or division in such ownership shall be binding on Lessee until thirty (30) days after Lessee shall have been furnished by registered U. S. mail at Lessee's principal place of business with a certified copy of recorded instrument or instruments evidencing same. In the event of assignment hereof in whole or in part liability for breach of any obligation hereunder shall rest exclusively upon the owner of this lease or of a portion thereof who commits such breach. In the event of the death of any person entitled to rentals hereunder, Lessee may pay or tender such rentals to the credit of the deceased or the estate of the deceased until such time as Lessee is furnished with proper evidence of the appointment and qualifications of an executor or administrator of the estate, or if there be none, then until Lessee is furnished with evidence satisfactory to it as to the heirs or devisees of the deceased, and that all debts of the estate have been paid. If at any time two or more persons be entitled to participate in the rental payable hereunder, Lessee may pay or tender said rental jointly to such persons or to their joint credit in the depository named herein; or, at Lessee's election, the proportionate part of said rental to which each participant is entitled may be paid or tendered to him separately or to his separate credit in said depository; and payment or tender to any participant of his portion of the rentals hereunder shall maintain this lease as to such participant. In event of assignment of this lease as to a segregated portion of said land, the rentals payable hereunder shall be apportionable as between the several leasehold owners ratably according to the surface area of each, and default in rental payment by one shall not affect the rights of other leasehold owners hereunder. If six or more parties become entitled to royalty hereunder, Lessee may withhold payment thereof unless and until furnished with a recordable instrument executed by all such parties designating an agent to receive payment for all.

Figure 6-16. Lease 2.

Producers 88-D9803 (Revised Oct. 1, 1948) With Pooling Provision. HEDERMAN BROS., JACKSON, MISS. 3

OIL, GAS AND MINERAL LEASE

THIS AGREEMENT made this 14 day of August 1979, between

Matthew Pickens, an unmarried man

Lessor (whether one or more) whose address is: P.O. BOx 23, Warren, MS 39789

and Joe Smart Lessee, WITNESSETH:

1. Lessor in consideration of ten and more Dollars ($________), in hand paid, of the royalties herein provided, and of the agreement of Lessee herein contained, hereby grants, leases and lets exclusively unto Lessee for the purpose of investigating, exploring, prospecting, drilling and mining for and producing oil, gas and all other minerals, laying pipe lines, building roads, tanks, power stations, telephone lines and other structures thereon to produce, save, take care of, treat, transport and own said products, and housing its employees, the following described land in Carroll County, Mississippi, to-wit:

Section 3, Township 16 North, Range 4 East: Lots 19 and 26 and all that part of lot 20 S and W of road, also all of lot 25 W of road, containing 89 acres more or less.

This lease also covers and includes all land owned or claimed by Lessor adjacent or contiguous to the land particularly described above, whether the same be in said section or sections, grant or grants, or in adjacent sections or grants, although not included within the boundaries of the land particularly described above. For the purpose of calculating the rental payments hereinafter provided for, said land is estimated to comprise 89 acres, whether it actually comprises more or less.

2. Subject to the other provisions herein contained, this lease shall be for a term of ten years from this date (called "primary term") and as long thereafter as oil, gas or other mineral is produced from said land or lands with which said land is pooled hereunder.

3. The royalties to be paid by Lessee are: (a) on oil, one-eighth of that produced and saved from said land, the same to be delivered at the wells or to the credit of Lessor into the pipe line to which the wells may be connected; Lessee may from time to time purchase any royalty oil in its possession, paying the market price therefor prevailing for the field where produced on the date of purchase, in either case such interest to bear its proportion of any expense of treating unmerchantable oil to render it merchantable as crude; (b) on gas, including casinghead gas or other gaseous substance, produced from said land and sold or used off the premises or in the manufacture of gasoline or other product therefrom, the market value at the well of one-eighth of the gas so sold or used, provided that on gas sold at the wells the royalty shall be one-eighth of the amount realized from such sale; where gas from a gas well is not sold or used, Lessee may pay as royalty $100.00 per well per year and if such payment is made it will be considered that gas is being produced within the meaning of Paragraph 2 hereof; and (c) on all other minerals mined and marketed, one-tenth either in kind or value at the well or mine, at Lessee's election, except that on sulphur mined and marketed, the royalty shall be fifty cents (50c) per long ton. Lessee shall have free use of oil, gas, coal, wood and water from said land, except water from Lessor's wells, for all operations hereunder, and the royalty on oil, gas and coal shall be computed after deducting any so used. Lessor shall have the privilege at his risk and expense of using gas from any gas well on said land for stoves and inside lights in the principal dwelling thereon out of any surplus gas not needed for operations hereunder.

4. Lessee, at its option, is hereby given the right and power to pool or combine the acreage covered by this lease or any portion thereof with other land, lease or leases in the immediate vicinity thereof, when in Lessee's judgment it is necessary or advisable to do so in order properly to develop and operate said premises in compliance with any lawful spacing rules which may be prescribed for the field in which this lease is situated by any duly authorized authority, or when to do so would, in the judgment of Lessee, promote the conservation of the oil and gas in and under and that may be produced from said premises. Lessee shall execute in writing an instrument identifying and describing the pooled acreage. The entire acreage so pooled into a tract or unit shall be treated, for all purposes except the payment of royalties on production from the pooled unit, as if it were included in this lease. If production is found on the pooled acreage, it shall be treated as if production is had from this lease, whether the well or wells be located on the premises covered by this lease or not. In lieu of the royalties elsewhere herein specified, Lessor shall receive on production from a unit so pooled only such portion of the royalty stipulated herein as the amount of his acreage placed in the unit or his royalty interest therein on an acreage basis bears to the total acreage so pooled in the particular unit involved.

5. If operations for drilling are not commenced on said land or on acreage pooled therewith as above provided on or before one year from this date the lease shall then terminate as to both parties, unless on or before such anniversary date Lessee shall pay or tender to Lessor or to the credit of Lessor in First National Bank at Warren, Mississippi (which bank and its successors are Lessor's agent and shall continue as the depository for all rentals payable hereunder regardless of changes in ownership of said land or the rentals) the sum of Forty-four and 50/100 Dollars ($44.50), (herein called rental), which shall cover the privilege of deferring commencement of drilling operations for a period of twelve (12) months. In like manner and upon like payments or tenders annually the commencement of drilling operations may be further deferred for successive periods of twelve (12) months each during the primary term. The payment or tender of rental may be made by the check or draft of Lessee mailed or delivered to Lessor or to said bank on or before such date of payment. If such bank (or any successor bank) should fail, liquidate or be succeeded by another bank, or for any reason fail or refuse to accept rental, Lessee shall not be held in default for failure to make such payment or tender of rental until thirty (30) days after Lessor shall deliver to Lessee a proper recordable instrument, naming another bank as agent to receive such payments or tenders. The down cash payment is consideration for this lease according to its terms and shall not be allocated as mere rental for a period. Lessee may at any time or times execute and deliver to Lessor or to the depository above named or place of record a release or releases covering any portion or portions of the above described premises and thereby surrender this lease as to such portion or portions and be relieved of all obligations as to the acreage surrendered, and thereafter the rentals payable hereunder shall be reduced in the proportion that the acreage covered hereby is reduced by said release or releases.

6. If prior to discovery of oil, gas or other mineral on said land or on acreage pooled therewith Lessee should drill a dry hole or holes thereon, or if after discovery of oil, gas or other mineral, the production thereof should cease from any cause, this lease shall not terminate if Lessee commences additional drilling or reworking operations within 60 days thereafter or if it be within the primary term, commences or resumes the payment or tender of rentals or commences operations for drilling or reworking on or before the rental paying date next ensuing after the expiration of 60 days from date of completion of dry hole or cessation of production. If at any time subsequent to sixty (60) days prior to the beginning of the last year of the primary term and prior to the discovery of oil, gas or other mineral on said land, or on acreage pooled therewith, Lessee should drill a dry hole thereon, no rental payment or operations are necessary in order to keep the lease in force during the remainder of the primary term. If at the expiration of the primary term, oil, gas or other mineral is not being produced on said land, or on acreage pooled therewith, but Lessee is then engaged in drilling or reworking operations thereon or shall have completed a dry hole thereon within sixty (60) days prior to the end of the primary term, the lease shall remain in force so long as operations are prosecuted with no cessation of more than sixty (60) consecutive days, and if they result in the production of oil, gas or other mineral, so long thereafter as oil, gas or other mineral is produced from said land or acreage pooled therewith. In the event a well or wells producing oil or gas in paying quantities should be brought in on adjacent land and within one hundred fifty (150) feet of and draining the leased premises, or acreage pooled therewith, Lessee agrees to drill such offset wells as a reasonably prudent operator would drill under the same or similar circumstances.

7. Lessee shall have the right at any time during or after the expiration of this lease to remove all property and fixtures placed by Lessee on said land, including the right to draw and remove all casing. When required by Lessor, Lessee will bury all pipe lines below ordinary plow depth, and no well shall be drilled within two hundred (200) feet of any residence or barn now on said land without Lessor's consent. Lessee shall be responsible for all damages caused by Lessee's operations hereunder other than damages necessarily caused by the exercise of the rights herein granted.

8. The rights of either party hereunder may be assigned in whole or in part, and the provisions hereof shall extend to their heirs, successors and assigns; but no change or division in ownership of the land, rentals or royalties, however accomplished, shall operate to enlarge the obligations or diminish the rights of Lessee; and no change or division in such ownership shall be binding on Lessee until thirty (30) days after Lessee shall have been furnished by registered U. S. mail at Lessee's principal place of business with a certified copy of recorded instrument or instruments evidencing same. In the event of assignment hereof in whole or in part liability for breach of any obligation hereunder shall rest exclusively upon the owner of this lease or of a portion thereof who commits such breach. In the event of the death of any person entitled to rentals hereunder, Lessee may pay or tender such rentals to the credit of the deceased or the estate of the deceased until such time as Lessee is furnished with proper evidence of the appointment and qualifications of an executor or administrator of the estate, or if there be none, then until Lessee is furnished with evidence satisfactory to it as to the heirs or devisees of the deceased, and that all debts of the estate have been paid. If at any time two or more persons be entitled to participate in the rental payable hereunder, Lessee may pay or tender said rental jointly to such persons or to their joint credit in the depository named herein; or, at Lessee's election, the proportionate part of said rental to which each participant is entitled may be paid or tendered to him separately or to his separate credit in said depository; and payment or tender to any participant of his portion of the rentals hereunder shall maintain this lease as to such participant. In event of assignment of this lease as to a segregated portion of said land, the rentals payable hereunder shall be apportionable as between the several leasehold owners ratably according to the surface area of each, and default in rental payment by one shall not affect the rights of other leasehold owners hereunder. If six or more parties become entitled to royalty hereunder, Lessee may withhold payment thereof unless and until furnished with a recordable instrument executed by all such parties designating an agent to receive payment for all.

Figure 6-17. Lease 3.

Producers 88-D9803 (Revised Oct. 1, 1948) With Pooling Provision.   HEDERMAN BROS., JACKSON, MISS.

4

OIL, GAS AND MINERAL LEASE

THIS AGREEMENT made this _____ 23 _____ day of _____ October _____ 19 84 ____, between

_____ International Paper Company _____

Lessor (whether one or more) whose address is: _____ P. O. Box 988, Red Bank, MS 39555 _____
and _____ P. L. Broker _____ Lessee, WITNESSETH:

1. Lessor in consideration of _____ Ten and more _____ Dollars

($ _____), in hand paid, of the royalties herein provided, and of the agreement of Lessee herein contained, hereby grants, leases and lets exclusively unto Lessee for the purpose of investigating, exploring, prospecting, drilling and mining for and producing oil, gas and all other minerals, laying pipe lines, building roads, tanks, power stations, telephone lines and other structures thereon to produce, save, take care of, treat, transport and own said

products, and housing its employees, the following described land in _____ Carroll _____ County, Mississippi, to-wit:

Township 17 north, Range 4 east

Section 4:   W/2 NW, S/2 SE NW, W/2 SE, SW/4-

Section 5:   E/2 SE

Section 8:   W/2 E/2, E/2 W/2, SW SW

Section 7:   SE SE

Section 17:   NW NE

Section 9: NE/4 and NW/4 less and except NW NW, also less and except

tract desc. as beginning at int. of Smith Rd. and Jones Rd.

go due N along Smith Rd. 110 yds., then E 110 yds., then S

110 yds. to north R/OW of Jones Rd., then W to POB,

containing 2.5 ac.

This lease also covers and includes all land owned or claimed by Lessor adjacent or contiguous to the land particularly described above, whether the same be in said section or sections, grant or grants, or in adjacent sections or grants, although not included within the boundaries of the land particularly described above. For the purpose of calculating the rental payments hereinafter provided for, said land is estimated to comprise _____ 1137.5 _____ acres, whether it actually comprises more or less.

2. Subject to the other provisions herein contained, this lease shall be for a term of five years from this date (called "primary term") and as long thereafter as oil, gas or other mineral is produced from said land or lands with which said land is pooled hereunder.

3. The royalties to be paid by Lessee are: (a) on oil, one-eighth of that produced and saved from said land, the same to be delivered at the wells or to the credit of Lessee into the pipe line to which the wells may be connected; Lessee may from time to time purchase any royalty oil in its possession, paying the market price therefor prevailing for the field where produced on the date of purchase, in either case such interest to bear its proportion of any expense of treating unmerchantable oil to render it merchantable as crude; (b) on gas, including casinghead gas or other gaseous substance, produced from said land and sold or used off the premises or in the manufacture of gasoline or other product therefrom, the market value at the well of one-eighth of the gas so sold or used, provided that on gas sold at the wells the royalty shall be one-eighth of the amount realized from such sale; where gas from a gas well is not sold or used, Lessee may pay as royalty $100.00 per well per year and if such payment is made it will be considered that gas is being produced within the meaning of Paragraph 2 hereof; and (c) on all other minerals mined and marketed, one-tenth either in kind or value at the well or mine, at Lessee's election, except that on sulphur mined and marketed, the royalty shall be fifty cents (50c) per long ton. Lessee shall have free use of oil, gas, coal, wood and water from said land, except water from Lessor's wells, for all operations hereunder, and the royalty on oil, gas and coal shall be computed after deducting any so used. Lessor shall have the privilege at his risk and expense of using gas from any gas well on said land for stoves and inside lights in the principal dwelling thereon out of any surplus gas not needed for operations hereunder.

4. Lessee, at its option, is hereby given the right and power to pool or combine the acreage covered by this lease or any portion thereof with other land, lease or leases in the immediate vicinity thereof, when in Lessee's judgment it is necessary or advisable to do so in order properly to develop and operate said premises in compliance with any lawful spacing rules which may be prescribed for the field in which this lease is situated by any duly authorized authority, or when to do so would, in the judgment of Lessee, promote the conservation of the oil and gas in and under and that may be produced from said premises. Lessee shall execute in writing an instrument identifying and describing the pooled acreage. The entire acreage so pooled into a tract or unit shall be treated, for all purposes except the payment of royalties on production from the pooled unit, as if it were included in this lease. If production is found on the pooled acreage, it shall be treated as if production is had from this lease, whether the well or wells be located on the premises covered by this lease or not. In lieu of the royalties elsewhere herein specified, Lessor shall receive on production from a unit so pooled only such portion of the royalty stipulated herein as the amount of his acreage placed in the unit or his royalty interest therein on an acreage basis bears to the total acreage so pooled in the particular unit involved.

5. If operations for drilling are not commenced on said land or on acreage pooled therewith as above provided on or before one year from this date the lease shall then terminate as to both parties, unless on or before such anniversary date Lessee shall pay or tender to Lessor or to the credit of Lessor

in _____ Red Bank _____ Bank at _____ Red Bank _____, Mississippi (which bank and its successors are Lessor's agent and shall continue as the depository for all rentals payable hereunder regardless of changes in ownership

of said land or the rentals) the sum of _____ One thousand one hundred thirty-seven and 50/100 _____ Dollars

($ 1137.50 ____), (herein called rental), which shall cover the privilege of deferring commencement of drilling operations for a period of twelve (12) months. In like manner and upon like payments or tenders annually the commencement of drilling operations may be further deferred for successive periods of twelve (12) months each during the primary term. The payment or tender of rental may be made by the check or draft of Lessee mailed or delivered to Lessor or to said bank on or before such date of payment. If such bank (or any successor bank) should fail, liquidate or be succeeded by another bank, or for any reason fail or refuse to accept rental, Lessee shall not be held in default for failure to make such payment or tender of rental until thirty (30) days after Lessor shall deliver to Lessee a proper recordable instrument, naming another bank as agent to receive such payments or tenders. The down cash payment is consideration for this lease according to its terms and shall not be allocated as mere rental for a period. Lessee may at any time or times execute and deliver to Lessor or to the depository above named or place of record a release or releases covering any portion or portions of the above described premises and thereby surrender this lease as to such portion or portions and be relieved of all obligations as to the acreage surrendered, and thereafter the rentals payable hereunder shall be reduced in the proportion that the acreage covered hereby is reduced by said release or releases.

6. If prior to discovery of oil, gas or other mineral on said land or on acreage pooled therewith Lessee should drill a dry hole or holes thereon, or if after discovery of oil, gas or other mineral, the production thereof should cease from any cause, this lease shall not terminate if Lessee commences additional drilling or reworking operations within 60 days thereafter or if it be within the primary term, commences or resumes the payment or tender of rentals or commences operations for drilling or reworking on or before the rental paying date next ensuing after the expiration of 60 days from date of completion of dry hole or cessation of production. If at any time subsequent to sixty (60) days prior to the beginning of the last year of the primary term and prior to the discovery of oil, gas or other mineral on said land, or on acreage pooled therewith, Lessee should drill a dry hole thereon, no rental payment or operations are necessary in order to keep the lease in force during the remainder of the primary term. If at the expiration of the primary term, oil, gas or other min-

Figure 6-18. Lease 4.

Producers 88-D9803 (Revised Oct. 1, 1948) With Pooling Provision.   HEDERMAN BROS., JACKSON, MISS.

OIL, GAS AND MINERAL LEASE

5

THIS AGREEMENT made this_____18_____day of_____August_____19__83____, between

_____B. J. Nelms and wife, Arlene P. Nelms_____

Lessor (whether one or more) whose address is:_____P.O. Box 15, Carollton, MS 39570_____

and _____P.L. Broker_____Lessee, WITNESSETH:

1. Lessor in consideration of_____Ten and more_____ Dollars

($_____), in hand paid, of the royalties herein provided, and of the agreement of Lessee herein contained, hereby grants, leases and lets exclusively unto Lessee for the purpose of investigating, exploring, prospecting, drilling and mining for and producing oil, gas and all other minerals, laying pipe lines, building roads, tanks, power stations, telephone lines and other structures thereon to produce, save, take care of, treat, transport and own said products, and housing its employees, the following described land in_____Carroll_____County, Mississippi, to-wit:

Township 18 North, Range 4 East

Section 35: SW SW, NE SW, NW SW east of road, and all of the

S/2 NW south & east of road, less & except a parcel described as

beginning at the NW corner of SE NW, thence S 900' to a stake, thence

N 56° E to a pt. where co. road crosses line between N/2 NW & S/2 NW,

thence W 1320' to POB, containing 187 ac., more or less.

Section 34: All that part of E/2 E/2 SE/4 south of co. road,

containing 28 ac., more or less.

This lease also covers and includes all land owned or claimed by Lessor adjacent or contiguous to the land particularly described above, whether the same be in said section or sections, grant or grants, or in adjacent sections or grants, although not included within the boundaries of the land particularly described above. For the purpose of calculating the rental payments hereinafter provided for, said land is estimated to comprise_____215_____acres, whether it actually comprises more or less.

2. Subject to the other provisions herein contained, this lease shall be for a term of ~~ten years~~ *five* from this date (called "primary term") and as long thereafter as oil, gas or other mineral is produced from said land or lands with which said land is pooled hereunder.

3. The royalties to be paid by Lessee are: (a) on oil, one-eighth of that produced and saved from said land, the same to be delivered at the wells or to the credit of Lessor into the pipe line to which the wells may be connected; Lessee may from time to time purchase any royalty oil in its possession, paying the market price therefor prevailing for the field where produced on the date of purchase, in either case such interest to bear its proportion of any expense of treating unmerchantable oil to render it merchantable as crude; (b) on gas, including casinghead gas or other gaseous substance, produced from said land and sold or used off the premises or in the manufacture of gasoline or other product therefrom, the market value at the well of one-eighth of the gas so sold or used, provided that on gas sold at the wells the royalty shall be one-eighth of the amount realized from such sale; where gas from a gas well is not sold or used, Lessee may pay as royalty $100.00 per well per year and if such payment is made it will be considered that gas is being produced within the meaning of Paragraph 2 hereof; and (c) on all other minerals mined and marketed, one-tenth either in kind or value at the well or mine, at Lessee's election, except that on sulphur mined and marketed, the royalty shall be fifty cents (50c) per long ton. Lessee shall have free use of oil, gas, coal, wood and water from said land, except water from Lessor's wells, for all operations hereunder, and the royalty on oil, gas and coal shall be computed after deducting any so used. Lessor shall have the privilege at his risk and expense of using gas from any gas well on said land for stoves and inside lights in the principal dwelling thereon out of any surplus gas not needed for operations hereunder.

4. Lessee, at its option, is hereby given the right and power to pool or combine the acreage covered by this lease or any portion thereof with other land, lease or leases in the immediate vicinity thereof, when in Lessee's judgment it is necessary or advisable to do so in order properly to develop and operate said premises in compliance with any lawful spacing rules which may be prescribed for the field in which this lease is situated by any duly authorized authority, or when to do so would, in the judgment of Lessee, promote the conservation of the oil and gas in and under and that may be produced from said premises. Lessee shall execute in writing an instrument identifying and describing the pooled acreage. The entire acreage so pooled into a tract or unit shall be treated, for all purposes except the payment of royalties on production from the pooled unit, as if it were included in this lease. If production is found on the pooled acreage, it shall be treated as if production is had from this lease, whether the well or wells be located on the premises covered by this lease or not. In lieu of the royalties elsewhere herein specified, Lessor shall receive on production from a unit so pooled only such portion of the royalty stipulated herein as the amount of his acreage placed in the unit or his royalty interest therein on an acreage basis bears to the total acreage so pooled in the particular unit involved.

5. If operations for drilling are not commenced on said land or on acreage pooled therewith as above provided on or before one year from this date the lease shall then terminate as to both parties, unless on or before such anniversary date Lessee shall pay or tender to Lessor or to the credit of Lessor in _____First Savings_____Bank at _____Carollton_____, Mississippi (which bank and its successors are Lessor's agent and shall continue as the depository for all rentals payable hereunder regardless of changes in ownership of said land or the rentals) the sum of_____two hundred fifteen and no/100_____ Dollars

($__215.00_____), (herein called rental), which shall cover the privilege of deferring commencement of drilling operations for a period of twelve (12) months. In like manner and upon like payments or tenders annually the commencement of drilling operations may be further deferred for successive periods of twelve (12) months each during the primary term. The payment or tender of rental may be made by the check or draft of Lessee mailed or delivered to Lessor or to said bank on or before such date of payment. If such bank (or any successor bank) should fail, liquidate or be succeeded by another bank, or for any reason fail or refuse to accept rental, Lessee shall not be held in default for failure to make such payment or tender of rental until thirty (30) days after Lessor shall deliver to Lessee a proper recordable instrument, naming another bank as agent to receive such payments or tenders. The down cash payment is consideration for this lease according to its terms and shall not be allocated as mere rental for a period. Lessee may at any time or times execute and deliver to Lessor or to the depository above named or place of record a release or releases covering any portion or portions of the above described premises and thereby surrender this lease as to such portion or portions and be relieved of all obligations as to the acreage surrendered, and thereafter the rentals payable hereunder shall be reduced in the proportion that the acreage covered hereby is reduced by said release or releases.

Figure 6-19. Lease 5.

Producers 88-D9803 (Revised Oct. 1, 1948) With Pooling Provision.   HEDERMAN BROS., JACKSON, MISS.

OIL, GAS AND MINERAL LEASE

THIS AGREEMENT made this ____8____ day of ____September____ 19_79_, between

____C. D. Saunders, G. Rodney Saunders, Greta S. Smith____

Lessor (whether one or more) whose address is: ____P. O. Box 1890, Winoka, MS 39876____

and ____Harold Beasley____ Lessee, WITNESSETH:

1. Lessor in consideration of ____Ten and more____ Dollars

($____), in hand paid, of the royalties herein provided, and of the agreement of Lessee herein contained, hereby grants, leases and lets exclusively unto Lessee for the purpose of investigating, exploring, prospecting, drilling and mining for and producing oil, gas and all other minerals, laying pipe lines, building roads, tanks, power stations, telephone lines and other structures thereon to produce, save, take care of, treat, transport and own said products, and housing its employees, the following described land in ____Carroll____ County, Mississippi, to-wit:

Township 17 North, Range 4 East

Section 5: SE/4 NW/4, also a tract of land described as beginning

at SW corner of SE NW, go E 850', then S 420', then in an easterly

direction along a fence row 900' to an iron stake, then N 1000',

then W 400', then S 550', then W 500' to POB. All containing

54.3 Acres.

This lease also covers and includes all land owned or claimed by Lessor adjacent or contiguous to the land particularly described above, whether the same be in said section or sections, grant or grants, or in adjacent sections or grants, although not included within the boundaries of the land particularly described above. For the purpose of calculating the rental payments hereinafter provided for, said land is estimated to comprise ____54.3____ acres, whether it actually comprises more or less.

2. Subject to the other provisions herein contained, this lease shall be for a term of ten years from this date (called "primary term") and as long thereafter as oil, gas or other mineral is produced from said land or lands with which said land is pooled hereunder.

3. The royalties to be paid by Lessee are: (a) on oil, one-eighth of that produced and saved from said land, the same to be delivered at the wells or to the credit of Lessor into the pipe line to which the wells may be connected; Lessee may from time to time purchase any royalty oil in its possession, paying the market price therefor prevailing for the field where produced on the date of purchase, in either case such interest to bear its proportion of any expense of treating unmerchantable oil to render it merchantable as crude; (b) on gas, including casinghead gas or other gaseous substance, produced from said land and sold or used off the premises or in the manufacture of gasoline or other product therefrom, the market value at the well of one-eighth of the gas so sold or used, provided that on gas sold at the wells the royalty shall be one-eighth of the amount realized from such sale; where gas from a gas well is not sold or used, Lessee may pay as royalty $100.00 per well per year and if such payment is made it will be considered that gas is being produced within the meaning of Paragraph 2 hereof; and (c) on all other minerals mined and marketed, one-tenth either in kind or value at the well or mine, at Lessee's election, except that on sulphur mined and marketed, the royalty shall be fifty cents (50c) per long ton. Lessee shall have free use of oil, gas, coal, wood and water from said land, except water from Lessor's wells, for all operations hereunder, and the royalty on oil, gas and coal shall be computed after deducting any so used. Lessor shall have the privilege at his risk and expense of using gas from any gas well on said land for stoves and inside lights in the principal dwelling thereon out of any surplus gas not needed for operations hereunder.

4. Lessee, at its option, is hereby given the right and power to pool or combine the acreage covered by this lease or any portion thereof with other land, lease or leases in the immediate vicinity thereof, when in Lessee's judgment it is necessary or advisable to do so in order properly to develop and operate said premises in compliance with any lawful spacing rules which may be prescribed for the field in which this lease is situated by any duly authorized authority, or when to do so would, in the judgment of Lessee, promote the conservation of the oil and gas in and under and that may be produced from said premises. Lessee shall execute in writing an instrument identifying and describing the pooled acreage. The entire acreage so pooled into a tract or unit shall be treated, for all purposes except the payment of royalties on production from the pooled unit, as if it were included in this lease. If production is found on the pooled acreage, it shall be treated as if production is had from this lease, whether the well or wells be located on the premises covered by this lease or not. In lieu of the royalties elsewhere herein specified, Lessor shall receive on production from a unit so pooled only such portion of the royalty stipulated herein as the amount of his acreage placed in the unit or his royalty interest therein on an acreage basis bears to the total acreage so pooled in the particular unit involved.

5. If operations for drilling are not commenced on said land or on acreage pooled therewith as above provided on or before one year from this date the lease shall then terminate as to both parties, unless on or before such anniversary date Lessee shall pay or tender to Lessor or to the credit of Lessor in ____Winoka____ Bank at ____Winoka____, Mississippi (which bank and its successors are Lessor's agent and shall continue as the depository for all rentals payable hereunder regardless of changes in ownership of said land or the rentals) the sum of ____Fifty-four and 30/100____ Dollars

($____54.30____), (herein called rental), which shall cover the privilege of deferring commencement of drilling operations for a period of twelve (12) months. In like manner and upon like payments or tenders annually the commencement of drilling operations may be further deferred for successive periods of twelve (12) months each during the primary term. The payment or tender of rental may be made by the check or draft of Lessee mailed or delivered to Lessor or to said bank on or before such date of payment. If such bank (or any successor bank) should fail, liquidate or be succeeded by another bank, or for any reason fail or refuse to accept rental, Lessee shall not be held in default for failure to make such payment or tender of rental until thirty (30) days after Lessor shall deliver to Lessee a proper recordable instrument, naming another bank as agent to receive such payments or tenders. The down cash payment is consideration for this lease according to its terms and shall not be allocated as mere rental for a period. Lessee may at any time or times execute and deliver to Lessor or to the depository above named or place of record a release or releases covering any portion or portions of the above described premises and thereby surrender this lease as to such portion or portions and be relieved of all obligations as to the acreage surrendered, and thereafter the rentals payable hereunder shall be reduced in the proportion that the acreage covered hereby is reduced by said release or releases.

6. If prior to discovery of oil, gas or other mineral on said land or on acreage pooled therewith Lessee should drill a dry hole or holes thereon, or if after discovery of oil, gas or other mineral, the production thereof should cease from any cause, this lease shall not terminate if Lessee commences additional drilling or reworking operations within 60 days thereafter or if it be within the primary term, commences or resumes the payment or tender of rentals or commences operations for drilling or reworking on or before the rental paying date next ensuing after the expiration of 60 days from date of completion of dry hole or cessation of production. If at any time subsequent to sixty (60) days prior to the beginning of the last year of the primary term and prior to the discovery of oil, gas or other mineral on said land, or on acreage pooled therewith, Lessee should drill a dry hole thereon, no rental payment or operations are necessary in order to keep the lease in force during the remainder of the primary term. If at the expiration of the primary term, oil, gas or other mineral is not being produced on said land, or on acreage pooled therewith, but Lessee is then engaged in drilling or reworking operations thereon or shall have completed a dry hole thereon within sixty (60) days prior to the end of the primary term, the lease shall remain in force so long as operations are prosecuted with no cessation of more than sixty (60) consecutive days, and if they result in the production of oil, gas or other mineral, so long thereafter as oil, gas or other mineral is produced from said land or acreage pooled therewith. In the event a well or wells producing oil or gas in paying quantities should be brought in on adjacent land and within one hundred fifty (150) feet of and draining the leased premises, or acreage pooled therewith, Lessee agrees to drill such offset wells as a reasonably prudent operator would drill under the same or similar circumstances.

7. Lessee shall have the right at any time during or after the expiration of this lease to remove all property and fixtures placed by Lessee on said land, including the right to draw and remove all casing. When required by Lessor, Lessee will bury all pipe lines below ordinary plow depth, and no well shall be drilled within two hundred (200) feet of any residence or barn now on said land without Lessor's consent. Lessee shall be responsible for all damages caused by Lessee's operations hereunder other than damages necessarily caused by the exercise of the rights herein granted.

8. The rights of either party hereunder may be assigned in whole or in part, and the provisions hereof shall extend to their heirs, successors and assigns; but no change or division in ownership of the land, rentals or royalties, however accomplished, shall operate to enlarge the obligations or diminish the rights of Lessee; and no change or division in such ownership shall be binding on Lessee until thirty (30) days after Lessee shall have been furnished by registered U. S. mail at Lessee's principal place of business with a certified copy of recorded instrument or instruments evidencing same. In the event of

Figure 6-20. Lease 6.

Producers 88-D9803 (Revised Oct. 1, 1948) With Pooling Provision.   HEDERMAN BROS., JACKSON, MISS.

7

OIL, GAS AND MINERAL LEASE

THIS AGREEMENT made this _____5_____ day of _____May_____ 19_85_, between

_____Emmy Walls Throckmorton and husband, W. B. Throckmorton_____

Lessor (whether one or more) whose address is: _____166 Sign Valley Rd., New Post, MS 39605_____
and _____Joe Smart_____ Lessee, WITNESSETH:

1. Lessor in consideration of _____Ten and more_____ Dollars

($_____), in hand paid, of the royalties herein provided, and of the agreement of Lessee herein contained, hereby grants, leases and lets exclusively unto Lessee for the purpose of investigating, exploring, prospecting, drilling and mining for and producing oil, gas and all other minerals, laying pipe lines, building roads, tanks, power stations, telephone lines and other structures thereon to produce, save, take care of, treat, transport and own said products, and housing its employees, the following described land in _____Carroll_____ County, Mississippi, to-wit:

Township 17 North, Range 4 East

Section 15: NE/4, E/2 NW, SW NW, N/2 NW SW, and a 15 acre

strip 300' wide off North side of SE/4.

Section 16: E/2 SE NE.

This lease also covers and includes all land owned or claimed by Lessor adjacent or contiguous to the land particularly described above, whether the same be in said section or sections, grant or grants, or in adjacent sections or grants, although not included within the boundaries of the land particularly described above. For the purpose of calculating the rental payments hereinafter provided for, said land is estimated to comprise_____335_____acres, whether it actually comprises more or less.

2. Subject to the other provisions herein contained, this lease shall be for a term of _three_ years from this date (called "primary term") and as long thereafter as oil, gas or other mineral is produced from said land or lands with which said land is pooled hereunder.

3. The royalties to be paid by Lessee are: (a) on oil, one-eighth of that produced and saved from said land, the same to be delivered at the wells or to the credit of Lessor into the pipe line to which the wells may be connected; Lessee may from time to time purchase any royalty oil in its possession, paying the market price therefor prevailing for the field where produced on the date of purchase, in either case such interest to bear its proportion of any expense of treating unmerchantable oil to render it merchantable as crude; (b) on gas, including casinghead gas or other gaseous substance, produced from said land and sold or used off the premises or in the manufacture of gasoline or other product therefrom, the market value at the well of one-eighth of the gas so sold or used, provided that on gas sold at the wells the royalty shall be one-eighth of the amount realized from such sale; where gas from a gas well is not sold or used, Lessee may pay as royalty $100.00 per well per year and if such payment is made it will be considered that gas is being produced within the meaning of Paragraph 2 hereof; and (c) on all other minerals mined and marketed, one-tenth either in kind or value at the well or mine, at Lessee's election, except that on sulphur mined and marketed, the royalty shall be fifty cents (50c) per long ton. Lessee shall have free use of oil, gas, coal, wood and water from said land, except water from Lessor's wells, for all operations hereunder, and the royalty on oil, gas and coal shall be computed after deducting any so used. Lessor shall have the privilege at his risk and expense of using gas from any gas well on said land for stoves and inside lights in the principal dwelling thereon out of any surplus gas not needed for operations hereunder.

4. Lessee, at its option, is hereby given the right and power to pool or combine the acreage covered by this lease or any portion thereof with other land, lease or leases in the immediate vicinity thereof, when in Lessee's judgment it is necessary or advisable to do so in order properly to develop and operate said premises in compliance with any lawful spacing rules which may be prescribed for the field in which this lease is situated by any duly authorized authority, or when to do so would, in the judgment of Lessee, promote the conservation of the oil and gas in and under and that may be produced from said premises. Lessee shall execute in writing an instrument identifying and describing the pooled acreage. The entire acreage so pooled into a tract or unit shall be treated, for all purposes except the payment of royalties on production from the pooled unit, as if it were included in this lease. If production is found on the pooled acreage, it shall be treated as if production is had from this lease, whether the well or wells be located on the premises covered by this lease or not. In lieu of the royalties elsewhere herein specified, Lessor shall receive on production from a unit so pooled only such portion of the royalty stipulated herein as his acreage placed in the unit or his royalty interest therein on an acreage basis bears to the total acreage so pooled in the particular unit involved.

5. If operations for drilling are not commenced on said land or on acreage pooled therewith as above provided on or before one year from this date the lease shall then terminate as to both parties, unless on or before such anniversary date Lessee shall pay or tender to Lessor or to the credit of Lessor in _____Coffeeville_____ Bank at _____Coffeeville_____, Mississippi (which bank and its successors are Lessor's agent and shall continue as the depository for all rentals payable hereunder regardless of changes in ownership of said land or the rentals) the sum of_____Three hundred thirty-five and no/100_____ Dollars

($__335.00__), (herein called rental), which shall cover the privilege of deferring commencement of drilling operations for a period of twelve (12) months. In like manner and upon like payments or tenders annually the commencement of drilling operations may be further deferred for successive periods of twelve (12) months each during the primary term. The payment or tender of rental may be made by the check or draft of Lessee mailed or delivered to Lessor or to said bank on or before such date of payment. If such bank (or any successor bank) should fail, liquidate or be succeeded by another bank, or for any reason fail or refuse to accept rental, Lessee shall not be held in default for failure to make such payment or tender of rental until thirty (30) days after Lessor shall deliver to Lessee a proper recordable instrument, naming another bank as agent to receive such payments or tenders. The down cash payment is consideration for this lease according to its terms and shall not be allocated as mere rental for a period. Lessee may at any time or times execute and deliver to Lessor or to the depository above named or place of record a release or releases covering any portion or portions of the above described premises and thereby surrender this lease as to such portion or portions and be relieved of all obligations as to the acreage surrendered, and thereafter the rentals payable hereunder shall be reduced in the proportion that the acreage covered hereby is reduced by said release or releases.

6. If prior to discovery of oil, gas or other mineral on said land or on acreage pooled therewith Lessee should drill a dry hole or holes thereon, or if after discovery of oil, gas or other mineral, the production thereof should cease from any cause, this lease shall not terminate if Lessee commences additional drilling or reworking operations within 60 days thereafter or if it be within the primary term, commences or resumes the payment or tender of rentals or commences operations for drilling or reworking on or before the rental paying date next ensuing after the expiration of 60 days from date of completion of dry hole or cessation of production. If at any time subsequent to sixty (60) days prior to the beginning of the last year of the primary term and prior to the discovery of oil, gas or other mineral on said land, or on acreage pooled therewith, Lessee should drill a dry hole thereon, no rental payment or operations are necessary in order to keep the lease in force during the remainder of the primary term. If at the expiration of the primary term, oil, gas or other mineral is not being produced on said land, or on acreage pooled therewith, but Lessee is then engaged in drilling or reworking operations thereon or shall have completed a dry hole thereon within sixty (60) days prior to the end of the primary term, the lease shall remain in force so long as operations are prosecuted with no cessation of more than sixty (60) consecutive days, and if they result in the production of oil, gas or other mineral, so long thereafter as oil, gas or other mineral is produced from said land or acreage pooled therewith. In the event a well or wells producing oil or gas in paying quantities should be brought in on adjacent land and within one hundred fifty (150) feet of and draining the leased premises, or acreage pooled therewith, Lessee agrees to drill such offset wells as a reasonably prudent operator would drill under the same or similar circumstances.

7. Lessee shall have the right at any time during or after the expiration of this lease to remove all property and fixtures placed by Lessee on said land, including the right to draw and remove all casing. When required by Lessor, Lessee will bury all pipe lines below ordinary plow depth, and no well shall be drilled within two hundred (200) feet of any residence or barn now on said land without Lessor's consent. Lessee shall be responsible for all damages caused by Lessee's operations hereunder other than damages necessarily caused by the exercise of the rights herein granted.

8. The rights of either party hereunder may be assigned in whole or in part, and the provisions hereof shall extend to their heirs, successors and assigns; but no change or division in ownership of the land, rentals or royalties, however accomplished, shall operate to enlarge the obligations or diminish the rights of Lessee; and no change or division in such ownership shall be binding on Lessee until thirty (30) days after Lessee shall have been furnished by registered U. S. mail at Lessee's principal place of business with a certified copy of recorded instrument or instruments evidencing same. In the event of assignment hereof in whole or in part liability for breach of any obligation hereunder shall rest exclusively upon the owner of this lease or of a portion thereof who commits such breach. In the event of the death of any person entitled to rentals hereunder, Lessee may pay or tender such rentals to the credit of the deceased or the estate of the deceased until such time as Lessee is furnished with proper evidence of the appointment and qualifications of an executor or administrator of the estate, or if there be none, then until Lessee is furnished with evidence satisfactory to it as to the heirs or devisees of the deceased, and

Figure 6-21. Lease 7.

MODEL
SECTION

Figure 6-22. Model section. Add lessees and lessors and net acres.

EXERCISE 6-3: FIGURING NET ACRES

Practice figuring net acres. Figure 6-22 is a "model" section. Read through the following exercise and divide the section into Tracts 1, 2, and 3. Then post the lease information, mineral ownership, and net acres in the respective tracts.

Tract 1: NE/4 NE/4
Mineral owners: B. C. Cook   1/2 int.
                A. Cook Davis   1/4 int.
                H. T. Lewis   1/8
                V. S. Hart   1/8

Tract 2: E/2 NW/4
Mineral owners: J. C. Penney   1/4 int.
                P. B. Daniel   1/4 int.
                J. C. Marx   1/6
                Scott Lbr. Co.   1/6
                B. C. Cook   1/6

Tract 3: SE/4
Mineral owners: J. C. Penney   2/5
                P. B. Daniel   1/10
                J. C. Marx   1/10
                Scott Lbr. Co.   1/5
                V. S. Hart   3/20
                B. C. Cook   1/20

These companies leased acreage in this section:

- Shell leased all of the interest held by B.C. Cook in Tracts 1, 2, and 3, as well as H. T. Lewis' interest in Tract 1.

- EXXON leased all the interest owned by these people: A. C. Davis, Tract 1; V. S. Hart, Tract 1; J. C. Penney, Tracts 2 and 3; J. C. Marx, Tracts 2 and 3.

- Chevron leased these interests: P. B. Daniel, E/2 NW; P. B. Daniel, SE/4.

Chapter 7
Cross Sections

Cross sections are diagrams or drawings that illustrate features transected by a given plane (Figure 7-1). They are important to exploration projects when used in conjunction with maps because they add a third dimension that is difficult to depict by maps alone.

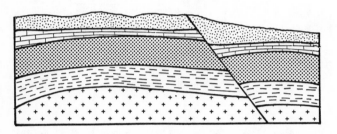

Figure 7-1. Cross section or profile showing a fault.

There are two types of geological cross sections: *structural* and *stratigraphic. Structural cross sections* are "hung" on a horizontal line which is related to mean sea level (Figure 7-2). A structural section shows the shape of the strata. Just as it is necessary to correlate the logs for a structure map, it is necessary to compare logs in the cross section from a common point. The log depths therefore must be adjusted for elevation relative to mean sea level. (For example: You might hang the logs on "−3000′," "−6000′," etc.)

DATUM SEA LEVEL

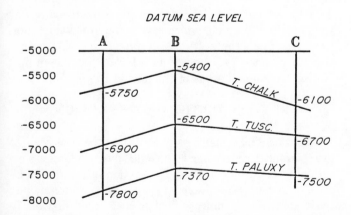

Figure 7-2. Structural cross section with a hang line datum of −5,000 ft. Note the subsea datum levels on the left.

Stratigraphic cross sections are hung on a stratigraphic marker which is common to each of the wells (Figure 7-3). It may be the top or bottom of a formation, or it may be a "marker" that is easily identified on the logs. (For example: You could hang a strat section on the "Top of Eutaw," the "Top Lower Tuscaloosa," or on the "Base Ferry Lake," etc.) This would make the formation appear flat. A strat section shows the arrangement of the "strata" or rock layers. It is hung without regard to sea level or the relative elevations of the wells. Although a stratigraphic section does not show structure directly, any thickening or thinning of the strata can be indicative of structural growth.

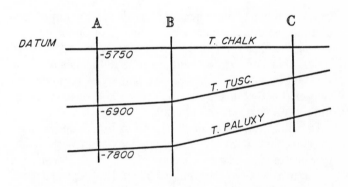

Figure 7-3. Stratigraphic cross sections are hung without regard to sea level. They are hung on the top of a formation or marker.

HANGING CONSIDERATIONS

Before setting the scale for the section, consider the distance covered by the wells and the log interval to be shown. Overall size is a major consideration. If one-inch logs are used, then the vertical scale of the section is 1″ = 100′. A log covering a mile of depth would be 52.8 inches long. If the same scale were used horizontally, a cross section covering wells over a twenty-mile distance would require 1,056 inches or 88 feet of length. As you can see, a distortion between the horizontal and vertical scales will always be present. Regional cross sections covering many miles cannot be drawn on the same horizontal scale as those sections covering only a local situation. To make a cross section covering ten miles in dis-

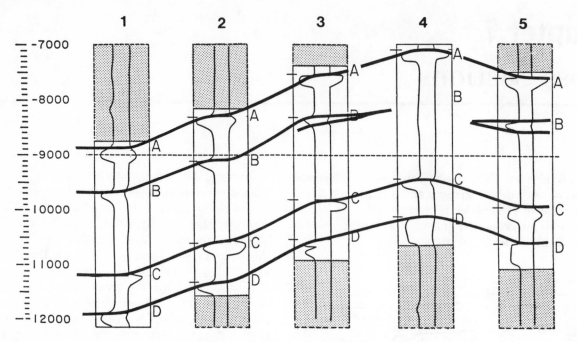

Figure 7-4. Actual structural cross section using the table of formation tops on this page.

tance, you might use a horizontal scale of 3″ = 1 mile. The distance could be covered by 30 inches of paper or film. If, on the other hand, the wells were spaced over 60 miles, this same scale would require 180 inches of material and be almost impossible to handle. A regional section of this distance might be drawn to a scale of 1″ = 1 mile, requiring 60″ of material.

Deciding how much of the log to include is much more of a problem with structural sections than with stratigraphic ones, since much depends on the difference in structural relief of the wells involved. If 1″ logs are used, there is 1 inch in length for every 100 feet of depth, so in order to cover 4,000 feet of depth, you will need 40 inches of log. Even though you may not need to show 4,000 feet of each well, there might be a 4,000-foot difference between the upper zone of the highest well to the lower zone of the lowest well.

In the following table of formation tops, the log depths have already been converted to subsea elevations. For a structural section we will use −9,000 feet for the hang line datum.

Formation	Well #1	Well #2	Well #3	Well #4	Well #5
A	−8,900	−8,300	−7,500	−7,100	−7,600
B	−9,700	−9,100	−8,300	n/a	−8,400
C	−11,200	−10,600	−9,800	−9,400	−9,900
D	−11,900	−11,300	−10,500	−10,100	−10,600

In this example note that the upper zone (Formation A) is at −7,100 feet in Well #4 (the highest well). The lower

zone (Formation D) is at −11,900 feet in Well #1, which is a difference of 4,800 feet. In order to show all the zones in all the wells it is necessary to show 4,800 feet of log, or 48 inches without even allowing for headings or notes (Figure 7-4). As you can readily see, this particular cross-section would be almost unmanageable. It would be necessary either to show less log or to reduce the vertical scale of the logs. Reducing the scale to less than 1″ = 100′ may make it difficult to see the features which the section was made to show. (See Figure 7-4.)

A stratigraphic section of the same logs could be hung at the top of Formation A and need only show 30 inches of log. See Figure 7-5.

In order to hang this structural section, it was necessary to find a datum point common to each well. In this case −9,000 feet fits nicely. It is permissible to show only the portion of each log which covers the interval in question. However, the section will appear more "presentable" if you show enough of each log to "line them up." Notice the shaded areas of the logs in Figure 7-4.

SETTING UP THE CROSS SECTION

After deciding which logs to show and the best scale to use, you must remember to include several elements essential to any cross section. The section in Figure 7-6 includes a few of these. Each log should be accompanied by the well symbol to indicate final disposition of the well. In this case, the first well was a dry hole, the second a gas well, etc. The vertical line in the middle is used to indi-

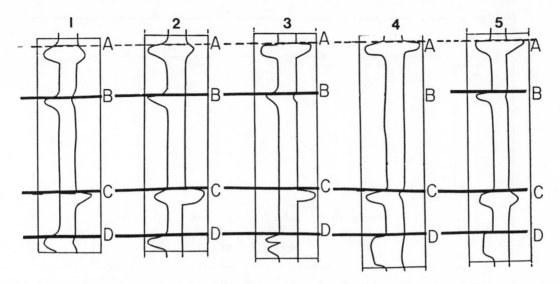

Figure 7-5. Actual stratigraphic cross section using the table of formation tops on page 105.

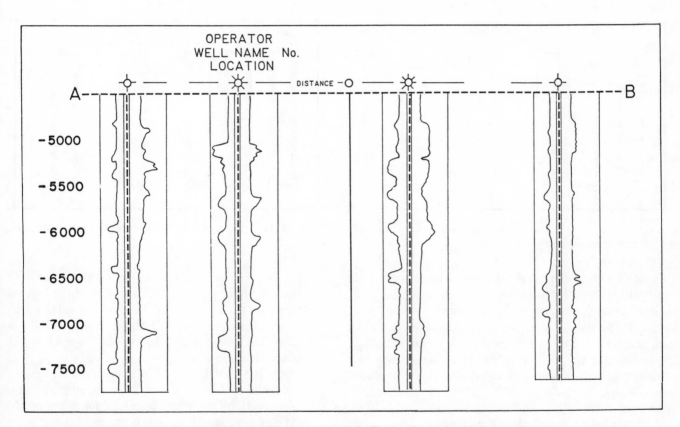

Figure 7-6. A structural section laid out and hung on − 5,000 ft. The location in the middle is indicated by a vertical line.

cate a location, either proposed or drilling, for which no log is available. On some cross sections the distance between wells is shown as indicated. The operator and well name and number, along with the location, should be indicated for each well. Sometimes log headings are used, but they are difficult to read. The line of cross section in this example is A to B, and should be indicated on a map of the area, which may or may not be included on the cross section itself. The subsea elevations shown on the left side are an indication that this one is set up for a structural section. They would not be necessary for a strat section.

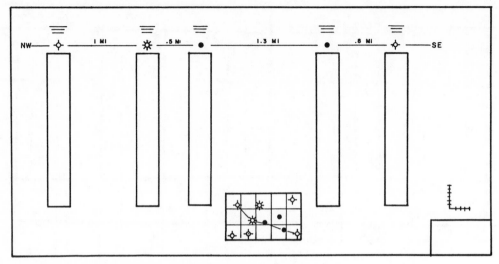

Figure 7-7. A pleasing layout of a cross section includes scale and index map, well symbols for each log, and distance between wells. The three short lines above each well symbol indicate placement of well names and locations.

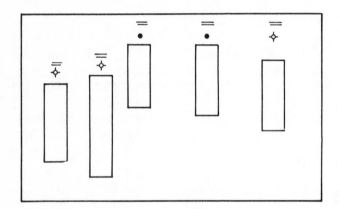

Figure 7-8. A cross section that includes only the essential portions of the logs presents a less-than-pleasing appearance.

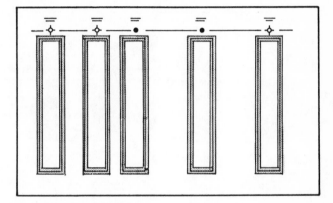

Figure 7-9. Logs spliced into the drafting medium are difficult to handle and difficult to print.

Figure 7-7 shows a typical set up for a cross section of any type. Enough log is present in each case to give a pleasing overall appearance. Symbols and distances are included. The line of cross section is indicated by direction, i.e., NW to SE. In this example the map showing the location of the wells involved is an index map included on the cross section itself. Above the title block the scale has been drawn with vertical and horizontal scale both indicated.

In Figure 7-8 we see what happens when we show only the particular portions of logs which are essential, without regard to aesthetics.

MAKING A REPRODUCIBLE CROSS SECTION

A few of the ways to make a cross section that can be reproduced are covered in the following:

1. Make a film of each log and splice it into a piece of drafting mylar (Figure 7-9). If done carefully, this process may make the best prints, although it is difficult to splice perfectly all four sides of the log, and there is a tendency for this type of original to buckle in the Diazo machine. If this is the method you choose, it is best to put the tape on the reverse side of the drafting film.

There is a kind of matte film available with a nonreproducible grid of light blue lines, called grid film or cross section film, which is helpful for lining up this type of section. Also a nonrepro grid tracing paper can be used effectively for this purpose and costs considerably less than the mylar. If paper is used the prints will not be as clear because of the different textures of the surface of the paper and the log film.

2. Attach clear films of the log on the back side of the cross section paper. Tape down only one side of each log (Figure 7-10). This prevents the curling that can result as the paper passes over the rollers in the Diazo machine. Clear film allows the light to penetrate fully for printing, but this kind of film does not

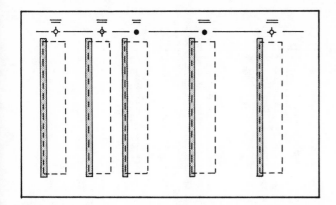

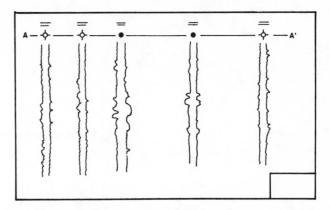

Figure 7-10. Log films taped on one side only to the back of the medium allow good prints but don't wrinkle in the Diazo machine. Better resolution is also achieved since the images of the curves are in direct contact with the print paper.

Figure 7-11. Sometimes it is more expedient to trace the curves of the log instead of showing the entire log on a cross section.

readily take ink. If the films of the logs are taped onto the back of the tracing paper, all drafting can be done on the tracing paper itself, which is designed for ink drafting. This method also puts the logs in direct contact with the print paper, which makes better prints.

3. Set up a preliminary cross section using white paper and photocopies of the logs. Then photocopy it (if it is not too large). Sometimes this will help you see if these particular logs effectively show what you are trying to portray.

4. Avoid splicing and taping and making films by tracing the curves onto the drafting surface (Figure 7-11). Since a long piece of log will usually have some stretch in the print, the scale will be a little off at the end. When tracing the curves, you must allow for this discrepancy.

Occasionally it is sufficient to make a schematic cross section as in Figure 7-12. In this type of section, only a representative line is shown in place of the log. It is used to show relative structure or thickness just to get an idea across. Figure 7-13 shows a typical regional cross section.

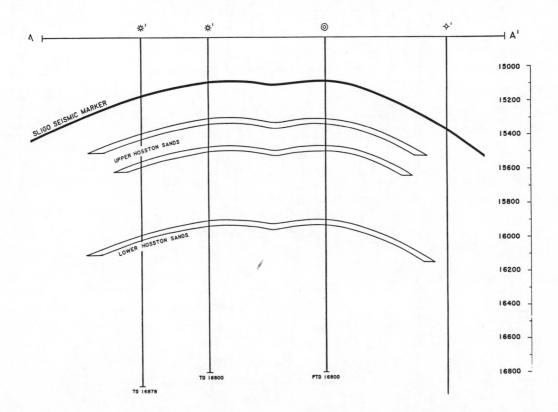

Figure 7-12. A schematic cross section may be used in some circumstances when only relationships between wells must be shown.

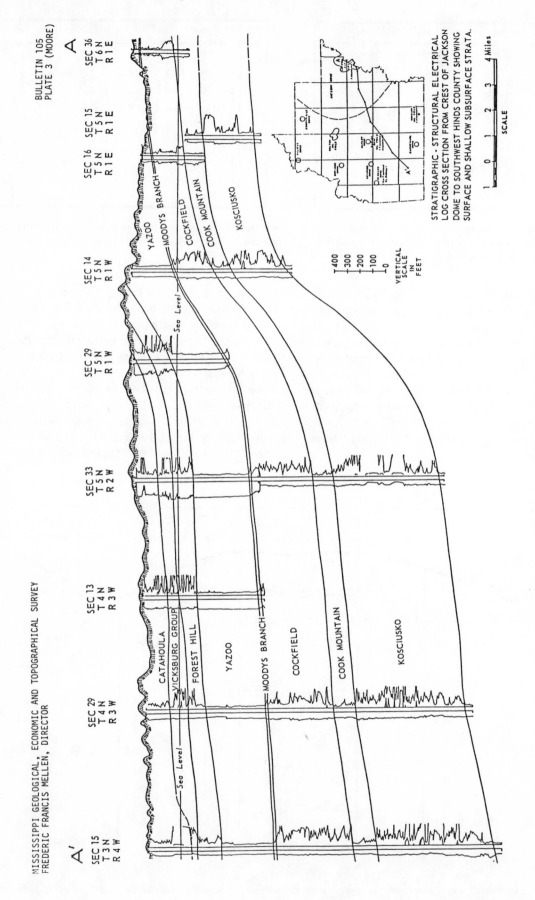

Figure 7-13. A typical cross section (Reprinted with permission of Mississippi Geological Survey.)

SYMBOLS FOR LOGS AND CROSS SECTIONS

A number of symbols used on logs and cross sections are more or less standard in the industry. Some of the common ones are shown in Figure 7-14. The mark used to indicate the fault also includes the "throw" and the subsea elevation, in this case 200 feet at −15,718. Sidewall cores are shown by either short horizontal lines or arrows. Diamond cores are indicated by a box with an X in it covering the correct interval. Perforations are indicated at the correct depth with a similar box with small circles inside. The labels are for identification in this example only, they are not necessary on the log or cross section, as the symbols are self explanatory.

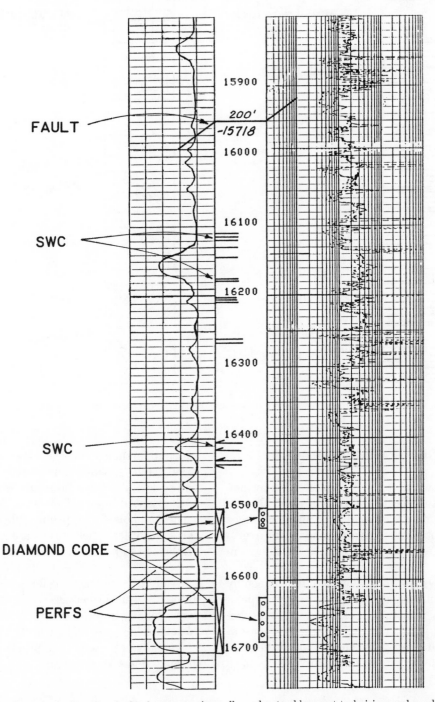

Figure 7-14. The symbols depicted on the log here are universally understood by most technicians and need not be labeled.

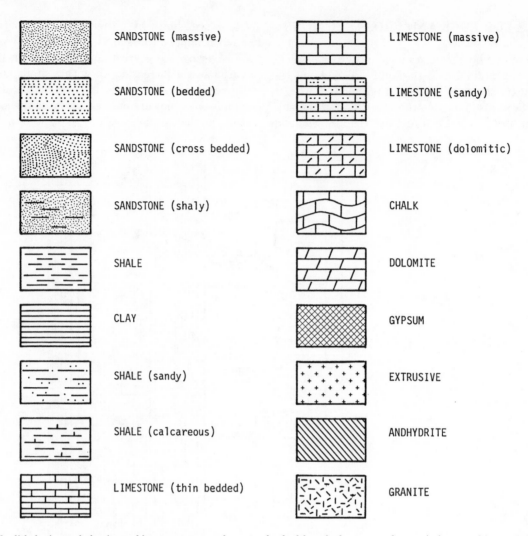

Figure 7-15. The lithologic symbols pictured here are more or less standard, although there are a few variations used in particular situations.

LITHOLOGIC GRAPHIC SYMBOLS

Situations arise in which it may be beneficial to include a lithologic symbol to indicate the type of rock. You see these symbols on sample logs, mud logs, and sometimes on cross sections. Not all symbols are standard for everybody, but some of the more common ones are shown in Figure 7-15.

Sandstone is always shown by dots, as you can see by the examples, even if the pattern differs for the type of sandstone. Symbols for other rocks may be superimposed on the dotted pattern to indicate the presence of shale, limestone, quartz, etc. The same is true of the standard symbol for shale. It may have dots or vertical lines added to further define the type of shale. Notice the limestone symbols: sandy limestone is indicated by the addition of dots, dolomitic limestone is shown by the addition of the slanted lines indicative of dolomite.

The symbols for gypsum, anhydrite, extrusive, salt, and some other types of rock are not standard. A copy of symbols used by the U.S.G.S. may be ordered from that office.

Different companies prefer various colors for shading in the different lithologies. In general, sandstones are always yellow; limestones are blue. Shales are shown in various colors, depending on the type of shale. Almost universally accepted is the practice of coloring oil shows green and gas shows red.

Chapter 8
Reprographics Systems and Applications

Reprographics is the duplication of flat documents, and covers everything from photocopying a letter on the office copying machine to the design of a complete set of construction and assembly drawings for ocean-going vessels or multistory skyscrapers.

New technology in reprographic systems, materials, and services introduce changes that can add to the confusion of users. It is a good idea to talk with your repro professional and keep up to date on the latest methods and materials.

Four factors—production time, reproducibility, permanence, and cost effectiveness—are the prime considerations in determining the best reprographic method. Lower costs may be sacrificed for speed, or production time may be lengthened to preserve quality.

Since redrafting (tracing) existing data is the most expensive, time-consuming, and error-prone reprographic system, and reduces the work of an expensive, skilled designer or drafter to a mundane and sometimes frustrating job, other alternatives need to be considered. A discussion of most of the common reprographic processes and materials follows.

TERMINOLOGY

Proper use of any system requires a thorough understanding of the terminology involved. Your local repro service center can provide you with further explanations of these terms and actual samples or demonstrations of their practical use. Ask questions! A "dumb" question is better than a costly mistake.

Acetate—A synthetic material similar to celluloid but not easily flammable. Available with smooth or matte surface. Used as a photographic base or as an overlay.

Ammonia process—See *Diazo process*.

Autopositive—Trade name of Eastman Kodak Co. for certain photographic direct positive intermediates. (See *Direct positive*).

Background—(1) Nonimage area of a print. (2) Density, discoloration, or tint noticed in the fully exposed areas of a print above the color and density of the base material. (3) For overlay drafting, the reference image.

Base stock—Any paper or other material, such as film or cloth, to which a chemical coating is to be applied.

Blocking out—The use of black or orange paper, photographic opaque, tape, or India ink to fill in areas on a negative so that they will not be reproduced on the positive print.

Blow back—Generic term for projected image.

Blue line—(Dry) See *Diazoprint*. (Wet) A white background, blue line print made on iron sensitized paper by printing only through a negative. Almost obsolete. See *Blueprint*.

Blueprint—A wet process negative image reproduction having white lines with a solid blue background on iron-sensitized paper. While not obsolete, this process has been largely superseded by the dry Diazo process. Usually today's "blueprint" is a blueline or blackline Diazo positive print.

Brown line—(Dry) See *Diazo process*.

Color transparency—A film positive, generally viewed by transmitted light, that portrays the subject in natural colors.

Composite printing—A combination of multiple exposures onto photographic material using more than one negative.

Contact frame—Device for making same-size reproductions from translucent material held in immediate contact with the original. Items in contact are exposed to light through a glass cover and usually held in position by a vacuum.

Contact print—Print produced by exposing a negative or positive original placed in immediate contact with the print paper. These prints are always the same size as the original.

Continuous tone copy—Photographic copy that contains a varying gradation of gray densities between black and white.

Contrast—Difference of tone between the darker and the lighter parts of an image.

Copyboard—That portion of a process camera on which the art copy, drawing, or object to be photographed is mounted.

Copy negative—A photographic negative made as an intermediate from which prints can be produced.

Density—In general terms, the relative darkness of an image area.

Diazo paper—A reproduction paper which depends on the light sensitivity of diazonium compounds to form an image when developed by means of aqueous ammonia, heat, or a specialized developing solution.

Diazoprint—A reproduction made by using the Diazo paper. Also referred to as a whiteprint, blue line, black line, etc.

Diazo process—A reproduction method using material coated with a light-sensitive Diazo compound that, after exposure, is subject to ammonia-vapor or moist development to produce a colored, positive image. A positive translucent or transparent original produces a positive image.

Diazo vellum—An intermediate on pre-transparentized paper, sensitized with a black or sepia diazo solution; sepia is most popular. See *Sepia intermediate*.

Diffusion transfer—A photographic method involving image transfer. A sheet of sensitized material is exposed to an image in a contact printing frame and processed in contact with a receiver sheet. The image is transferred during processing.

Dimensional stability—Term applied to the relative ability of photographic materials to maintain their size and shape before, during, and after processing.

Direct positive—A generic term for prints made on either paper or film by means of a positive to positive silver type emulsion.

Direct print—A positive reproduction on Diazo sensitized paper printed directly from a translucent original without the use of a negative.

Drawing—Generally a pencil or ink drawing on vellum, tracing paper, or polyester matter film. Also a reproduction copy on translucent material. See *Original*.

Dry mount—Mounting of print on cardboard or pressed board for display.

Duplicate—(Noun) In microcopying, a copy usually made by contact printing from a master or an intermediate. In reprographics, an intermediate used to replace an original drawing in producing future reproductions. A second original. (Verb) To make multiple copies of a document, usually with the aid of a master.

Electrostatic process—Reproduction method in which image formation depends on electrical, rather than chemical, changes induced by light.

Emulsion—A single or multilayered coating of gelatinous material on a high quality base carrying radiant energy reactive chemicals that create a latent image upon exposure. Processing techniques produce a final, visible, usable image.

Eradicator—A one-, two-, or three-solution preparation used for making changes on intermediates and prints.

Specific preparations are required for either photographic or Diazo intermediates.

Facsimile—(1) An exact copy of an original document. (2) The process or result of the process by which fixed graphic images are scanned, transmitted electronically, and reproduced either locally or remotely.

Fading—Loss in density in an image.

Film positive—A positive reproduction made on photographic film.

Fixline—A photographic film image requiring a two-solution eradicating process.

Format—The layout area or boundary of artwork, drawings, or film copy.

Generation—Each succeeding stage in reproduction from the original copy.

Ghost—A second or retained image, not usually desired.

Image—A likeness of the subject matter which appears on the reproduced copy.

Intermediate—A translucent reproduction from an original drawing or a print used in place of the original for making other copies.

Line copy—Originals containing only lines and solids and with no intermediate tone (generally black and white only).

Line negative—A high-contrast negative used when continuous tone is not needed.

Masking—Using opaque material to cut off exposures to certain areas of reproductions to produce desirable effects.

Master—Original from which reproductions are made.

Matte—Dull, gloss-free finish. Also, the drafting surface on polyester film.

Microfiche—Transparent film approximately $4'' \times 6''$ containing micro-images in a group pattern with a title heading large enough to be read by the naked eye.

Microfilm—(1) A fine-grain, high-resolution film containing an image greatly reduced in size from the original. (2) The recording of microphotographs on film. (3) Raw film with characteristics as in definition (1). (4) Also a generic term relating to an entire family of films with images that cannot be discerned by the unaided eye.

Mylar—DuPont Company trade name for polyester-type film of high strength and dimensional stability, used as a base stock for light-sensitive photographic coatings and drafting films.

Negative—A reverse-reading, black background copy with white or clear images on paper or film used for subsequent printing.

Negative print—An image, usually on opaque base stock, in which the light and dark areas are reversed from those of the original.

Nonreproducible—Not intended for use as an intermediate master, generally opaque (usually blue or light violet in color).

Offset printing—Indirect photo-lithography in which the ink image is transferred to a rubber blanket which in turn offsets the image onto a sheet of paper.

Opacity—The property of a sheet of paper or other material that prevents dark objects on or in contact with the back of the sheet from being seen. Nontranslucent.

Opaque copy—Material which is impervious to transmitted light and consequently must be reproduced by reflected light.

Opaquing—Handwork done on a negative or original to remove spots or unwanted images. See *Blocking out.*

Original—Material from which copies, such as handwritten copy, typed copy, printing matter, tracings, drawings, and photographs, are made. See *Master.*

Overlay—Transparent or translucent prints, which when placed one on the other form a composite picture.

Overlay drafting—Separation of common data images onto several sheets of drafting film (not paper) to allow multiple use of those images.

Paste-up—Composite drawings produced by pasting or taping the individual segments into a format before reproduction; scissors drafting.

Photocopy (photostat copy)—Usually a black, right-reading photographic paper copy of any document made in a special machine. Also, white copies made from such black copies.

Photodrafting—Combining sections of several drawings onto one new or revised drawing by the use of photographic techniques.

Photodrawing—The technique of combining a photograph and drawing detail to form a finished engineering drawing.

Pin bar—A strip of metal with precisely placed pins. Used for overlay alignment.

Pin registered overlays—Precise mechanical alignment of separate film overlays by means of prepunched holes and a standard pin bar.

Polyester film—A type of film with high strength and dimensional stability used as a base stock for light-sensitive coating and drafting material. Used for pin-registered overlay drafting.

Positive—A print which is normal reading and made from any type of negative or in the Diazo process from a positive or original.

Print—In this chapter "print" is used to designate a positive reading reproduction.

Projection image—Photographic print made through a lens, enlarged, reduced, or kept the same size.

Reader—A projection device for viewing an enlarged micro-image with the naked eye.

Reader-printer—A microfilm reader which also has the capability of producing a hard copy reproduction from the microfilm image.

Registration—Precision alignment, using targets or pin bars, of several overlay images.

Register marks—Marks used to ensure that individual prints will line up correctly when making a composite.

Reprodrafting—Any combination of photo or mechanical reproduction methods used to save drafting time or to enhance the drawn image.

Reprographic processes—All of the copying and duplicating processes.

Resolution—The ability of the optical systems and photomaterials to render visible fine detail of an object; a measure of the sharpness of an image.

Reproducible—Capable of producing copies in Diazo or photographic methods.

Reverse reading—Letters reading from right to left as observed in a mirror instead of left to right. Such letters will be right reading when observed through the back of a transparent medium.

Right reading—A photographic image that is readable from the front or image side of the material.

Screen (halftone)—A negative having a pattern of various dots and white spaces, which are used to maintain the gray scale ranges and continuous appearance of a photo image.

Screen tint—A negative having a uniform dot pattern in various gray scale percentages, which are used to subdue a normally full tone image.

Scribing—A drawing process in which a stylus is used to cut lines on a suitably prepared base stock.

Sepia intermediates—Printing intermediates made on Diazo intermediate paper, cloth, or film that have a light brown image.

Text—Written matter on a page as distinguished from the photographs, drawn lines, etc.

Tracing—Translucent original drawn or traced by hand or a reproduction made on transparent sensitized material and called an intermediate.

Translucent—Admitting the passage of light. Partially transparent.

Transmitted light—Light that has passed through a material such as film or paper. Intermediates and transparent negatives are reproduced by transmitted light in most cases.

Transparency—A monochrome or color positive, the image to be viewed or reproduced by transmitted light.

Turn-around time—The time required from start to finish for the reproduction of an image.

Vacuum frame—See *Contact frame.*

Vellum—A chemically treated translucent paper used for original drawings in pencil or ink.

Wash-off material—A photographic film with a wet erasable image. No eradication fluid is needed.

Whiteprint—See *Diazoprint.*

Xerography—An electrostatic reproduction method for copying and duplicating.

CAMERA READY COPY

Most presentations require "camera ready copy," meaning simply that the material must be good enough to print or photograph. This artwork or text is the foundation for any reprographics program or presentation, and it is important to understand how to prepare it, as certain kinds of images photograph better than others. The following are some of the things to consider in deciding whether the material is "ready."

- *Pencil*—Graphite lines on paper provide good production time and a low cost factor but reproduce poorly. It is best if pencil drawings are used for preliminary study only.
- *Technical pen*—Ink on drafting film is permanent, produces copy with excellent reproducibility, and requires a production time not much more extensive than that of pencil work.
- *Scribing*—Scribed line work allows for precise width control with few flaws, but it requires more complex production techniques. The result is exceptionally good for reproduction.
- *Graphic tapes*—Using graphic tapes with adhesive backing saves production time, and there are many patterns available, but, as with any applique, such tape is not very permanent.
- *Automated drawing machines*—There are several electronically controlled lettering machines on the market which can place high-quality inked letters and symbols directly on drafting media. These are expensive, but allow high-speed, high-quality work to be done by the nonprofessional.
- *Pattern films*—Acetate pattern films save repetitive drawing of patterns or the need for shading. They are great for reproduction but not very permanent.
- *Templates*—Mechanical production of lettering utilizing templates or guides makes excellent uniform lettering. When used with ink on film, these provide excellent permanence, good reproducibility, but

naturally has a little slower production time than free-hand drawing.

- *Dry transfer*—Pressure-sensitive transfer lettering with limited symbols requires that individual letters be positioned one at a time, which lengthens production time. It is not permanent, yet involves considerable cost.
- *Custom I.N.T.*—Custom-made dry transfer sheets prepared from selected artwork are a considerable time saver when producing repetitive symbols or characters. These may be made in the office on a standard photocopy machine using special sheets, or they may be ordered in certain quantities, but the are not very permanent.
- *Kroy*—Using this machine-produced lettering placed on an adhesive-backed carrier for ease in placement, eliminates wasted lettering and results in excellent production time. The machines are quite expensive and use costly consumable tape cartridges. Also the lettering is not permanent, and unless care is taken, fingerprints and ghosts will appear on the prints.
- *Phototypeset*—Photo-mechanical typesetting is good for large quantities of body copy and is best for large volume printings.

PROJECT CONSIDERATIONS

A number of variables determine how a project should be prepared. Proper planning and communication with the reprographics specialist can result in superior copy produced in less time for less cost.

Some of the elements to be considered include the following.

Type of Original

Some questions about the condition of the original need to be answered before certain decisions can be made about the method of reprographics.

- Is the base material translucent, transparent, or opaque?
- What is the scale? If the required copy is to be a different size or scale than the original, then a reprographics process using optical lenses must be used. Contact processes such as Diazo can only produce a copy the same size and scale as the original.
- Is the image contrast a "line" (high contrast) copy, black and white with no gradations of tone or "continuous tone," with variations of tone from black through white, or are there colors?
- Is the image positive, where the original image is identical to the desired copy?

- Is the image negative, where the original image is opposite to the image of the needed copy?
- What is the image quality? Originals with faded lines, discolored background, creases and tears, or other "problem copy" usually require a two-step copying technique—negative to positive. Direct positive contact reprographic systems record all the undesirable bits along with the required image.
- What is the size of the original? Available equipment and/or materials determine the maximum size original that can be copied in one piece. Originals may be copied in sections, then spliced. Width is defined as the shortest dimension of an original, length as the longer dimension, regardless of the horizontal or vertical orientation of the image.

Ultimate Purpose of the Copy

Before deciding on the type of reprographics you should consider what the copy will be used for. Some of the purposes for copies are discussed in the following.

Final Distribution Copy

Distribution prints are produced for the primary purpose of communications, and not for recopying. These copies should be complete as to information and meet all the requirements as to longevity, usage, and format. The quantity, quality, size, life-span, eventual obsolescence, and environmental conditions all determine the type of copy needed. Typical uses include:
- Construction drawings and specifications.
- Assembly and machine drawings.
- Maps for distribution, utilities, locations, ownership, zoning, etc.
- Progress and check prints for agency, consultants, or client approval.
- Reports, legal briefs, catalogs, and price lists.

Intermediates

These are copies produced to be recopied. They are always translucent if they are to be recopied by Diazo or contact methods. They may also be a different scale than the original, and may have additional data added prior to being recopied. They are typically used for:

- "Machine" originals, for producing distribution prints, particularly when copies are made by Diazo methods. Thus the original drawing can be kept by the designer for updating and revising and is not subject to wear from handling and copying in the Diazo machines.
- A duplicate set of reproducibles for a branch office, client, contractor, or partner at a different location.
- Reduced size intermediates so that drawings can be drafted at the size most convenient for the designer but be distributed at the size most convenient for the user.
- Base drawings, which are intermediates containing commonly used data reprographically produced rather than traced and redrawn. They are produced on a translucent material with a drafting surface so new data may be added for a complete drawing. The image can also be modified by changing scale or screening for a subordinate image.
- Conversion of an opaque original to a translucent intermediate for Diazo production.
- Pin-graphic slicks, which are clear base films copied in exact registration with the original using a precise pin-register bar and prepunched stable base polyester film.

Camera Ready Art

This is reproductions made to be recopied by photo, Lithographic or Xerographic processes. Image type, size, and scale are modified as needed to produce a high-contrast, best quality copy. Examples are graphics for paste-ups, photo-mechanicals, offset, and Xerox copying.

Appliqués

These are images produced on an adhesive-backed material which can be attached to a master drawing as desired. They have the same features and modifications as camera ready art. The material can be either opaque or translucent for compatability to the repro method used for the final copy.

Presentation Prints

These are usually produced in limited quantities with an emphasis on appearance rather than technical accuracy of detail and reusability. Colors, shading, and notations are added for impact.

Graphics Exhibits and Displays

These are similar to presentation copies, but more emphasis is placed on permanence and sizing to fit exhibits, wall space. They are usually dry-mounted to a rigid base for exhibiting.

Overhead Transparencies

These clear base films with images in a variety of transparent colors convert copy to desired size and color on a transparent base for use with overhead transparency projectors or to overlay base data on opaque copy.

Microfilm Copy Quality

Microfilm originals require a high contrast image (dense black on white base) to produce a quality reduced image. Reductions of 20–30 times are common and require excellent originals. Most originals cannot meet the requirements for microfilm copy.

Processes Available

Some companies have in-house reproduction departments which are usually limited to electrostatic or Diazo processes. If this is the case, the manager of this department will discuss options and limitations with you. The different processes available are discussed in detail under the heading "Reprographic Processes." Communication with whoever will be responsible for the final product is the key to flawless prints.

Base Materials

Usually either paper or polyester, stable-base film is used as a base. Both paper and film are available in an opaque or translucent variety.

Translucent films are also available in a completely clear form or with a matte surface added to one or both sides. Films vary in thickness from .0015 inches to .007 inches.

Opaque base materials are generally used for distribution or for final prints. Translucent base materials are selected when future copying by a contact method will be needed. If additional data are to be drafted, 100% rag content vellum tracing papers or matte sided films are needed.

Image Characteristics

The image characteristics must be considered since they limit the processes available for both original and the uses of the copies. Different images require different eradication methods, including friction with a soft eraser, moistened erasers, or chemical liquids that react with and bleach out the sensitized image. The method used must match the kind of image to be removed. The following are some of the types of images and their limitations.

- *Permanent (archival) images* are not subject to fading or discoloration due to exposure to light, heat, humid-

ity, or pollution. Documents needed for long periods of time should be archival quality. Photo, Litho, and Xerographic processes produce permanent images if done properly. Diazo and diffusion transfer images are not considered archival as they will eventually fade and discolor with time. Polyester films will meet archival standards, but most papers will not.
- *Direct images* produce a duplicate copy from a positive original (e.g., Diazo prints).
- *Negative working images* produce a negative (opposite) image from a positive original, or a positive image from a negative original.
- *High contrast images* do not produce a tone image (meaning shades of gray) but the exposed emulsion develops to its maximum density.
- *Continuous tone images* reproduce with various shades of gray, from black to almost white.
- *Right reading images* are oriented on the sheet the same way as the original image, capable of being read in the usual manner from left to right (e.g., Diazo prints, Xerox prints, offset prints).
- *Reverse reading images* are read in a manner opposite that of the original image, and are preferred for copying with intermediates. These result from the exposure technique and not necessarily the product. Intermediates to be used as second originals for Diazo copying are usually reverse reading so as to produce the sharpest copy.

Special Applications Required

At times there are situations that require special handling procedures because of the condition of the original or because of a change in budget or leadership or schedule. The following are some of the special processes that may be utilized in these instances.

- *Restoration (image enhancement)* is improving the legibility, contrast, and usability of the copied original. This can be achieved by using high contrast images, retouching negatives as needed, and then printing to a high contrast positive material.
- *Paste-up or scissors drafting* is not drafting at all, nor is it a reprographics process. "Paste-up" is taking portions of graphic data from several originals and positioning them on a format sheet to be copied. "Scissors drafting" is removing unwanted data prior to reproduction. Projection exposure systems and materials must be used.
- *Continuing revisions.* Certain copies cannot have images removed without damaging the base. Materials with erasable images should be used to reproduce "active" drawings. If additional drafting is required, repro materials with a good drafting surface and a re-

verse image opposite the drafting surface should be used.

- *Photo drawings* utilize photography rather than drafting. Additional data can be added to the reproduction.
- *Pin-graphics* or *overlay drafting* is a reproduction method in which the various data are separated onto different sheets of film according to repetitive usage or type of information. Each piece of film is punched to fit an industry standard pin bar to ensure precise registration of all the overlays. Reproductions are made using an identical pin register bar in a contact frame or on a camera copyboard so the various sheets are held in a registered sandwich. As the sheets are placed together, different sets of data can be combined. This method eliminates redrawing of common material, but requires a tremendous amount of planning.
- *Scaling* is producing an enlarged or reduced copy of the original document to match the user's requirements.
- *Subordinate image* is a shadow or screened image produced by placing a dotted screen between a negative image intermediate and positive copy during exposure. The dots block out segments of line and solid image, producing the appearance of a gray image on the final copy.
- *Reformatting* means taking the design data from one drawing and transferring it to a different format (to meet particular specifications of size, contract, job or customer's standard format). This is a real time saver.
- A *mirror image* means the copy is oriented in a manner opposite to that of the original drawing. Such images are used in compositing a complete drawing from partial drawings and for paste-up and step-and-repeat when components of a design are repetitive and identical except for the orientation.
- *Multiple color images* require separation of artwork and offset copying. Producing these is expensive unless large numbers of copies are needed. Clear films with different color images overlaid and in register to each other can be used for one-time presentations.

REPROGRAPHIC PROCESSES

Diazo Process

This reproduction method uses material coated with a light-sensitive Diazo compound and a translucent or transparent original. After contact exposure, the material is developed by being subjected to ammonia vapors, heat, or moisture. This method produces copy that is sensitive to sunlight, moisture, and heat, and the image will fade in time. Because the copies are made from contact with the original, the scale cannot be changed.

The Diazo process may be used to make several different kinds of copies, depending on the material used and the developing time. These include the following.

Blue or Black Line Paper Prints

The main function of these prints is for final distribution. They hold scale better than the wet paper processes and notations can be made easily on the white background. Also the image can be eradicated. They can be produced on paper that comes in various weights, colors, and speeds, as well as with such special characteristics as adhesive backs, plastic coatings (which make it possible to wipe the paper clean with a damp cloth), and plastic impregnation (which allows the paper to withstand heavy usage and repeated folding).

The limitations to this process are that no scale change is possible and the image will fade in time. The width is limited only by machine and material available, and the length is more or less unlimited.

Intermediates

These may be made of paper, matte film, or clear film. The main function of such prints is for use as second originals from which other prints may be made. They are recommended for making prints to preserve the original and for mailing to other locations to help with print distribution. They can also be used as a base so that certain pertinent information may be added or deleted.

They have good scale retention, depending on material used (especially if a vacuum frame is used). Polyester film is extremely stable, and comes in a variety of colors. It can be drafted upon and the image can be eradicated or erased. It also can be adhesive-backed for applique.

The limitations of these intermediates, however, are the same as those for paper Diazo prints.

Specialties

There are many specialized products which need complicated equipment to produce, but some different kinds of material can be used with a Diazo machine to produce distinctive prints. These include: Repro-proof paper, art-grain brown line paper, technisheen (for report covers and displays), card weight material, color transparency film, opaque cloth (rare) or film, and nonreproducible grid paper or film.

Small clear films mounted in viewgraph frames can be used for visual aids in overhead projectors for classroom situations. Films can also be used for engineering and graphic arts work, for color proofing, overlay drawings, and backlighted displays. Cardstock products are good for displays, flipcharts, and report covers.

Gummed back film can be added to other translucent originals for additional information, title blocks, repetitive drawings. Nonreproducible blue grid paper or film is useful as a masking guide when making visual aids, or as guidelines for lettering, or for hanging cross sections. Some people even call it cross section paper.

Photographic Processes

These are the most versatile, accurate, and expensive reprographic systems. The products can have a positive or negative image, be reduced or enlarged from an opaque or translucent original, are available on a variety of materials, and are permanent. These products require development, fixing, washing, and drying, so they require longer turn-around-times than other processes. Two different photographic methods are available, and each has its own characteristics.

Contact Photo Process

This uses high-contrast material and print-through or reflex techniques. These materials require a high-density light source and are intended for reproduction of line copy only. The products include:

- *Direct positive paper or film,* which is used to make duplicate originals (intermediates) from which other prints may be made. They may be made from either translucent or opaque originals without a negative. Direct positives produce high quality copies, and the image can be eradicated. They are usually made reverse reading to improve reproduction quality, and it is possible to improve the quality of drawings used as originals. Weak pencil lines or dirty backgrounds can also be improved through this process. The only limitations are that the scale cannot be changed, and the width is usually limited to 42 inches.
- *Fixed line films and wash-off films,* which are used to make second originals (intermediates) and are good for additional drafting or continuous revisions. These films are from a translucent base or negative. If the original is poor quality, the negative can be cleaned up to produce excellent intermediates. It is also microfilm quality copy. Its limitations are that the maximum width is usually 42 inches (length is not a critical concern), and the scale cannot be changed.
- *Other contact photo processes* include translucent paper negative or positive, opaque paper positive, continuous tone (mural). Consult your repro professional for specific uses and limitations of these processes.

Projection Photo Processes

These involve the use of a camera, require a darkroom, and include a number of products. Most positive products must be made from a negative, so this is a two-step process. The projection photo process can be used to produce repro-draft negatives, repro-draft halftone negatives, continuous tone negatives, opaque or translucent projection paper, clear or matte polyester film, wash-off film, white opaque film, camera line negatives, and halftone film negatives. Selection of the base material will depend on the end use. Opaque material is used for work prints; translucent or transparent material is used for intermediates. Glossy surface material is used if future reproductions will be made by a camera.

These processes permit scale changes, print restoration is possible by opaquing and scribing negatives, and a permanent image results. They are used for producing enlargements from microfilm, for applications that require extreme reduction of art work, and for restoration work. These projection photo processes are the most expensive processes available, but the size of the prints is limited only by equipment and space. The material can be spliced if necessary. Scale retention is usually adequate but depends on the material used.

Diffusion Transfer Process

This is a photographic method also known as "PMT" or "copyproof" involving image transfer. Sensitized material is exposed in a contact frame or process camera and processed in contact with a receiver sheet. If the original is a positive image, the result is a positive image. The same applies for a negative image.

This process is recommended for screened prints from continuous tone reflection copy or film positive, and type resizing from repro proofs, phototype, or artwork. The prints can be made adhesive-backed for use as paste-up art or applique, and they can be used as photodrawings.

There are some size limits, and scale retention depends on the base material.

Electrostatic (Xerographic) Process

Electrostatic systems produce both final and intermediate copies including offset plates, opaque paper prints, translucent and transparent film, and translucent paper prints. The size of the original that can be used and size of the copy produced are limited by the available equipment.

This process is recommended for making office copies, direct production of large drawings, reduced in size, and the production of visual aids. Producing translucent copies from opaque material by this method allows low-cost copies to be made on Diazo equipment. Some systems now copy in color.

There are many different brands of equipment with various limitations.

Lithographic Process (Offset)

This is a very versatile process that makes it possible to produce thousands of copies from a single master. Because making the master may be expensive, it is not recommended for producing small quantities of copies. It is the fastest way to produce large quantities depending on the equipment.

If more than one color is needed on the finished product, either a separate negative must be made for each color, or masking and multiple exposing techniques must be used. Increasing the number of colors increases the cost because in most cases each sheet must be run through the press for each color involved.

Size limitations vary with the equipment, but the exact scale can be held and the image is as permanent as the material on which it is printed.

Chapter 9
Presentations

Most people do not want to *read* about a product or service; they want to *see* it. Specifically, the boss doesn't want you to tell him how great the prospect is; he wants you to prove it! How well you present the pictures determines whether you communicate with your audience.

Presentations come in all sizes and shapes, and in planning for them you should ask what, who, when, where, and how. The answers to all of these questions determine how you begin, how long the presentation will take, and how much it will cost. The key is communication—among the boss who ordered it, the people who are responsible for actually planning and preparing it, the one who is to present it, and ultimately, the ones who must be persuaded by it.

PLANNING

Careful planning is the most important aspect of making a good presentation. Of course, even the best plan may fail if not properly executed, but the project is *sure* to fail without a plan. There are a number of questions to consider in developing a comprehensive scheme for a worthwhile presentation including:

1. *What* is the objective?
   a. To gain approval for continuing study?
   b. To secure funds, for leases, drilling, exploring, etc?
   c. To sell a product, an idea, a deal?
   d. To train new employees or students?
2. *Who* will be in the audience?
   a. Colleagues?
   b. Company brass?
   c. Client or customer?
   d. Technical or nontechnical personnel?
   e. Students?
3. *When* does it have to be ready?
   a. Unlimited time?
   b. Reasonable time?
   c. Rush job?
4. *Where* is the presentation to be delivered?
   a. Own local office?
   b. Home office?
   c. Many different locations?
   d. Other cities?
   e. Large auditorium?
   f. Conference room?
5. *How* can we best present our case?
   a. Wall displays?
   b. Brochures?
   c. Overhead transparencies?
   d. Slides?

As you can see, all of these considerations must be taken into account as we formulate an overall plan. Let's begin with the ultimate objective.

If the geologists must convince their superior to allow them to continue to study a certain area or trend, they may be able to get by with a few work maps and cross sections. On the other hand, if they must convince the board to include their project in next year's budget, they must go to greater lengths and make a real presentation with expertly drafted maps and sections backed up with plenty of pertinent data. After getting the money allocated for their project, they may still have to refine the presentation to show to outside clients to secure leasing funds, to get the necessary farmouts, or to promote drilling costs. All of these situations require a different kind of plan.

When we know who the audience will be, then we know the quality of presentation expected of us. Less explanation is required when dealing with colleagues, but company brass naturally expect to see quality data. Also, a presentation that is to be part of the technical session at a national convention should be as professional as possible. In both cases, the presenter is actually selling himself as well as his idea. Certainly you should tailor your material to fit the audience and their level of understanding (e.g., what is appropriate for technical personnel may be incomprehensible to students or clients).

A third consideration is the time factor. If you have unlimited time to prepare, which is highly unlikely, you still must have a plan, although you have more options. The usual situation requires a definite schedule, which greatly affects the plan. A reasonable time limit provides an opportunity for a quality presentation with controlled costs. Rush jobs are usually self-defeating. Besides sacrificing quality, they generally cost at least half again as much, sometimes several times the cost requirements of a more reasonable schedule.

The location of the presentation is very important. In familiar surroundings such as your own office, you know beforehand how much wall space is available for hanging maps and displays and whether you need magnets or thumbtacks. Also you do not have to transport the exhibits. If it is necessary to take the material to many different locations, such as the offices of various clients, streamlining the presentation might be helpful. Certainly it would be unwise to dry mount large maps or charts. Putting the material into a booklet that can be hand carried or mailed may be a good idea.

Once all the previous questions have been answered, the options for the final form of the presentation are limited. It is difficult to design exhibits that would be appropriate for wall display as well as brochures and for brochures as well as for slides. Each form has a unique set of parameters and must be planned accordingly.

Other factors must be weighed before final planning decisions are made. Among these considerations are how many copies will be needed, who will actually conduct the presentation, what special equipment is necessary, and what is the budget for the project? As you can see, a good plan requires a great deal of thought.

PREPARING

Once the overall plan has been decided, preparation can begin. The direction this takes is totally dependent on the final form expected for the exhibits. At this point, you should know if there are qualified in-house personnel and adequate equipment to handle the job, or if you must hire outside help. Any external assistance required must be carefully scheduled and integrated.

Wall exhibits

These are probably the easiest kind of exhibits to prepare. The maps and cross sections used every day in an oil company can usually be adapted for use in presentations. Several factors must be considered here.

Every exhibit begins with a reproducible original drawing, and the quality of the exhibit depends on the quality of the original. If acceptable originals are not available, new ones must be prepared. Certain properties of the original limit the reprographic processes you can use, and the processes available in-house or at the local reprographics company may limit your options further (see Chapter 8).

Since wall exhibits usually must be colored individually, the material used for final prints must be considered. Knowing the ultimate use, quality, longevity, and cost requirements helps to narrow the choice of reprographics processes even further. If available, airbrush painting is best for wall presentations. The color is smooth and permanent, and rolling the maps doesn't affect the color. Color tapes and appliqué films will wrinkle when rolled, but provide excellent color on mounted maps.

Usually dry mounted maps are reserved for easel presentations. Of course, size is a significant factor. This is especially true if the exhibit must be transported to different locations.

Brochures

When used in presentations, brochures can be extremely effective. They allow the material to be kept for consideration and study after the initial presentation. It is unrealistic to assume that the wall maps can just be reduced to fit into a brochure. Exhibits which are to be reduced significantly must be drawn with reduction in mind. See "Reduction of Maps" in Chapter 3 for details.

35mm Slides

These are increasingly popular for quality presentations, but they are costly and require more planning and more expertise. For this reason we will go into more detail about preparing slides. Some slides may be made from ordinary photographs, but the ones used most in oil company presentations involve graphics instead. Maps, diagrams, sketches, and cartoons are perfect candidates for slide presentations. Titles should be short and easy to remember, and changeable facts or figures should be on individual slides so they can be easily updated.

Each illustration should convey a single idea, with information limited to essential elements. If a map or diagram is complicated, it is best to produce a series rather than a single graphic. Letters should be bold and simple, large enough to be seen in the back row.

Artwork should be standardized. If a uniform size is adopted, then the same size pens, symbols, markers, etc. can be used for all. Artwork must always be in a ratio of 2 to 3 for 35mm slides (i.e., $6'' \times 9''$, $4'' \times 6''$, or any other dimensions in the same ratio). Purists demand that all slides be prepared in a horizontal format, that is, that the long dimension is the horizontal dimension. It is convenient to make the artwork $6'' \times 9''$ and mount it on a $10'' \times 12''$ artboard, which fits easily in a standard filing cabinet. Drawing the artwork a little larger than 6×9 leaves a little "safe" area around in case the camera is not precisely registered.

Black or dark colored backgrounds with light graphics are recommended, instead of white or very light backgrounds which are hard on viewers' eyes.

In a typical situation, viewers should not be seated further away than eight times the height of the projected image (meaning the height of the picture, not the screen). For example, if the image on the screen is 4 feet high, the viewers should not be seated more than 4×8, or 32, feet away. The same principle can be applied to wall maps also.

To test the artwork for legibility, back away from the graphic six inches for each inch of the largest dimension of the graphic. For example, if the original artwork is 6 inches high and 9 inches wide, you must be able to read it from 6×9, or 54, inches away.

There are at least two excellent manuals with instructions for making 35mm slides. One which is especially useful in preparing slides for oil industry use is entitled "35-mm Slides—A Manual for Technical Presentations," by Dan Pratt and Lev Ropes, published in 1978 by the American Association of Petroleum Geologists, Box 979, Tulsa, Oklahoma 74101.

Another source of information is called "Slides—Planning and Producing Slide Programs," written by Ann Bishop for Eastman Kodak Company. This is Kodak's publication S-30, available at the local photographic supply store, or from Eastman Kodak Company, Dept. 412L, Rochester, N.Y. 14650. This book goes into great detail about the entire process, including creating the artwork, planning the entire presentation, photographing your own slides, and many other areas.

Overhead Transparencies

These make for an excellent presentation, depending on the size of the audience and the viewing area. A number of products are made especially for this kind of project, including projectable color films, tapes and lettering, special markers, and ready-made mounting frames. Almost any art supply store or reprographics firm can supply the products and expert advice on how to use them. Sometimes the transparencies may be made on the office copy machine from opaque originals with color added to them later. Recent technology allows some copy machines to reproduce color copies or color transparencies.

Regardless of the kind of graphic presentation, an accompanying narration or explanation is needed. The presentation should have three main parts: the introduction, the body of material, and the conclusion. Quality is preferred to quantity, and a few conclusions, well documented and illustrated, will be remembered long after the presenter has left. Simplicity is the key.

CONSIDERATIONS FOR A TYPICAL OIL COMPANY PRESENTATION

1. Base map
   a. Do you have a good base map?
   b. Is it the correct scale?
   c. If you enlarge it, will it still look good?
   d. If you reduce it, will you be able to read it?

2. Contoured maps
   a. How many horizons will you need to show?
   b. Do you need to make isopachs?
   c. Are all the logs (or tops) available to you? If not, do you know where to get them?
   d. Can you utilize overlays for any of these?

3. Cross sections
   a. What types of cross sections do you need? How many?
   b. Have you chosen a scale which will allow a reasonably sized finished product?
   c. Do you have *good* copies of the logs you need?

4. Land map
   a. Have you all the information you need to make it?
   b. How much detail must be shown?
   c. Do you know the unit or area of mutual interest?
   d. Is the acreage outline on all other maps (structure or isopach)?

5. Regional map
   a. If using a portion of the regional map, is there sufficient information to identify the location?

6. Time factor
   a. Do you have a reasonable length of time to make a fantastic presentation?
   b. Will you need outside help?
   c. Is there anything you can do to save time, such as using stick-ons, pattern tapes, or films?
   d. Have you arranged your work so that you can be working on one part while another is out for prints?
   e. Could you paste it up and let the repro people make the finals photographically and save time and money too?

7. Final form of presentation
   a. Is this to be a wall presentation?
   b. Do you need overheads or slides?
   c. Do the data have to go into a binder? If so, have you allowed for the margin on the bound side?

Remember: The key is communication!

IN CONCLUSION
OR
DISASTERS WAITING
TO HAPPEN

If you must use notes (not text to be read), it is wise to clip them into a loose leaf notebook, or punch one hole in a stack of note cards and secure with one ring. In this manner, the notes may be turned over out of the way, yet remain in order. It is very distracting, embarrassing, catastrophic, and maybe fatal to drop a stack of notes off the lectern and have them scatter in all directions. A hundred and forty slides in an unlocked carousel can produce the same result.

Examine the meeting room in advance. Check for electrical outlets, seating arrangements, overhead lighting, uncovered windows, etc. On a sunny day uncovered windows can cancel an excellent slide show. A lecturn without a lamp may preclude the use of note cards. A short cord from the projector may not reach the only electrical outlet in the room.

Hints: Always carry an extension cord, an extra projector bulb, and an adapter that allows a three-prong cord to fit into a two prong outlet. Hand carry the maps or slides to the presentation; airlines and shipping companies occasionally lose things. Also note that push pins won't stick into a wall made for magnets. In summary, *be prepared.*

Answers to Exercises

EXERCISE 3-1: MAPS AND SURVEYS
(Page 46)

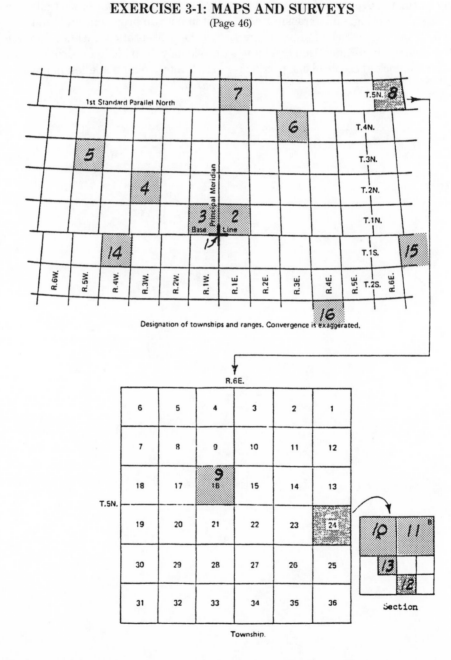

Figure 3-34. Township and range worksheet with locations as indicated in Exercise 3-1 shaded.

EXERCISE 3-2: INDEX MAPS
(Page 47)

A. M-102   K. M-103
B. M-202   L. M-103
C. M-202   M. M-203
D. M-202   N. M-203
E. M-202   O. M-203
F. M-204   P. M-203
G. M-103   Q. M-103
H. M-103   R. M-103
I. M-103   S. M-103
J. M-103   T. M-103

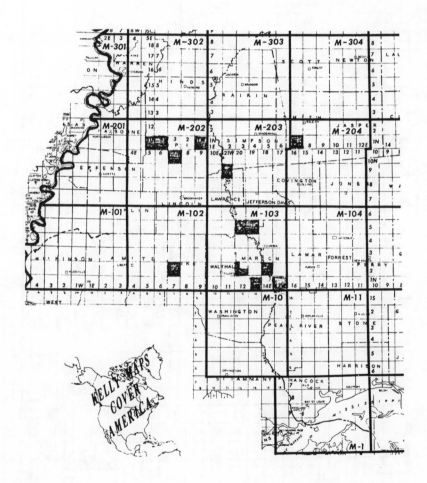

Figure 3-35. Index map showing available base maps in the area with townships and ranges from Exercise 3-2 shaded. (Courtesy George Kelly Map Co., Geological Consulting Services.)

EXERCISE 3-3: SPOTTING TOWNSHIP AND RANGE
(Page 48)

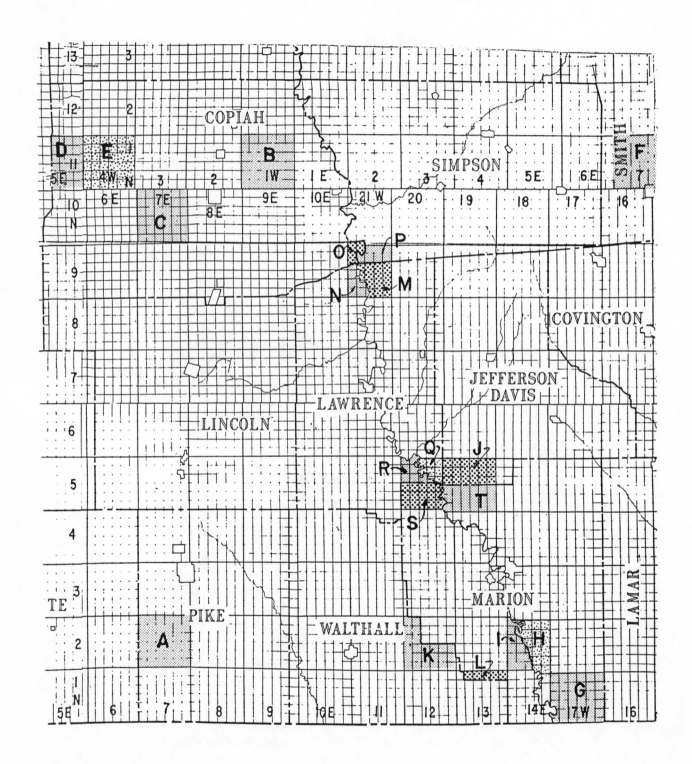

Figure 3-36. Map with township and range spotted as listed in Exercise 3-2.

EXERCISE 4-1: WELL SPOTTING
(Page 70)

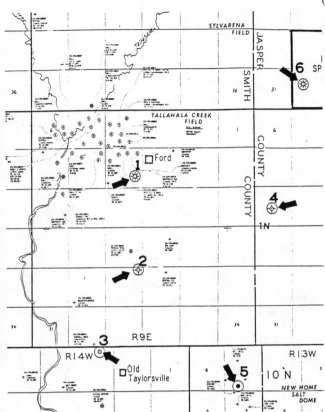

Figure 4-39. Map A with the six wells spotted as indicated in the exercise. (Courtesy of Geological Consulting Services.)

Figure 4-40. Map B with the five wells spotted as indicated in the exercise. (Courtesy Tobin Map Company.)

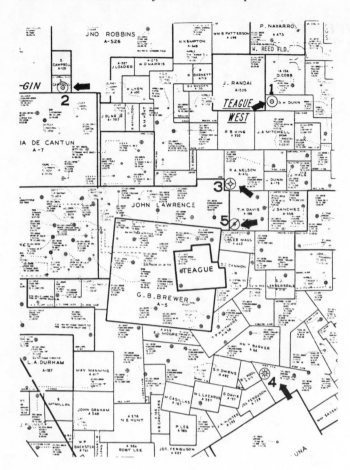

Figure 4-41. Map C with the five wells spotted as indicated in the exercise. (Courtesy of Geological Consulting Services.)

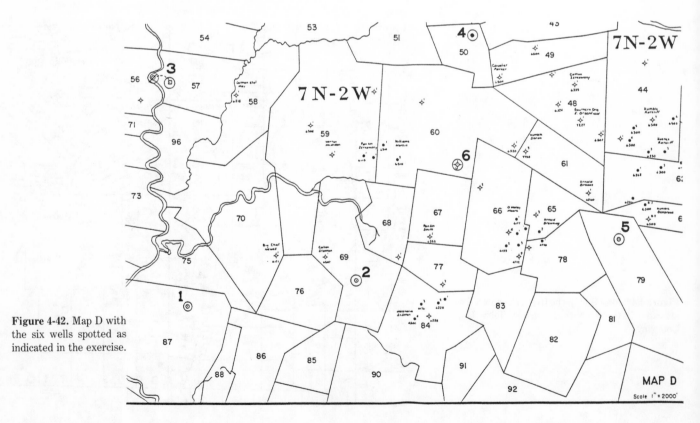

Figure 4-42. Map D with the six wells spotted as indicated in the exercise.

EXERCISE 4-2: CONTOURING
(Page 76)

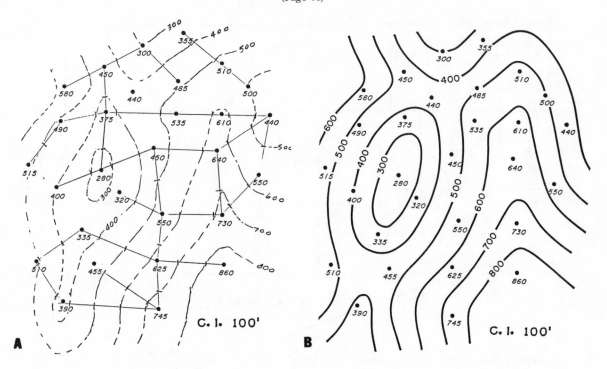

Figure 4-43: (A) A possible interpolation of the contour points indicated in Exercise 4-2. (B) The finished contour map.

EXERCISE 6-1: PLOTTING METES AND BOUNDS
(Page 92)

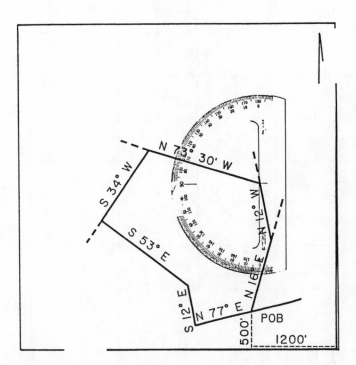

Figure 6-13. The metes and bounds description of Exercise 6-1 plotted with a protractor.

EXERCISE 6-2: PLOTTING LEASES
(Page 93)

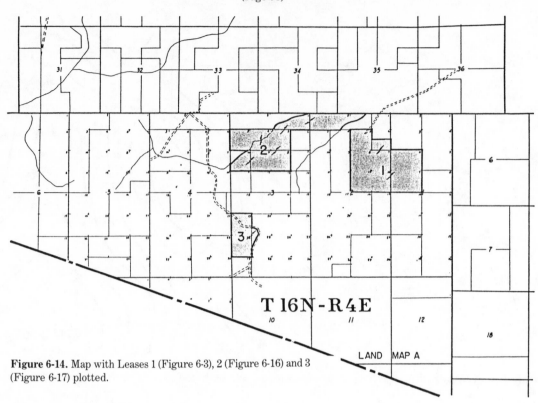

Figure 6-14. Map with Leases 1 (Figure 6-3), 2 (Figure 6-16) and 3 (Figure 6-17) plotted.

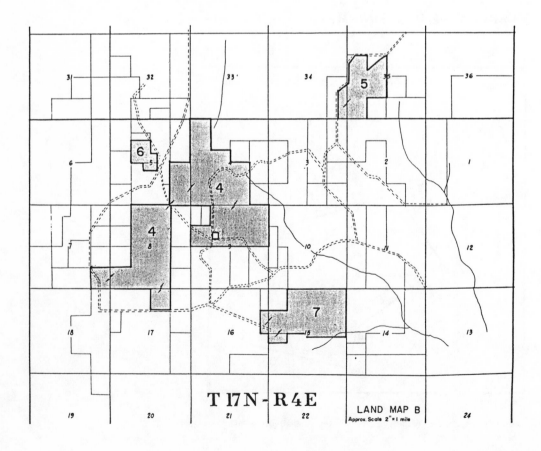

Figure 6-15. Map with Leases 4 (Figure 6-18) through 7 (Figure 6-21) plotted.

EXERCISE 6-3: FIGURING NET ACRES
(Page 102)

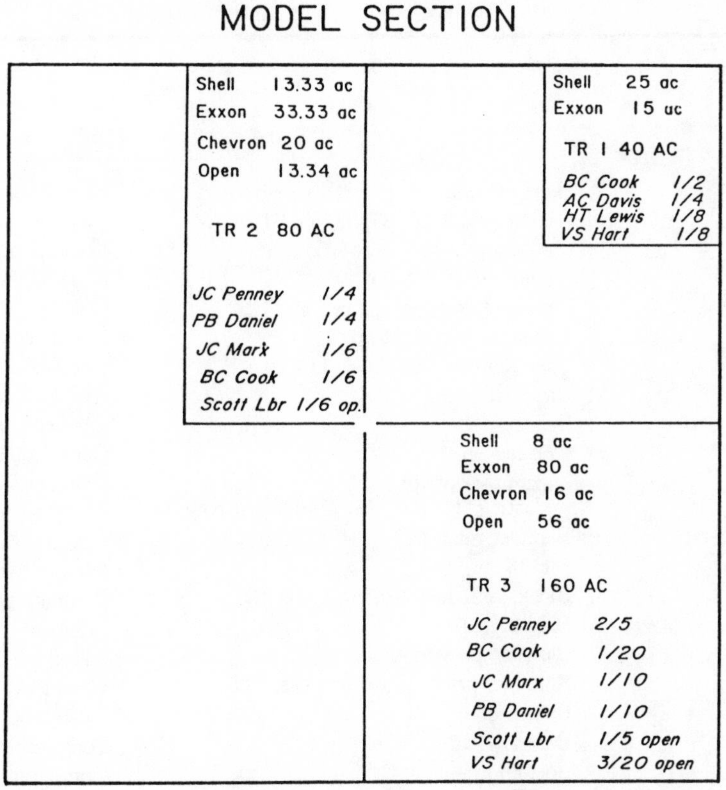

MODEL SECTION

	Shell 13.33 ac Exxon 33.33 ac Chevron 20 ac Open 13.34 ac TR 2 80 AC JC Penney 1/4 PB Daniel 1/4 JC Mark 1/6 BC Cook 1/6 Scott Lbr 1/6 op.		Shell 25 ac Exxon 15 ac TR 1 40 AC BC Cook 1/2 AC Davis 1/4 HT Lewis 1/8 VS Hart 1/8
		Shell 8 ac Exxon 80 ac Chevron 16 ac Open 56 ac TR 3 160 AC JC Penney 2/5 BC Cook 1/20 JC Marx 1/10 PB Daniel 1/10 Scott Lbr 1/5 open VS Hart 3/20 open	

Figure 6-22. The model section divided into tracts as described in Exercise 6-3 with lease information, mineral ownership, and net acres posted.

Index